THE NEW AMERICAN APARTMENT

Innovations in Residential Design and Construction

30 Case Studies

THE NEW AMERICAN APARTMENT

**Innovations in Residential Design
and Construction**

30 Case Studies

**Edited by
OSCAR RIERA OJEDA**

**Whitney Library of Design
an imprint of
Watson-Guptill Publications/New York**

HALF-TITLE PAGE: *View of renovation by David Guthrie*
TITLE PAGE: *Views of renovation by Lee Mindel*

Senior Editor: Ziva Freiman
Editor: Micaela Porta
Designer: Abigail Sturges
Production Manager: Ellen Greene

Copyright © 1997 by Oscar Riera Ojeda

Published in the United States in 1997 by Whitney Library of
Design, an imprint of Watson-Guptill Publications, a division of
BPI Communications, Inc., 1515 Broadway, New York, NY 10036.

Library of Congress Cataloging-in-Publication Data

The new American apartment: innovations in residential design and
construction: 30 case studies / edited by Oscar Riera Ojeda.
     p. cm.
     Includes index.
     ISBN 0-8230-3166-7
     1. Apartment houses—United States—Designs and plans—Case
studies. 2. Apartment houses—United States—Remodeling—Case
studies. I. Riera Ojeda, Oscar.
     NA7861.N48 1997
     728'.314'0222—dc21   97-23273
                                                            CIP

Manufactured in China
First printing, 1997

2 3 4 5 6 7 8 9 / 02 01 00 99 98

*It takes a long time to realize a book like this. As with every
large project, during its production there were ups and
downs. A lot of people have been crucial during this process.
I am grateful to all, but one person in particular, Michele
Tsakonas, deserves my special gratitude. She has given me
the best of herself without asking anything in return. Thank
you Michele for all your love and support.*

Oscar Riera Ojeda

Contents

Detail of fireplace by
Machado and Silvetti

Foreword

To approach a definition of the contemporary apartment one has to look at some of the challenges particular to urban life in the nineties. Naturally, what we want today is not what we wanted in the pre- and post-war years, or even in the sixties and seventies. The realities—more people working from home, high premiums on space coupled with dramatic fluctuations in the cost of living, and the increasing diversity of building types becoming available for residential conversion, to cite a few—call for greater imagination and versatility in the design of our residential spaces. At the end of the millenium, apartment design must accommodate a greater *number* of uses adapted to a broad variety of structures. Moreover, housing the technological component—such as computers and sophisticated communications systems—is no longer in the province of isolated aficionados, but has become a commonplace requirement. Accordingly, the search for the "totally functional" home is driving more clients to consult architects for clear solutions to their complex and often contradictory programs.

Apartments, in a sense, are becoming ingenious instruments for living. A pair of examples in the book depict this trend at its extreme: in their design for a model apartment in a former police building in lower Manhattan, Smith-Miller + Hawkinson provide a complete array of services and elements, cleverly tucked into a single two-story cabinet that dominates the loftlike space (pages 148-55). Across town in Tribeca, architects Kathryn Dean and Charles Wolf explore a parallel concept, in which three utilitarian mobile components (workroom/wall, bedroom/table, and bathroom/ladder) also define and organize a compact space (pages 156-63).

By making flexibility a priority, however, apartment dwellers are not casting their votes for spartan accommodations. Luxury and austerity may appear irreconcilable to some, but not to Gabellini Associates, whose minimalist duplex apartment for Barbara Dente (pages 232-39) offers sensuous expanses of cool marble and a meditative palette of whites.

As is often the case, some of the more inventive designs shown in this volume arose in response to imposed constraints. New York architect Joseph Giovannini saw in the co-op board's restrictions on a venerable East Side apartment the opportunity to salvage many of its traditional features while injecting it with the clients' special taste for the modern (pages 96-103). Here, modernity becomes a second architectural order that negotiates the existing structure in an electrifying example of coexistence.

This reconciliation of the old and the new is doubtless one of the more accepted current tendencies. Maintaining the structure and the existing spatial qualities, restoring moldings and original floors in order to introduce within them a new modernist vocabulary and spirit, are seductive endeavors for many architects that once had no qualms about imposing their own vanguardist postures. Lauretta Vinciarelli understood that in order to sustain the sense of her loft, she needed to allow the space to speak for itself, and so restricted her intervention to rescuing its most salient features (pages 256-61). Rodolfo Machado and Jorge Silvetti's remodeling of an apartment in Boston's historic Back Bay neighborhood (pages 256-61) focused on refining and formalizing the existing spatial order while incorporating a series of new elements, such as the fireplace, that become points of reference.

A common problem in apartments is storage, but how does one resolve it without compromising comfort or style? In his own apartment in San Francisco (pages 24-31), architect David Weingarten (an avid collector) makes each architectural element work overtime by serving as a repository for mementos from his many trips. On the other side of the spectrum, architects Calvin Tsao and Zach McKown specified a Palladium-leafed wall of floating cabinets along the length of their living room (pages 180-91) to simply and stylishly contain hidden treasures.

The quest for peace and serenity, contrasted against the chaos of the street, is yet another objective of today's apartment dweller. For George Suyama Architects this is made possible through a wood and stone palette's evocation of nature (pages 16-23). In other examples, the architecture provides a contemplative environment for art, as in the apartment architect Jim Olson designed for himself and his wife in Seattle (pages 8-15).

Conversely, some wish to see the rhythms of the city brought into their homes, as in the designs conceived by Shelton, Mindel, Pasanella Klein Stolzman Berg, and Agrest and Gandelsonas, which in various ways respond to visible and invisible urban elements.

Like *The New American House,* the first book in this series, *The New American Apartment* features thirty of the best and most timely examples of apartment design in the United States. If there is one conclusion that can be drawn from such a stylistically (and economically) diverse body of work, it is that American apartment dwellers are coming to appreciate the boons of interior architecture—moving beyond the mindset of "decorating" a passive container toward the genuine integration of architecture, furnishings, and ornament. As exemplified throughout this book, an apartment's skin and bones can be powerfully expressive in building a home's character.

View of staircase in renovation by Lee Mindel

Infinite Confines *1987*
OLSON SUNDBERG ARCHITECTS

BELOW AND FACING PAGE:
Views of living room
BOTTOM: *View of kitchen*

Owner: Jim and Katherine Olson
Architect: Olson Sundberg Architects, Seattle, Washington
Design Team: Jim Olson (architect)
Contributing Artists: Rik Adams, Jeffery Bishop,
Ann Gardner, Nancy Mee, Walter White.
General Contractor: Jerry Fulks & Company
Photography: Eduardo Calderon, Michael Jensen,
© Dick Busher

Site: Seattle, Washington
Program: Master bedroom, bathroom, kitchen, gallery, study.
Square Footage: 1400
Structural System: Steel frame construction
Mechanical System: Forced air heating and cooling
Major Interior Materials: Painted gypsum board walls and
ceilings, glass, medium density fiberboard floors.
Furnishings and Storage: Custom by architect.
Doors and Hardware: Sargent
Windows: Belknap glass
Fixtures: American Standard, Grohe
Appliances and Equipment: Sub-Zero (refrigerator/freezer),
Gaggenau (oven, cooktop, dishwasher).
Cost: $200 per square foot

Site/Context

The apartment is located in the Olympic Building in
historic Pioneer Square, a lively, mixed-use neighborhood
in downtown Seattle. The unit occupies a two-story space
on the eighth floor and penthouse with views to Pioneer
Square, downtown Seattle, and across Elliott Bay.

Design

The apartment represents the owner's exploration of
ideas about architecture, context, urban life, and space.
Despite the views, the relatively small, sparsely furnished residence turns inward, eschewing views in favor
of internal reflection. The apartment is designed to serve
as a retreat from the bustle of the city.

The concept alters traditional spaces and order through
both physical and illusory means. Art and architecture
are married in support of the creation of a spiritual
space. The perimeter of the apartment contains "real
life" rooms such as the kitchen, living room, and master
bedroom. The core of the apartment is a transitional
area, a point of entry as well as a refuge for mental
restoration. A thirty-foot vertical lightwell in the core
links the two levels and serves to orient the activities of
the apartment.

The lightwell is the apartment's most symbolically spiritual architectural device. A prism, designed by the artist Walter White, is located at the top of the lightwell. It refracts light into its visible component colors that trace the sun's path across the apartment. For the architect interacting with this space, moving around it, looking into it, and having its effects enter different rooms at different times are a constant reminder of the importance of reflection and contemplation.

Construction

The materials used in construction were basic: metal studs, sheetrock, plaster, medium density fiberboard, and glass. However, they were sculpted to create spaces and illusions of space that go beyond their physical limits. Materials were used simply to set the framework in which to experience light, space, and art.

Existing conditions

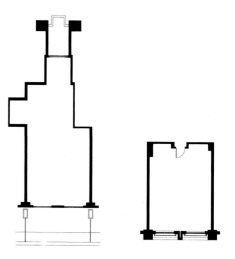

Upper level floor plan

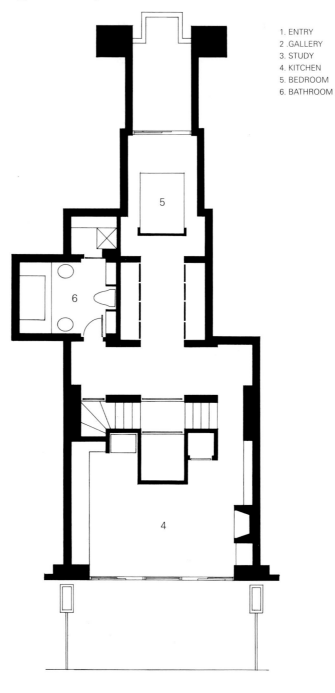

1. ENTRY
2. GALLERY
3. STUDY
4. KITCHEN
5. BEDROOM
6. BATHROOM

Lower level floor plan

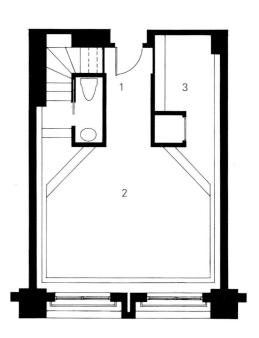

0   5   10

Cross section

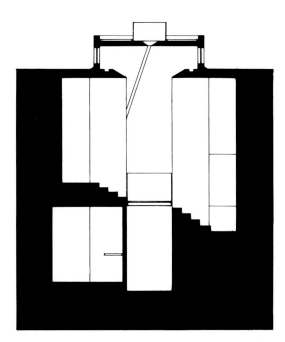

Longitudinal perspectival section

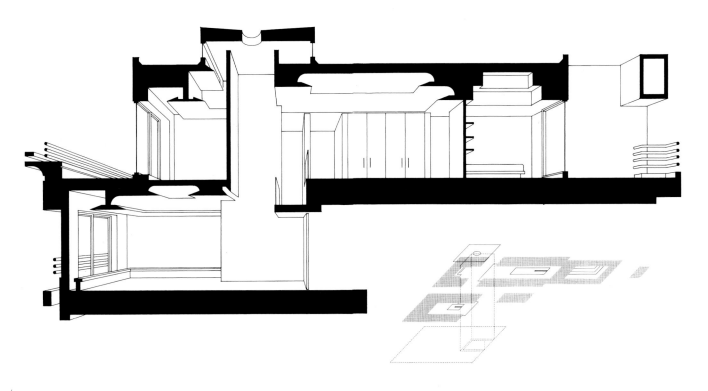

ABOVE: *View of stair to second level; sculpture by Nancy Mee, mural by Jeffrey Bishop*

ABOVE : *Second level landing*
FACING PAGE: *View of stair and landing from lightwell*

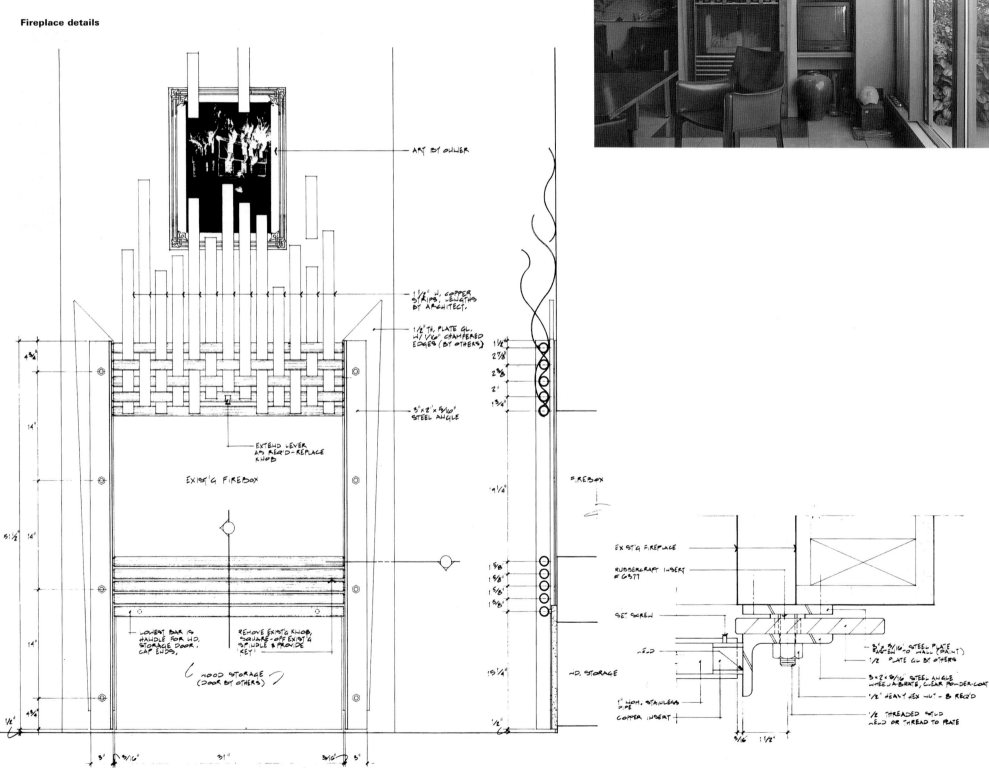

Fireplace details

ART BY OWNER

1 1/2" H. COPPER STRIPS, LENGTHS BY ARCHITECT.

1/2" TH. PLATE GL. W/ 1/16" CHAMFERED EDGES (BY OTHERS)

3"x2"x 3/16" STEEL ANGLE

EXTEND LEVER AS REQ'D - REPLACE KNOB

EXIST'G FIREBOX

LOWEST BAR IS HANDLE FOR H.D. STORAGE DOOR, CAP ENDS.

REMOVE EXIST'G KNOB, SQUARE-OFF EXIST'G SPINDLE & PROVIDE KEY.

WOOD STORAGE (DOOR BY OTHERS)

FIREBOX

H.D. STORAGE

1 1/2"
2 7/8"
2 3/8"
2"
1 3/4"

1 3/8"
1 3/8"
1 3/8"
1 3/8"

EX ST'G F.REPLACE

RUMFORDCRAFT INSERT # 6377

SET SCREW

WELD

1" NOM. STAINLESS P.PE

COPPER INSERT

3"x 2x 3/16" STEEL PLATE FASTEN'G TO WALL (PAINT)

1/2" PLATE GL. BY OTHERS

3"x 2"x 3/16" STEEL ANGLE W/FEE JA-BRATE, CLEAR POWDER-COAT

1/2" HEAVY HEX NUT - 8 REQ'D

1/2" THREADED STUD WELD OR THREAD TO PLATE

3/16" : 1/2"

Detail of recessed ceiling with light fixture

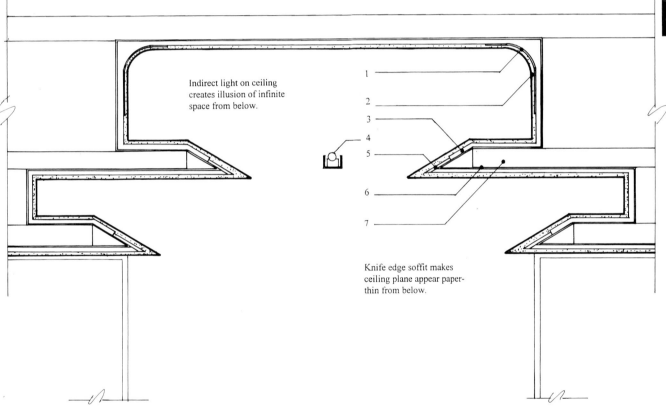

Indirect light on ceiling creates illusion of infinite space from below.

Knife edge soffit makes ceiling plane appear paper-thin from below.

1. Thin plastic cove
2. 1/2 " veneer plaster
3. 5/8 " GWB
4. Miniature low voltage light
5. 3/8" GWB
6. Fabricated sheet metal
7. Metal studs

Pike Place Market High Rise Condominium *1987-1989*
GEORGE SUYAMA ARCHITECTS

Owner: Name withheld at owner's request.
Architect: George Suyama Architects, Seattle, Washington
Interior Designer: Judy Davison
Design Team: George Suyama, Jeff Wilson, Bill Haas, Coleen Miller.
Engineers: Swenson Engineers (structural), Aungst Engineering (mechanical)
Consultants: Swift & Co. Landscape Architects, Christopher Thompson (lighting)
General Contractor: Flemming Sorensen
Photography: © 1994 Michael Shopenn Photography, David Story Photography, Michael Jensen

Site: Seattle, Washington; Marketplace Tower by NBBJ Architects
Program: Full-time downtown residence including 3 bedrooms, 2 bathrooms, powder room, living room, dining room, family room, kitchen, laundry, wine room, exercise room, office.
Square Footage: 5000 in one floor; 1000 in deck.
Structural System: Steel frame building structure, steel-framed raised floors and walls.
Mechanical System: Heat pump forced air supplemented by hydronic baseboard heating.
Major Exterior Materials: Glass fiber-reinforced concrete panels, aluminum and glass window walls, concrete pavers.
Major Interior Materials: Oak (cabinetry, floors, doors, and trim), cedar (columns, beams, and ceilings), sandstone (floors), marble (floors), granite (countertops), ash (paneling).
Furnishings and Storage: Custom designed and built furniture and antiques.
Doors and Hardware: Custom by GSA, fabricated by O.B. Williams; Corbin hardware.
Windows: Commercial rectangular section aluminum frames
Fixtures: Kroin, Grohe, custom plated
Appliances and Equipment: Sub-Zero, Dacor, Gaggenau, Kitchen Aid
Cost: $275 per square foot

Site/Context

This residence occupies the north half of the fifteenth floor in a glass- and concrete-clad mixed-use tower. The seventeen-story building is sited on the east bank above Elliott Bay within the Pike Place Market Historic District, one of the most active neighborhoods in Seattle.

Above the underground parking garage and street level retail are twelve stories of offices and four stories of residential condominiums comprising eight units. The residence looks west across the water, toward the islands and Olympic Peninsula beyond, and north and east to Lake Union and surrounding neighborhoods.

LEFT: *View of apartment building*

Design

The clients' charge to create a Northwestern home of timelessness and stability and the architects' reverence for natural materials combined to create the design for a serene residence, evocative of a traditional lodge but possessing a refined, highly detailed urban quality, intensified by its location in the sky. The inserted structural order and the treatment of materials throughout the residence invests the spaces with a sense of calm and transforms the raw shell into a familiar, grounded environment.

The building shell imposed a number of constraints that ultimately informed the condominium design. Among these were the building's structural steel frames and random array of flues rising from condominium units below. The primary fireproofed steel frame elements and fireplace flues determined the location of certain cedar-clad columns and beams, which now provide the structural order through which the spaces unfold. In the interest of placing ceilings as high as possible, the trabeated colonnade was overlaid with cedar purlins and planks, and steel-wire cloth panels line the shell structure.

Construction

Western Red Cedar was left to age naturally, with no sealers or varnish, sandblasted steel plates separate the stone floor from the columns, elevating and protecting the wood. Cabinets, doors and trims are all of rift sawn white oak. Steel and stone surround the four fireplaces in the residence and all hardware and plumbing fittings are nickel plated sandblasted brass, hand rubbed to a dull finish.

Because of acoustical isolation requirements for the condominium, all floor systems—including Pennsylvania bluestone, white oak, marble, ceramic tile, and carpet—float above a synthetic wire mat placed below the build-up for each floor finish. Lighting, audio, and sprinklers are integrated within sound-absorbing acoustical ceiling panels flanking the cedar ceiling, and are concealed by a refined steel-wire cloth finish.

Existing conditions

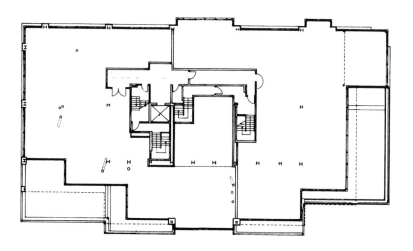

Floor plan

1. ENTRY
2. DINING ROOM
3. LIVING ROOM
4. STUDY
5. KITCHEN
6. MASTER BEDROOM
7. BEDROOM
8. MASTER BATHROOM
9. BATHROOM

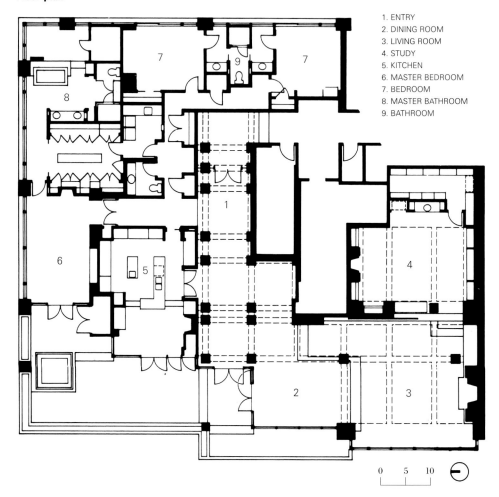

0   5   10

Perspective rendering

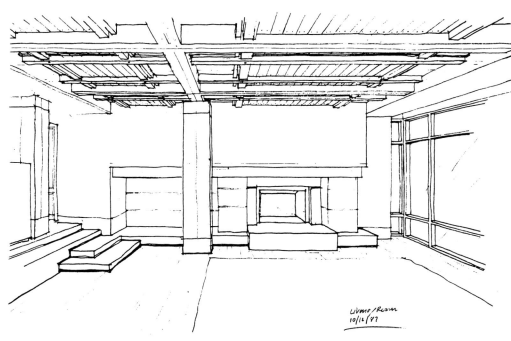

Living Room
10/12/87

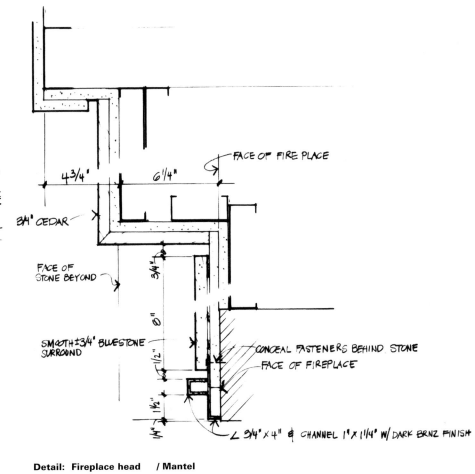

FACE OF FIRE PLACE

4 3/4"   6 1/4"

3/4" CEDAR

FACE OF
STONE BEYOND

3/4"

8"

CONCEAL FASTENERS BEHIND STONE
FACE OF FIREPLACE

SMOOTH ± 3/4" BLUESTONE
SURROUND

1 1/2"

1 1/2"

1/4"

∠ 3/4" X 4" & CHANNEL 1" X 1 1/4" W/ DARK BRNZ FINISH

Detail: Fireplace head   / Mantel

ABOVE: *View of kitchen*

ABOVE: *Art piece in entry vestibule*

FACING PAGE: *View of hallway with cedar-boxed columns and beams*

RIGHT: *View of ceiling and colonnade*

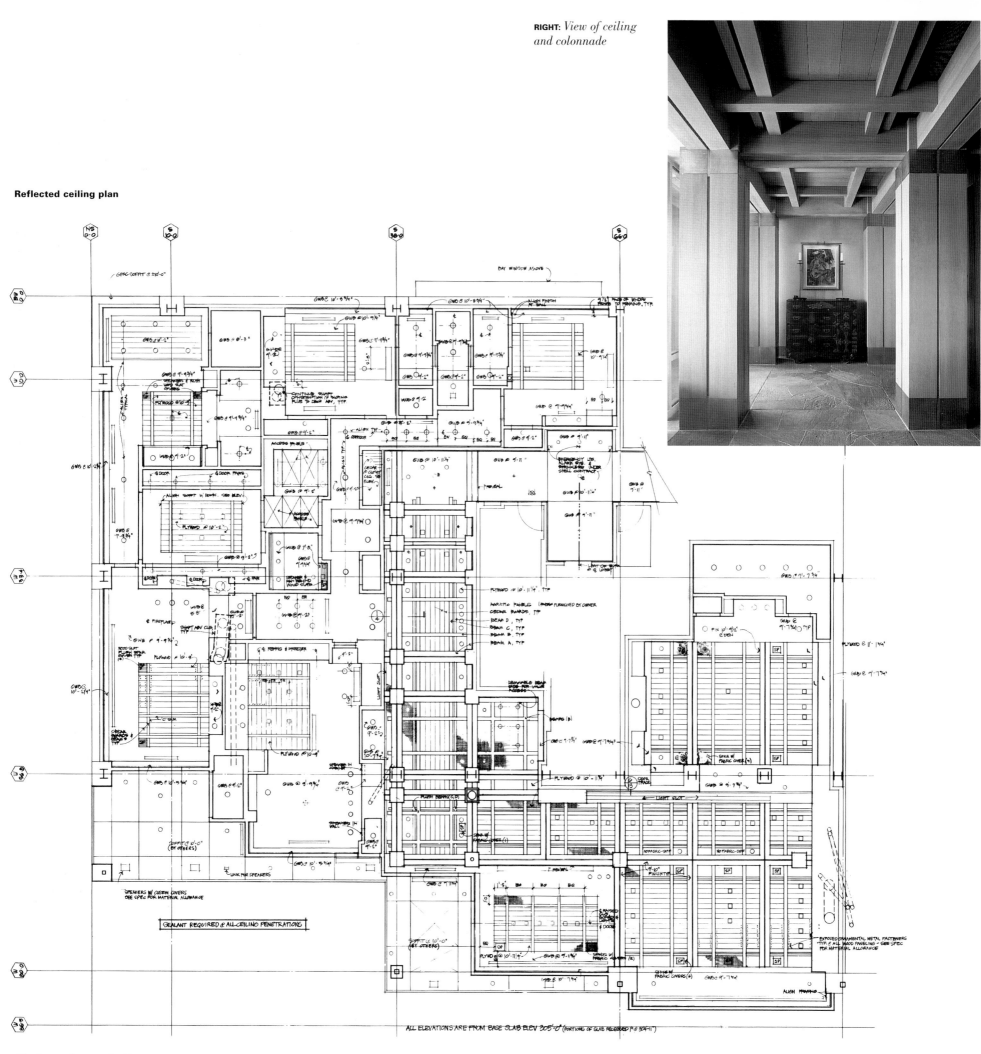

Reflected ceiling plan

SEALANT REQUIRED @ ALL CEILING PENETRATIONS

ALL ELEVATIONS ARE FROM BASE SLAB ELEV 305'-0" (PORTIONS OF SLAB RECESSED 1" @ 304'-11")

RIGHT: *Ceiling detail*

Ceiling construction drawings

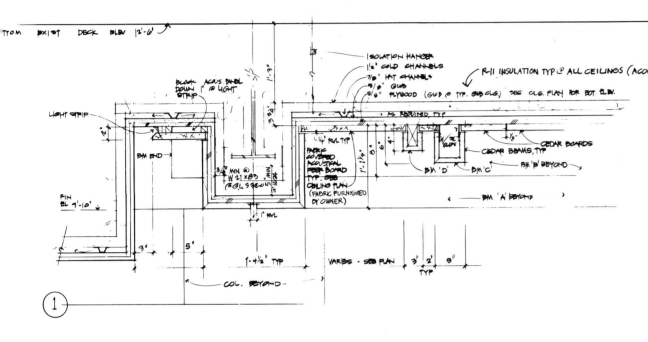

Section through cedar-boxed columns

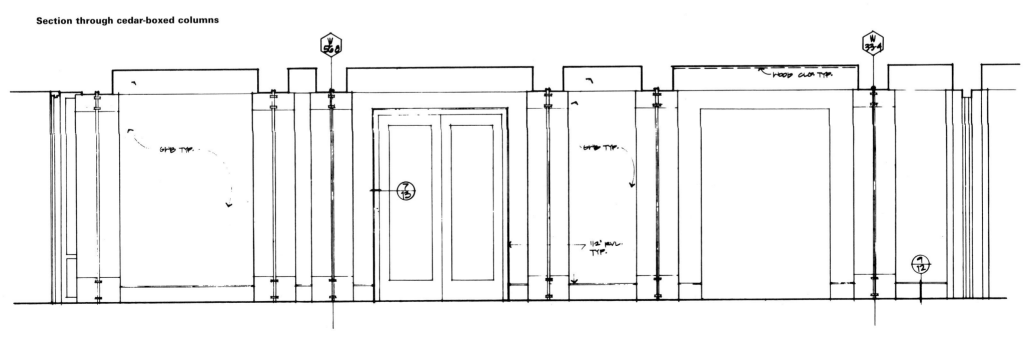

⑥ GALLERY 121·NORTH

36 Darrell Place *1986-87*
ACE ARCHITECTS

BELOW: *View of library toward entry*
FACING PAGE: *View of living room with Bay Bridge to the east*

Owner: David Weingarten
Architect: Ace Architects, Oakland, California
Design Team: David Weingarten (senior designer), Lucia Howard (project architect), Scott Glendinning (designer), Judy Choi (muralist), Mary Jo Sutton (finish artist).
Engineer: Ray Lindahl
Consultant: Barbara Meacham (landscape architect)
General Contractor: Creative Spaces
Photography: Alan Weintraub Photography

Site: Telegraph Hill, San Francisco
Program: Lower unit of a two-unit condominium on a 56' x 22' site including 1 bedroom, 2 bathrooms, study, open livingroom, dining and kitchen.
Square Footage: 1200
Structural System: Wood frame with steel posts and beams.
Major Interior Materials: Redwood (paneling and kitchen cabinets and counter), painted and textured gypboard (walls and ceilings), ceramic tile (bathroom walls and floors), oak (upstairs floor), marble and slate (downstairs floor), formica "metal-mica," brushed stainless steel (island).
Furnishings and Storage: Dining table, chairs, and bed designed by architect; antiques selected by architect; prints by Piranesi.
Doors and Hardware: Wood and wood and glass doors, custom steel and glass doors; hardware by Baldwin.
Windows: Bonetti
Fixtures: American Standard
Appliances and Equipment: Jennaire (cooktop and oven), Kohler (kitchen sink), GE (refrigerator).
Cost: Withheld at owner's request.

Site/Context

Along the Filbert Steps on Telegraph Hill in San Francisco stands 36 Darrell Place, with Coit Tower marking the top of the hill above and the Bay Bridge and Treasure Island to the east. Accessible only by a narrow lane (Darrell Place) crossing the Filbert Steps, the building— among the oldest in San Francisco—survived the 1906 earthquake and fire that destroyed much of the city.

Design

The Bay Region Style has defied definition ever since Lewis Mumford suggested there was one. Rather than attempt to define the style, the architects chose to reconstruct the three periods that together form the Bay Region Style.

Lower level floor plan

Upper level floor plan

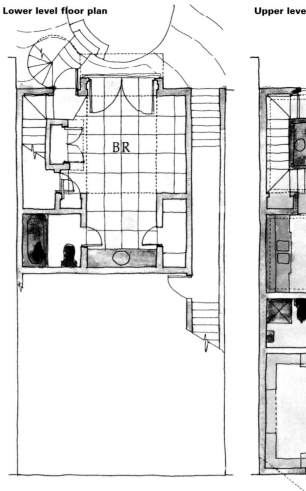

F. ENTRY FOYER
S. LIBRARY
K. KITCHEN
D. DINING ROOM
L. LIVING ROOM
BR. BEDROOM

Visible only from Darrell Place, the five-story building's west front fills a narrow gap between two apartment buildings. This façade is a fanciful reconstruction of a building that might have been assembled over time. Intersecting pieces from each period of the Bay Region Style happily coexist, as the style itself is a collection of other architectural motifs reconfigured in local materials and proportions. The two lower levels are informed by an early-twentieth-century aesthetic, while the middle two and upper floors become progressively more modern.

The owner, architect David Weingarten, occupies the building's lower level and a portion of the second level. He views the design of his unit in terms of a larger idea about the house as an "excavation" of the Bay Region Style. Even the bathroom has a view of San Francisco Bay in the mirror. Weingarten considers the bay "part of the architecture."

Construction

The project's materials are drawn from the vocabulary of the Bay Region Style at three different periods. The building was then assembled as if it had been constructed over time.

The first and second level are the earliest, made of stucco and detailed in a whimsical Beaux-Arts style. The third and fourth levels correspond to the Bay Region's modern era, and are constructed of horizontal painted redwood boards with large double-hung windows. A curved room is walled in glass brick beneath the big arch that faces the street. The fifth level is executed in a shed-roofed cabin style, also in redwood. A big skylight through the roof deck lights a two-story aedicula below.

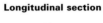

0   5   10

Longitudinal section

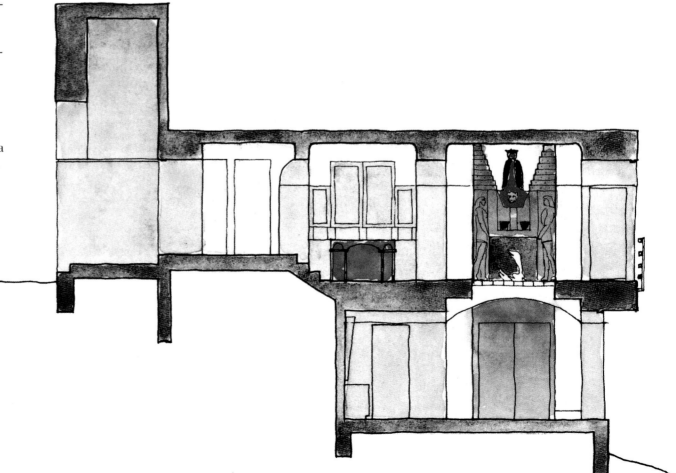

Views of building exterior as if constructed over time

c. 1887   1946   1970

Conceptual rendering with portraits of key Bay Region architects

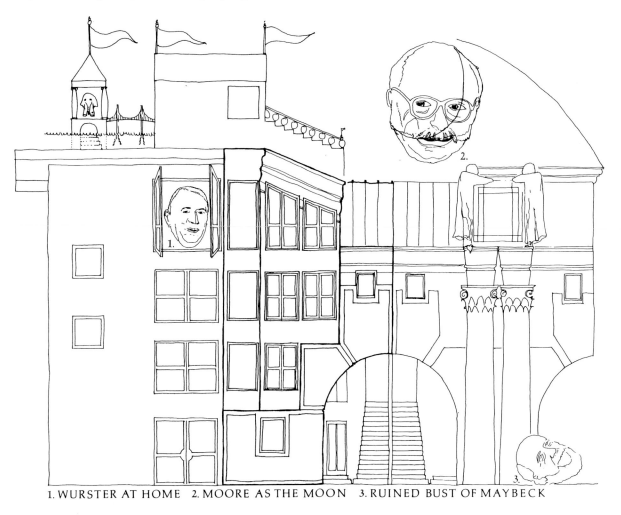

1. WURSTER AT HOME   2. MOORE AS THE MOON   3. RUINED BUST OF MAYBECK

LEFT: *View of bathroom and library*
FACING PAGE, CLOCKWISE FROM TOP LEFT: *View of kitchen toward entry; living room; bathroom; view of kitchen and dining area*

Interior elevations

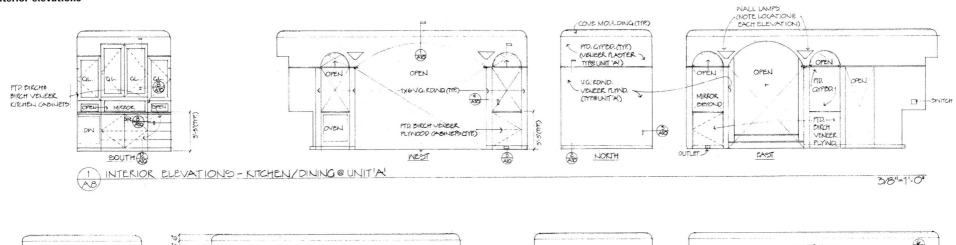

① ⟨A8⟩ INTERIOR ELEVATIONS - KITCHEN/DINING @ UNIT 'A' 3/8"=1'-0"

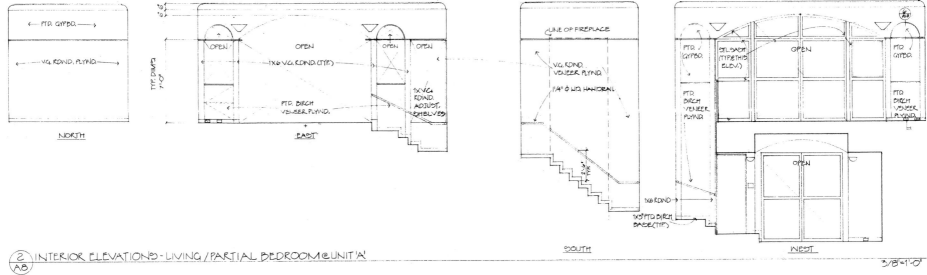

② ⟨A8⟩ INTERIOR ELEVATIONS - LIVING/PARTIAL BEDROOM @ UNIT 'A' 3/8"=1'-0"

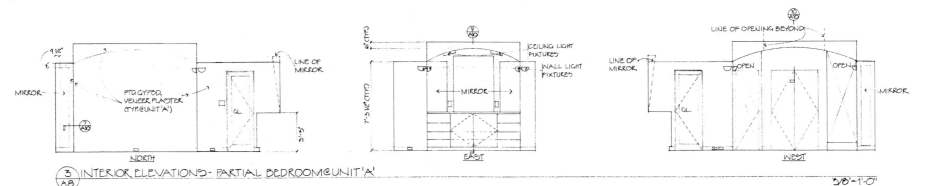

③ ⟨A8⟩ INTERIOR ELEVATIONS - PARTIAL BEDROOM @ UNIT 'A' 3/8"=1'-0"

Details

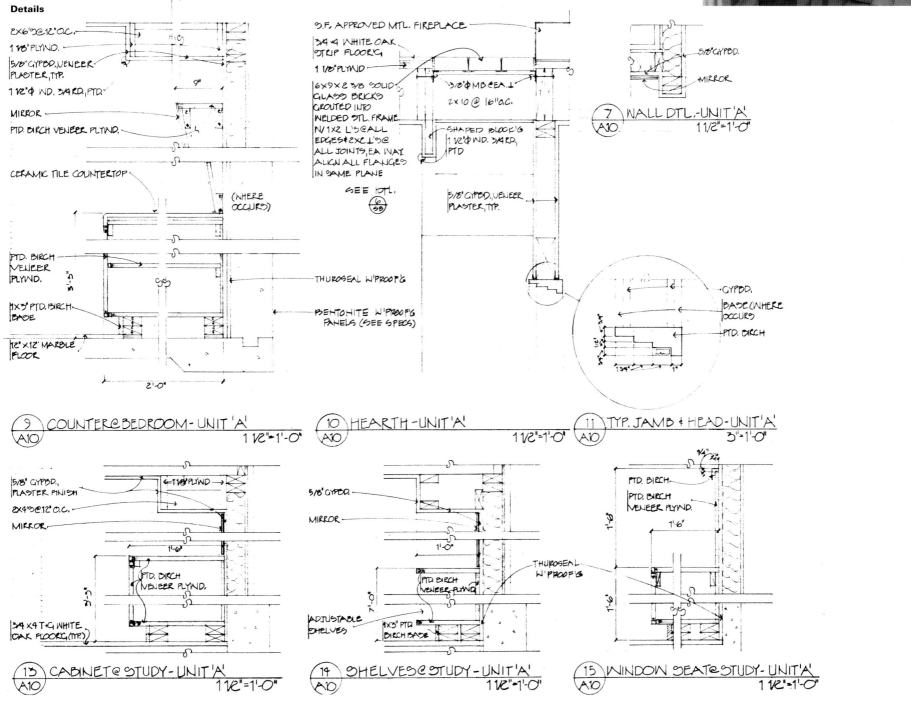

2X6'S@12'O.C.
1 1/8' PLYWD.
5/8' GYPBD., VENEER PLASTER, TYP.
1 1/2'∅ WD. 3/4 RD, PTD.
MIRROR
PTD. BIRCH VENEER PLYWD.

CERAMIC TILE COUNTERTOP

(WHERE OCCURS)

PTD. BIRCH VENEER PLYWD.

1X3' PTD. BIRCH BASE

12" X 12" MARBLE FLOOR

2'-0"

⑨ COUNTER @ BEDROOM - UNIT 'A'
A10   1 1/2"=1'-0"

S.F. APPROVED MTL. FIREPLACE
3/4 X 4 WHITE OAK STRIP FLOOR'G
1 1/8' PLYWD
6X9X2 3/8 SOLID GLASS BRICKS GROUTED INTO WELDED DTL. FRAME W/ 1X2 L'S @ ALL EDGES & EXC'L'S @ ALL JOINTS, EA WAY. ALIGN ALL FLANGES IN SAME PLANE

SEE DTL. ⑥/39

3/8'∅ MB @ EA ⊥
2X10 @ 16"O.C.

SHAPED BLOCK'G
1 1/2'∅ WD. 3/4 RD, PTD

5/8' GYPBD., VENEER PLASTER, TYP.

THUROSEAL W'PROOF'G

BENTONITE W'PROOF'G PANELS (SEE SPECS)

⑩ HEARTH - UNIT 'A'
A10   1 1/2"=1'-0"

5/8' GYPBD.
MIRROR

⑦ WALL DTL. - UNIT 'A'
A10   1 1/2"=1'-0"

GYPBD.
BASE (WHERE OCCURS)
PTD. BIRCH

⑪ TYP. JAMB & HEAD - UNIT 'A'
A10   3"=1'-0"

5/8' GYPBD., PLASTER FINISH
2X4'S @ 12' O.C.
MIRROR

1 1/8' PLYWD

1'-0"

PTD. BIRCH VENEER PLYWD.

3'-5"

3/4 X 4 T+G WHITE OAK FLOOR'G (TYP.)

⑬ CABINET @ STUDY - UNIT 'A'
A10   1 1/2"=1'-0"

5/8' GYPBD.
MIRROR

1'-0"

PTD. BIRCH VENEER PLYWD.

7'-0"

ADJUSTABLE SHELVES

1X3" PTD. BIRCH BASE

⑭ SHELVES @ STUDY - UNIT 'A'
A10   1 1/2"=1'-0"

PTD. BIRCH
PTD. BIRCH VENEER PLYWD.

1'-6"
1'-6"

THUROSEAL W'PROOF'G

1'-6"

⑮ WINDOW SEAT @ STUDY - UNIT 'A'
A10   1 1/2"=1'-0"

Live/Work Studio *1989*
INTERIM OFFICE OF ARCHITECTURE

Owner: Tom Bonauro
Architect: Interim Office of Architecture, San Francisco, California
Design Team: John Randolph, Bruce Tomb (partners); Mearyta Medrano (project manager); Vanessa Belli, Ben King (assistants).
Engineer: Neil Marshall (electrical)
Consultants: Pacassa Studios (woodwork), South Park Fabricators (metalwork)
General Contractor: Makerstudio
Photography: Paul Warchol

Site: Potrero Hill, San Francisco, California
Program: Residence and graphic design studio including bathroom, entry foyer, kitchen, dining area, walk-in storage, sleeping area, design production area.
Square Footage: 1500 including mezzanine
Structural System: Existing wood frame
Mechanical System: Existing wall heater
Major Interior Materials: Stucco cement, steel, Douglas fir, Filon fiberglass, aluminum, maple, glass.
Furnishings and Storage: Custom by architect and Phillip Agee.
Doors and Hardware: Custom by architect
Fixtures: Custom by architect, Chicago (plumbing).
Appliances and Equipment: Custom by architect.
Cost: Withheld at owner's request.

Site/Context

The apartment is located in what was originally part of an airplane wheel and tire manufacturing factory. When the factory vacated the premises, artists moved in and illegally inhabited their studios. The city of San Francisco came under pressure to create a new category in its city planning codes to include a living/working type space for professional artists, which they called live/work lofts. This building houses one of the first such complexes.

Design

The designers sought to redefine the conventions of "home," which become vague and problematic with the incorporation of one's livelihood into private life. Presented with a blank interior space, IOOA stripped the existing shell by removing a staircase to an existing mezzanine that interrupted the main room, and in some areas, exposed the existing construction. By subdividing the 1500-square-foot rectangular space into three unequal bays, different uses were distinguished: a double-height work area at the rear, a more intimate kitchen/dining area beneath the bedroom, and a stairwell, closet storage, and bathroom packed into a tall narrow "service alley" at the front, through which one enters the living and work spaces.

TOP: *View of main room*
BOTTOM: *Steel frame fiberglass panels enclosing mezzanine*
FACING PAGE: *View of main floor from mezzanine bedroom*

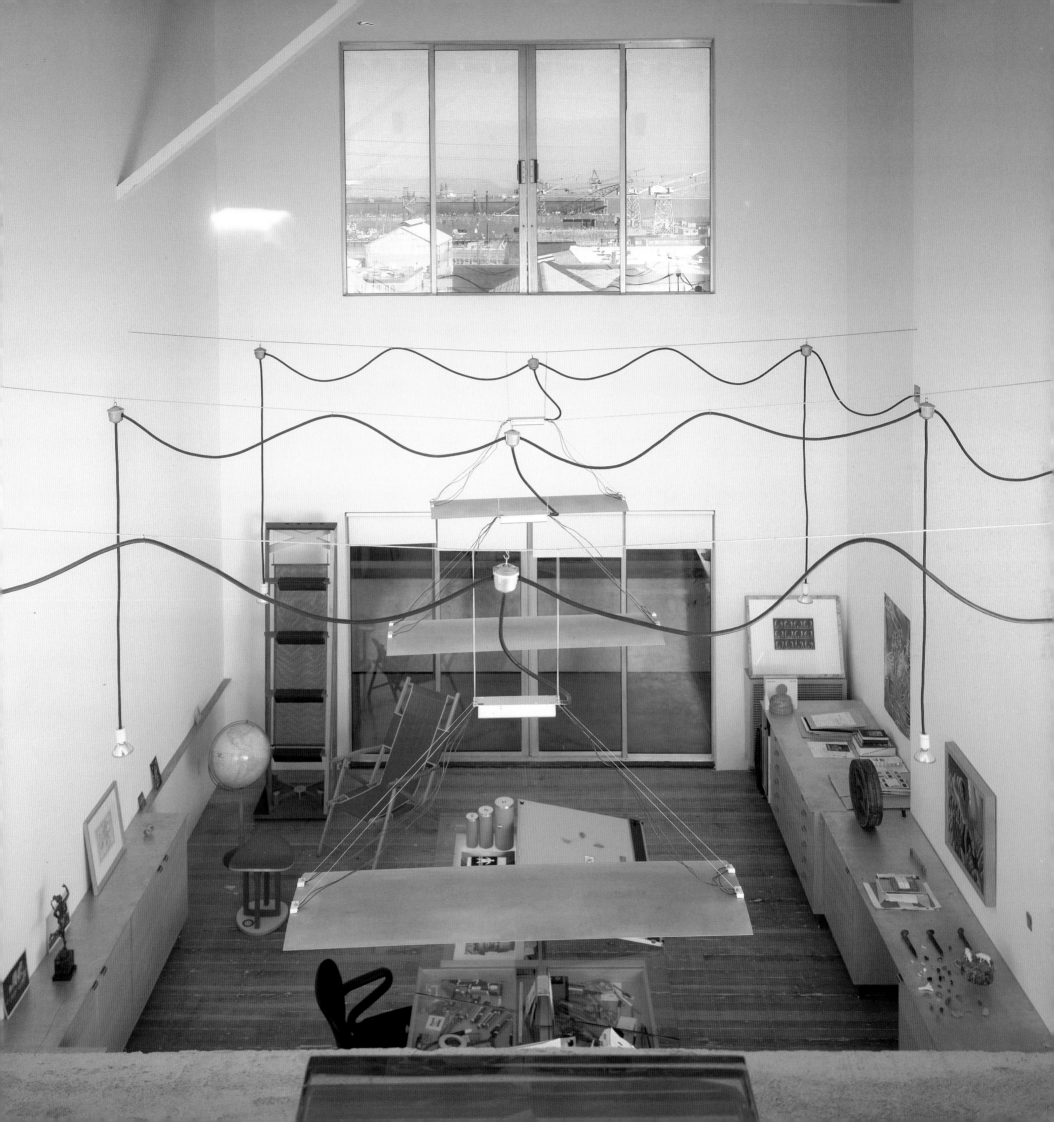

Axonometric sketch of existing space

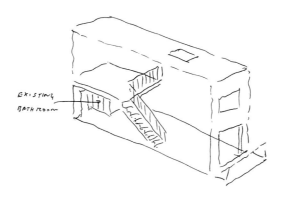

To connect the levels, the designers sculpted stairs from
thick stucco walls that turn to wood steps and conceal a
cabinet, then lead up to an aluminum ramp which turns
again to another stair sculpted into a stucco wall, and so
on. A well defined private sanctuary above the kitchen
and dining area is distanced from the rest of the space
by way of a convoluted ascent.

Within this condensed contrast of compression and
release, the designers provided multipurpose furnishings
and lighting, as well as storage for the client's collection
of visual icons. A thirteen-foot-long glass-topped desk-
conference table has built-in light boxes, and white-
washed mahogany perimeter cabinets with aluminum
counter tops provide a work surface as well as display
space. For the client's most treasured possessions, IOOA
designed a translucent, thick glass "reliquarium", which
is placed upstairs in the sleeping area.

Construction

At the top of the "service alley," a new skylight was cut
in over the narrow stairwell and closet to bring daylight
down through the glass floor of the closet, into the otherwise dark bathroom. The bathroom and kitchen are situated back to back and are separated by textured glass
panels, emphasizing their proximity and borrowing light
from one another.

Mezzanine floor plan

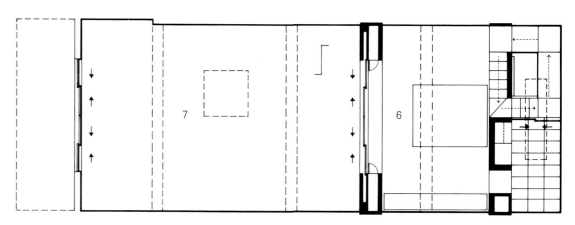

Lower level floor plan

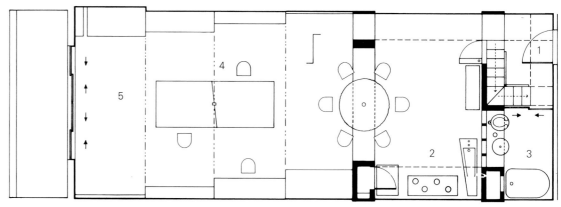

1. ENTRY
2. KITCHEN
3. BATHROOM
4. WORK AREA
5. BALCONY
6. SLEEPING AREA
7. OPEN

0   5   10

Cross section

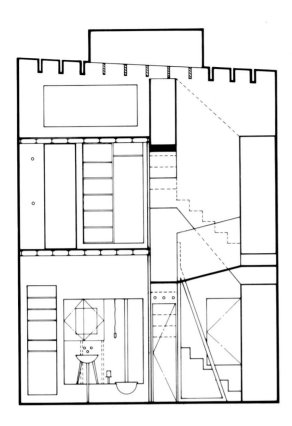

Longitudinal section

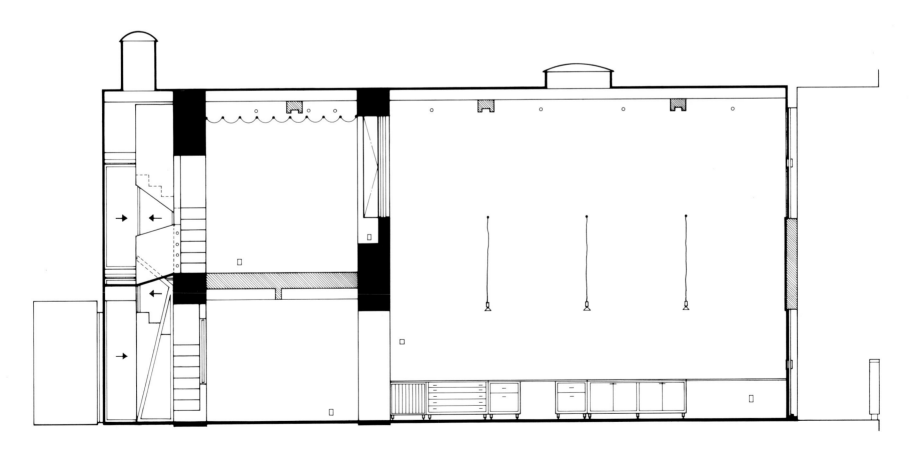

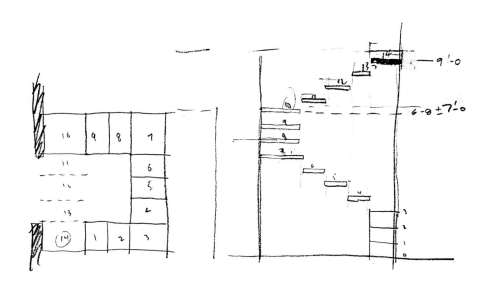

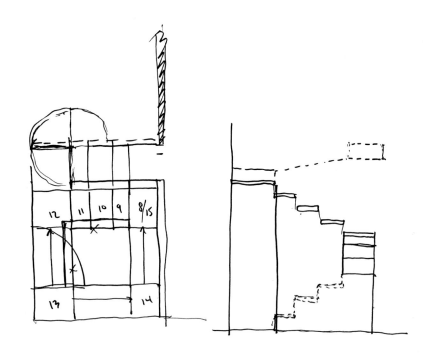

Section

Section study

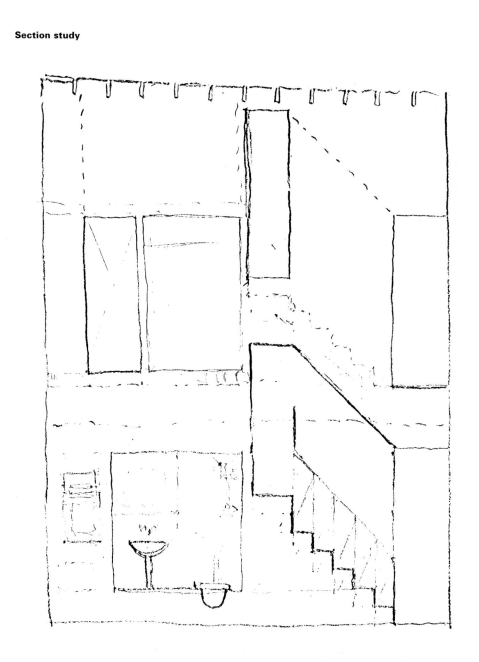

Penthouse Apartment at Greenway Plaza *1991-1994*
DAVID GUTHRIE

Owner: Name withheld at owner's request.
Architect: David Guthrie, Houston, Texas
Assistants: Rebecca Bearss, John Herrera, Karl Jensen, Christian Schmidt, Mat Greer.
Engineers: Wilson Wan (structural); Day, Brown, Rice (M.E.P.)
Consultants: T. Kondos & Associates (lighting)
General Contractor: Goodland Construction
Photography: © Richard Barnes, David Guthrie

Site: Houston, Texas
Program: Entry box, living room, study, dining room, kitchen, laundry, storage, service, bathroom, bar, guest bedroom and bathroom, master bedroom and bathroom, balcony.
Square Footage: 3300
Structural System: 2 x 6 and 2 x 4 metal studs
Mechanical System: Sub-floor forced air with linear diffusers, chill water air conditioning, electric heat element.
Major Interior Materials: Heavy gauge metal studs and metal clips (floor framing), plywood decking and maple (floors), painted sheet rock and stained particle board (walls), ceramic and glass mosaic tile, marble, 5/8" rubber (bathrooms), sandblasted glass, stainless steel (kitchen cabinets, counters, and hood), birch plywood with dyed lacewood veneer (pantry), zinc-coated metal studs and fire-rated fiberglass panels (entry).
Furnishings and Storage: Custom by architect.
Doors and Hardware: Doors custom by architect; Edward R. Butler and Co., Perko (nautical), and custom by architect.
Windows: Interior windows custom by architect.
Fixtures: Acorn "Dura-Ware" (toilets and shower controls), Chicago (kitchen faucet and rinse), Kohler (bathroom faucets).
Appliances and Equipment: Traulsen "Ultra" line (refrigerator/freezer), Thermador (wall oven), Kitchen Aid (trash compactor, dishwasher), GE (modular stove), Sharpe (convection/microwave), Sub-Zero (wine cooler), Asko (washer/dryer).
Cost: $775,000

TOP: *Entry box*
BOTTOM: *Boxes containing guest and master bathrooms along corridor toward master bedroom*
FACING PAGE: *View of dining room and aquaria toward living room*

Site/Context
Situated on the 28th floor of a thirty-story tower, the L-shaped apartment overlooks the city with a sweeping 280-degree vista across the northern horizon. The building is one of a pair of residential towers located in Greenway Plaza, one of Houston's several urban nodes, near the geographic center of the city. The towers stand among a cluster of glass-skinned office blocks and sports facilities, mediated by a series of modernist plazas. Built circa 1975, the two concrete-frame skyscrapers are rotated forty-five degrees, defying the established orthogonal grid.

LEFT: *View of apartment building*

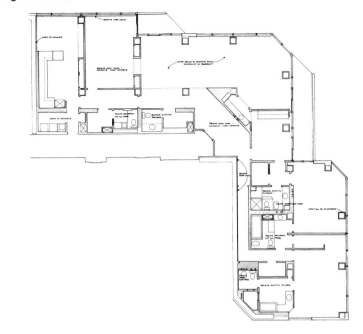

Design

Prior to the architect's intervention, the apartment was ordered as a series of small, compartmentalized spaces. To achieve the illusion of Palladian load-bearing walls, ersatz solids absorbed most of the structural columns, while those left free-standing were wrapped in camouflage. This plan restricted the space's sweeping views of the city, thereby mitigating the greatest asset of skyscraper dwelling. A central motive driving the new design was the rejection of the traditional domestic arrangement, whereby space—regardless of its structure—is manipulated to mimic a house. Instead, the architect sought to develop a design plan that offered a more appropriate fit between the idea of domesticity and physical context.

To liberate the space, the existing interior was stripped down to its naked, essential structure and the framework of concrete columns and slabs left exposed. The new construction, with its highly refined materials and complex details, establishes a certain tension between the crude structural envelope and the crafted, transitory quality of the new architecture.

Several devices were used to challenge the traditional boundaries between public and private. A group of floating boxes containing bathrooms, mechanical equipment, and storage modulates what is essentially a large, single space. Because the bathrooms push out into the public space, they act as primary elements in defining the space. The strategic placement of interior windows between the public and private areas allows shared views while it also preserves privacy. The fiberglass and sandblasted windows dematerialize both the public/private boundary and dissolve the mass of the boxes, while filling their interior space with natural light.

Construction

From the beginning, nearly every aspect of construction was subject to reevaluation; although the plan emerged early in the process, the details evolved over the course of construction. Concrete slabs, shear walls, columns, and a glass and metal skin form the basic container. The entire interior skin, like make-up thickly smeared over unsightly blemishes, obscured virtually any trace of the underlying structure that potentially interfered with the desired reading of house. The location of existing plumbing risers determined the placement of the bathrooms and kitchen.

1. CORRIDOR
2. ENTRY BOX
3. LIVING ROOM
4. STUDY
5. DINING ROOM
6. KITCHEN
7. LAUNDRY
8. STORAGE
9. SERVICE
10. TOILET
11. BAR
12. GUEST BEDROOM
13. MASTER BEDROOM
14. GUEST BATHROOM
15. MASTER BATHROOM
16. HALL
17. RETRACTABLE BED
18. BALCONY
19. AQUARIA
20. PANTRY BOX

Floor plan

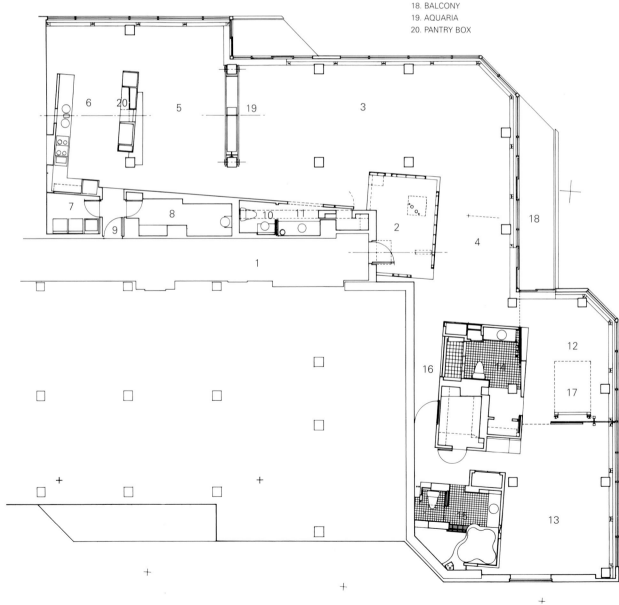

0 5 10

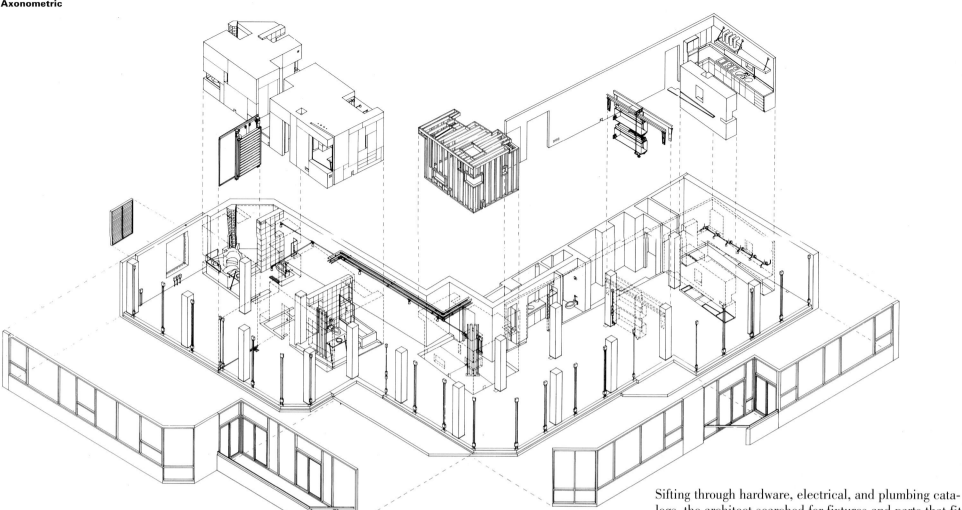

Sifting through hardware, electrical, and plumbing catalogs, the architect searched for fixtures and parts that fit a kind of engineering vernacular—undecorated, straightforward, utilitarian. The idea was to avoid simulations and elements otherwise distorted by some stylistic intent. The most fruitful catalogs turned out to be institutional (especially prison) for plumbing fixtures, industrial for electrical parts, and nautical for hardware (the kitchen drawer pulls are boat cleats). While building a framework of mass-produced elements, custom-made parts were used to fill in the gaps.

The MDF millwork was constructed on site, but most components were fabricated in respective shops. Most of the stainless and aluminum fabrication took place in a machine shop on the Rice University campus that produces research apparatus for Rice labs and NASA. (The aquarium lights were inspired by the explosion-proof fixtures used in refineries.) The heavy steel was fabricated in a small one-man shop that produces off-shore equipment for the oil industry.

Three air conditioning units are mounted above the ceilings of the "boxes." To eliminate exposed duct work or furred down ceilings, conditioned air is fed through a network of channels constructed in a six-inch space between the existing floor slab and a raised floor. To achieve this result, a frame of structural steel channels was constructed, forming a network of air channels calculated to deposit the air at the proper velocity. The supply registers are located in a continuous metal strip along the exterior perimeter. Electrical wiring and other utilities are run below the floor as well.

RIGHT: *View of entry box from public space*
BOTTOM: *View of entry box from private space*
FACING PAGE: *View of living room*

LEFT: *Aquarium seen from below*
FACING PAGES: *Views of kitchen*

Aquaria construction drawings

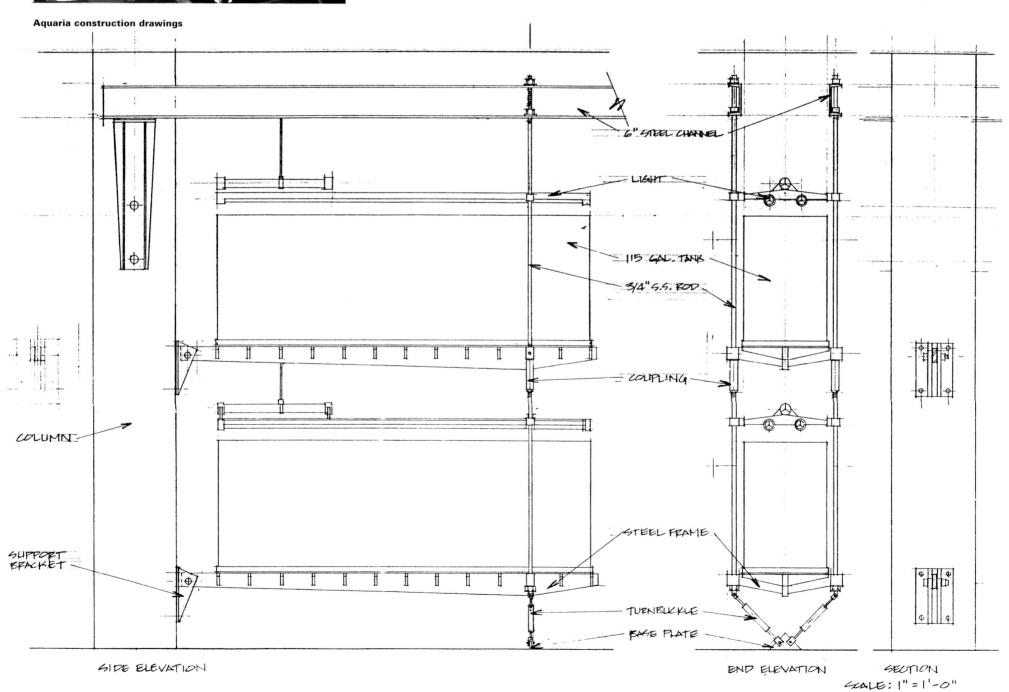

6" STEEL CHANNEL

LIGHT

115 GAL. TANK

3/4" S.S. ROD

COLUMN

COUPLING

SUPPORT BRACKET

STEEL FRAME

TURNBUCKLE

BASE PLATE

SIDE ELEVATION

END ELEVATION

SECTION
SCALE: 1" = 1'-0"

Details of pot rack and hood

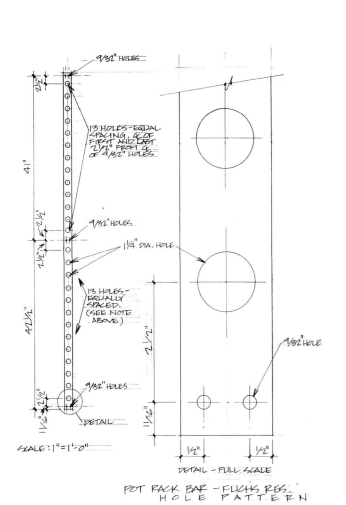

9/32" HOLES

13 HOLES-EQUAL
SPACING. ₵ OF
FIRST AND LAST
2½" FROM ₵
OF 9/32" HOLES

9/32" HOLES

1¼" DIA. HOLE

13 HOLES-
EQUALLY
SPACED.
(SEE NOTE
ABOVE)

9/32" HOLES

9/32" HOLE

DETAIL

SCALE: 1"=1'-0"

½"   ½"

DETAIL - FULL SCALE

POT RACK BAR - FLICKS RES.
H O L E   P A T T E R N

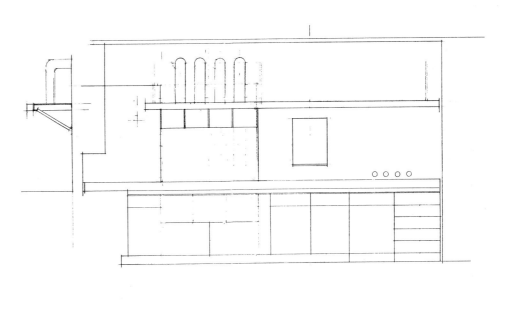

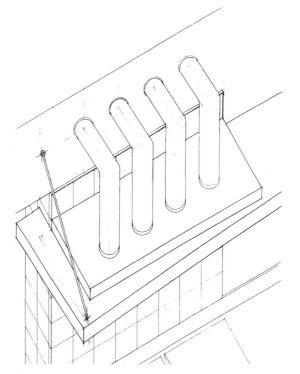

 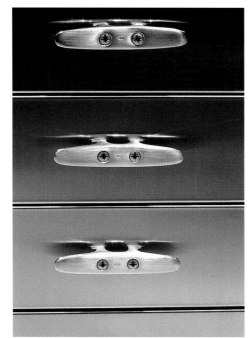  

 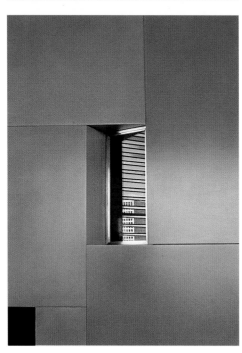  

 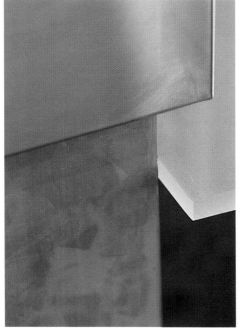  

RIGHT: *Guest bathroom*
BOTTOM: *Master bathroom*
FACING PAGE: *Details and finishes*

Exploded axonometric of bed trolley and pivot arm assembly

‡SITS UP   ‡OUT OF BED, WALKING   ‡BACK INTO BED, SITTING   ‡LIES DOWN

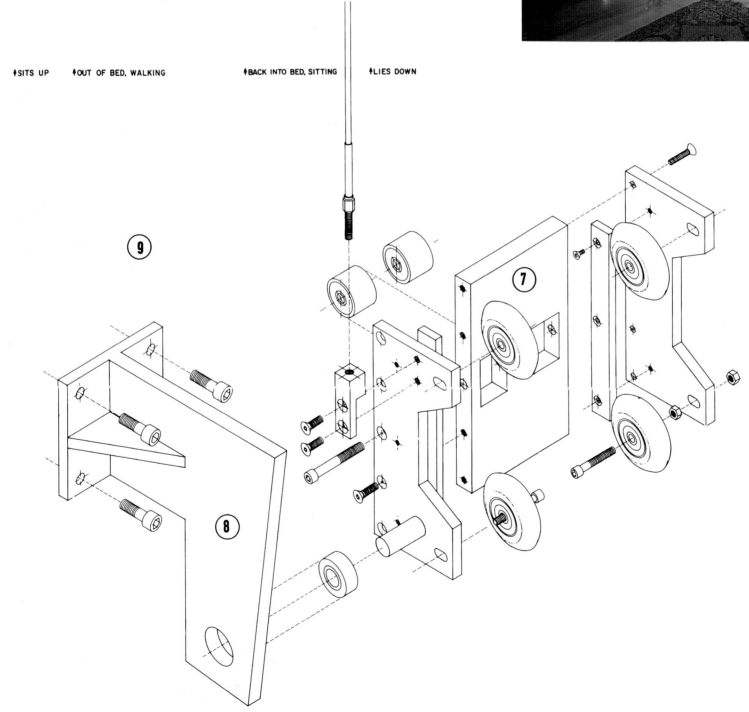

Exploded axonometric of bed assembly

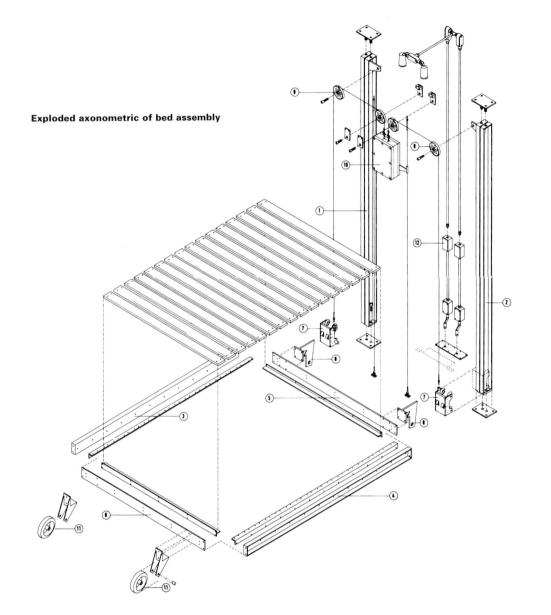

Rotating elevation of bed retraction from down to up position

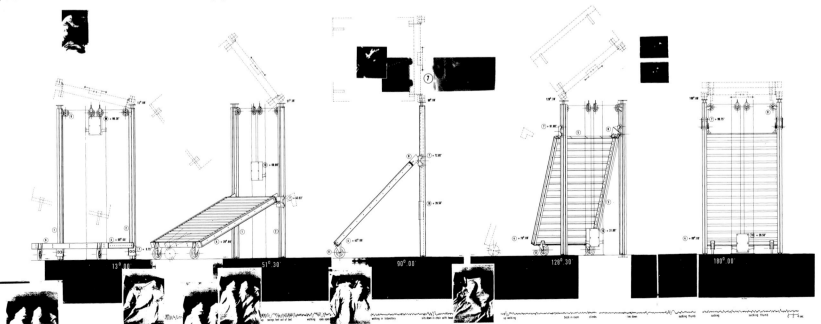

Gardner Apartment _1993–1995_
VALERIO DEWALT TRAIN ASSOCIATES

Owner: Tracy Gardner
Architect: Valerio Dewalt Train Associates, Chicago, Illinois
Design Team: Joseph Valerio (design principal), Michael Cygan, Randall Mattheis, Shawn Trentlage, Sarah Morie, Nancy Willert.
Engineers: Robert Darvas Associates (structural), WMA Consulting Engineers, Inc. (M.E.P)
General Contractor: Turner SPD
Photography: Barbara Karant, Karant + Associates

Site: Chicago, Illinois
Program: Highrise condominium with foyer, kitchen/dining space, living space, bedroom, bathroom, dressing room, study with bathroom, laundry room.
Square Footage: 800 on 2 levels
Structural System: Existing poured in place concrete frame and floor slabs.
Mechanical System: Building-supplied hot and cold water to local air handling units and baseboard radiators along windows.
Major Interior Materials: Plate aluminum (wall panels, pivot doors, suspended ceiling, floor, stair), terrazzo (floors and stair), clear finished maple (wall cabinets, wall panels, suspended ceiling, floor).
Furnishings and Storage: Built in by architect.
Doors and Hardware: Custom by architect.
Fixtures: Kroin, Elkay, American Standard; "Lucy" light fixture by Flos, "Logo" light fixtures by Italiana Luce (living space/study); "YaYaHo" cable-hung light fixture by Ingo Mauer, Pasini "Robbia Full" light fixture by Artemide (sleeping space); Citterio "Enniea" light fixtures by Artemide (kitchen).
Appliances and Equipment: Sub-Zero (refrigerator), Gaggenau (cooktop and oven).
Cost: Withheld at owner's request.

Site/Context

The apartment is located on the 64th floor of a condominium building just off Chicago's North Michigan Avenue. The windows open north to a dramatic view of Chicago's Gold Coast neighborhood and the shore line of Lake Michigan. The view is also dominated by the John Hancock Tower.

Design

The two-story apartment is divided between "ceremonial" and "functional" spaces. Into a single space the architect inserted two idealized boxes: one of metal on the first level and one of wood on the second. These containers define the ceremonial space within the apartment. The boxes are extremely thin, barely substantial enough to retain their form. In homage to the nearby John Hancock Tower, each box is "warped" by the Tower's gravitational pull. The aluminum shell is defined by a series of straight lines that are orthogonal to either the city grid or the angled sides of the Tower. The curves of the wood shell run tangent to an imagined circle passing through the four outer corners of the Hancock.

LEFT: *View of apartment building*

The leftover space between the walls of these new containers and the apartment's outer walls provides space for sleeping, cooking, bathing, and storage. The surface of each container is hinged to provide access to the different functional areas. The media center, for instance, is both idealized and functional, having attached itself to one of the pivoting metal panels with access to the sleeping and bathing area as well as the ceremonial space.

Construction

The key spaces in the apartment are finished in materials that have a pure iconic quality. Eight-foot-high aluminum rotating panels were fabricated from single-thickness aluminum plate. Aluminum ribs were welded to the back side to add rigidity. Custom pivot hinges are located at the top and bottom of the moving panels. Aluminum panels are adhered to the ceiling and floor, while aluminum plate is folded and then welded on edge to an aluminum wall panel.

The curving wood wall at the study is made of maple veneer plywood. Plywood panels are held together by metal tabs that have been slotted into the edge of the panel. The panels are hung from a series of brackets made of square aluminum tubing. Brackets are bolted to the concrete deck above.

Upper mezzanine floor plan

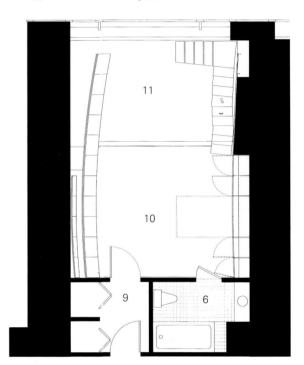

1. ENTRY
2. KITCHEN
3. DINING ROOM
4. LIVING ROOM
5. BEDROOM
6. BATHROOM
7. DRESSING ROOM
8. CLOSET
9. EXISTING CLOSET
10. STUDY
11. OPEN

Lower floor plan

0   5   10

LEFT: *View of wood wall in mezzanine study*

Sketch of wood wall's structural elements

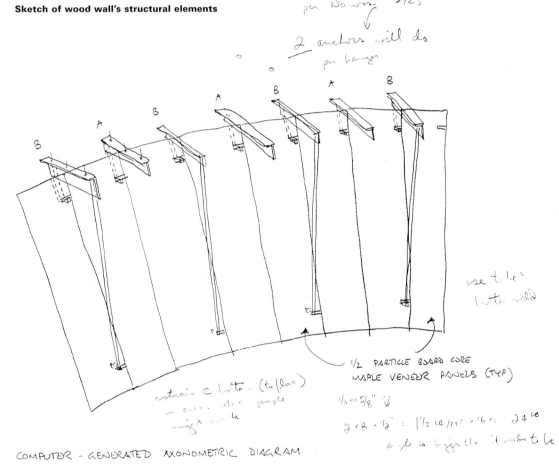

½ PARTICLE BOARD CORE
MAPLE VENEER PANELS (TYP)

COMPUTER - GENERATED AXONOMETRIC DIAGRAM

Rendering of wood and metal containers

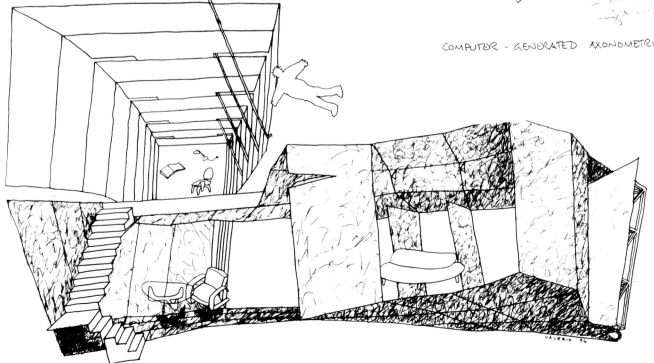

55

TOP: *View of stair from living room*
BOTTOM: *Bathroom; pivoting media center*
FACING PAGE: *View from entry toward living room*

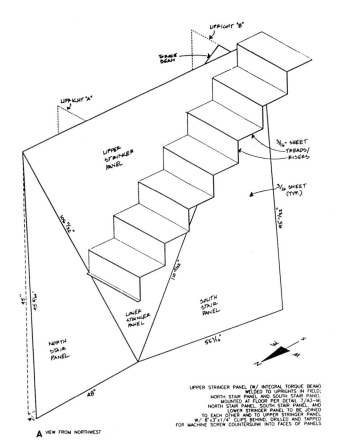

Axonometric diagrams of stair assembly

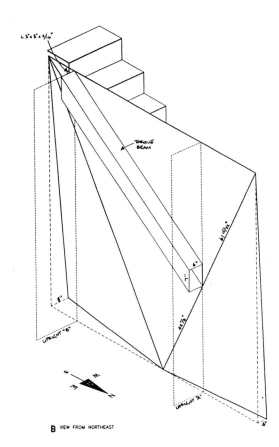

UPPER STRINGER PANEL (W/ INTEGRAL TORQUE BEAM)
WELDED TO UPRIGHTS IN FIELD;
NORTH STAIR PANEL AND SOUTH STAIR PANEL
MOUNTED AT FLOOR PER DETAIL 7/A3-M;
NORTH STAIR PANEL, SOUTH STAIR PANEL, AND
LOWER STRINGER PANEL TO BE JOINED
TO EACH OTHER AND TO UPPER STRINGER PANEL
W/ 6"x3"x1/4" CLIPS BEHIND, DRILLED AND TAPPED
FOR MACHINE SCREW COUNTERSUNK INTO FACES OF PANELS

A VIEW FROM NORTHWEST

B VIEW FROM NORTHEAST

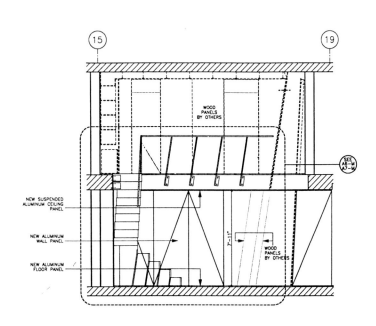

ABOVE: *View of stair*

Section

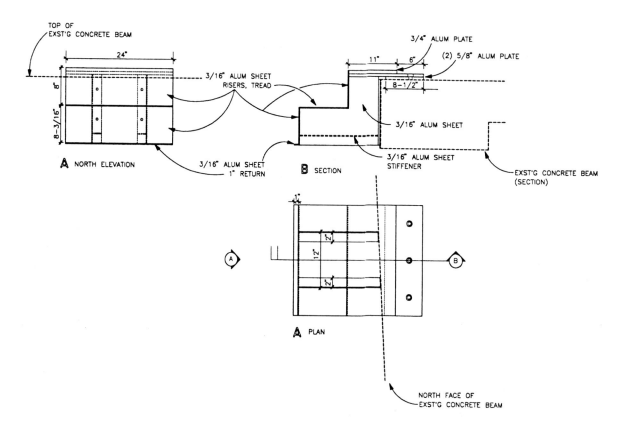

Stair plan details

A NORTH ELEVATION

B SECTION

A PLAN

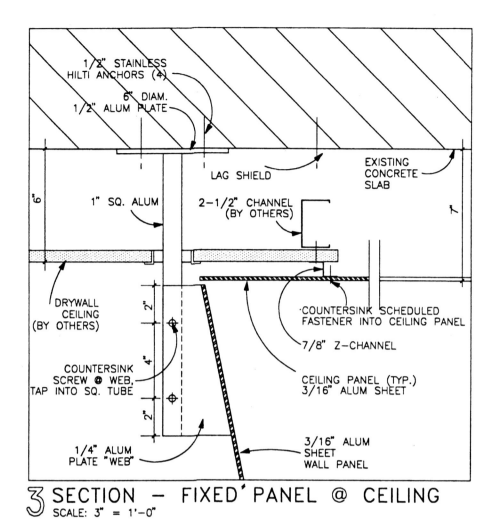

3 SECTION – FIXED PANEL @ CEILING
SCALE: 3" = 1'-0"

Labels (top-left detail):
- 1/2" STAINLESS HILTI ANCHORS (4)
- 6" DIAM. 1/2" ALUM PLATE
- LAG SHIELD
- EXISTING CONCRETE SLAB
- 6"
- 1" SQ. ALUM
- 2-1/2" CHANNEL (BY OTHERS)
- 1"
- DRYWALL CEILING (BY OTHERS)
- COUNTERSINK SCHEDULED FASTENER INTO CEILING PANEL
- 2"
- COUNTERSINK SCREW @ WEB, TAP INTO SQ. TUBE
- 4"
- 7/8" Z-CHANNEL
- CEILING PANEL (TYP.) 3/16" ALUM SHEET
- 2"
- 1/4" ALUM PLATE "WEB"
- 3/16" ALUM SHEET WALL PANEL

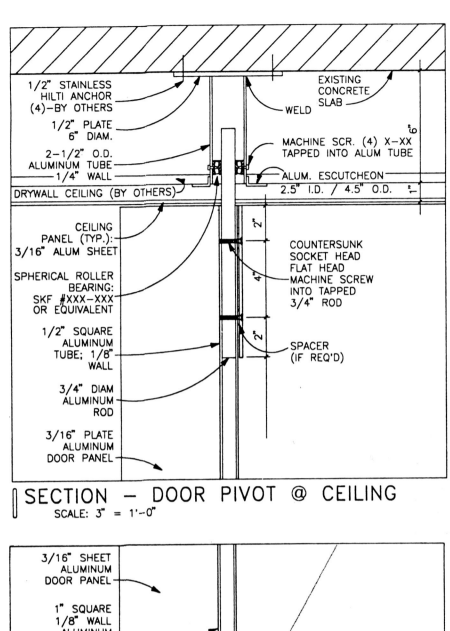

1 SECTION – DOOR PIVOT @ CEILING
SCALE: 3" = 1'-0"

Labels (top-right detail):
- 1/2" STAINLESS HILTI ANCHOR (4)-BY OTHERS
- 1/2" PLATE 6" DIAM.
- 2-1/2" O.D. ALUMINUM TUBE
- 1/4" WALL
- DRYWALL CEILING (BY OTHERS)
- EXISTING CONCRETE SLAB
- WELD
- MACHINE SCR. (4) X–XX TAPPED INTO ALUM TUBE
- ALUM. ESCUTCHEON 2.5" I.D. / 4.5" O.D.
- 6"
- 1"
- CEILING PANEL (TYP.): 3/16" ALUM SHEET
- 2"
- SPHERICAL ROLLER BEARING: SKF #XXX–XXX OR EQUIVALENT
- COUNTERSUNK SOCKET HEAD FLAT HEAD MACHINE SCREW INTO TAPPED 3/4" ROD
- 4"
- 1/2" SQUARE ALUMINUM TUBE; 1/8" WALL
- 2"
- SPACER (IF REQ'D)
- 3/4" DIAM ALUMINUM ROD
- 3/16" PLATE ALUMINUM DOOR PANEL

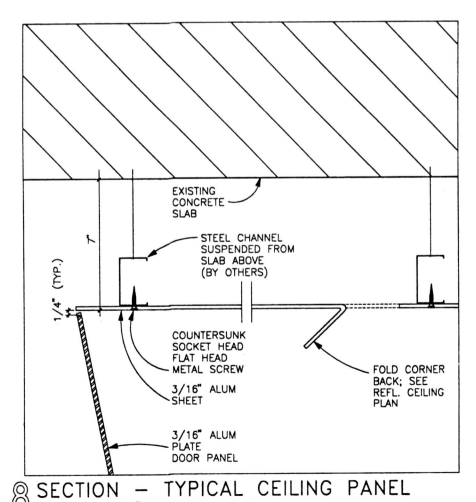

8 SECTION – TYPICAL CEILING PANEL
SCALE: 3" = 1'-0"

Labels (bottom-left detail):
- EXISTING CONCRETE SLAB
- 1"
- 1/4" (TYP.)
- STEEL CHANNEL SUSPENDED FROM SLAB ABOVE (BY OTHERS)
- COUNTERSUNK SOCKET HEAD FLAT HEAD METAL SCREW
- 3/16" ALUM SHEET
- FOLD CORNER BACK; SEE REFL. CEILING PLAN
- 3/16" ALUM PLATE DOOR PANEL

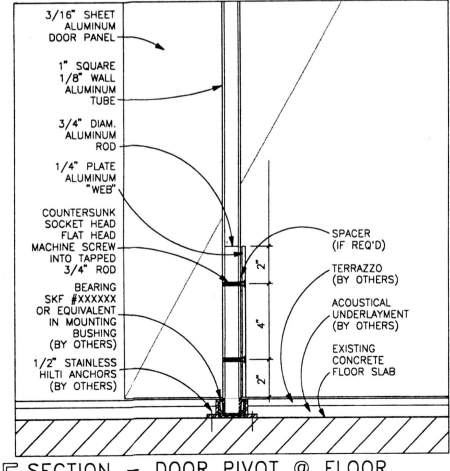

5 SECTION – DOOR PIVOT @ FLOOR
SCALE: 3" = 1'-0"

Labels (bottom-right detail):
- 3/16" SHEET ALUMINUM DOOR PANEL
- 1" SQUARE 1/8" WALL ALUMINUM TUBE
- 3/4" DIAM. ALUMINUM ROD
- 1/4" PLATE ALUMINUM "WEB"
- COUNTERSUNK SOCKET HEAD FLAT HEAD MACHINE SCREW INTO TAPPED 3/4" ROD
- BEARING SKF #XXXXXX OR EQUIVALENT IN MOUNTING BUSHING (BY OTHERS)
- 1/2" STAINLESS HILTI ANCHORS (BY OTHERS)
- SPACER (IF REQ'D)
- TERRAZZO (BY OTHERS)
- ACOUSTICAL UNDERLAYMENT (BY OTHERS)
- EXISTING CONCRETE FLOOR SLAB
- 2"
- 4"
- 2"

Stainless Steel Apartment

1993-1995

KRUECK & SEXTON ARCHITECTS

Owner: Name withheld at owner's request.
Architect: Krueck & Sexton Architects, Chicago, Illinois
Design Team: Ronald Krueck (design principal), Mark P. Sexton (project principal), Miles Linblad (project architect).
Engineer: Tylk Gustafson & Associates
General Contractor: Fraser Construction
Photography: Paul Warchol, Marco Lorenzeti/Korab Hedrich-Blessing

Site: Chicago, Illinois
Program: Entry, living room, dining room, kitchen, study, office, 2 powder rooms, service, master bedroom, bath, and closet, 2 children's bedrooms with bathroom, storage.
Square Footage: 3400
Structural System: Steel structure with composite concrete and steel deck
Mechanical System: Existing baseboard heat and Space-Pak air conditioning
Major Interior Materials: Glass chip terrazzo, stainless steel, colored stainless steel.
Furnishings and Storage: Custom by architect, Ateier International
Doors and Hardware: Custom by architect, Schlage, Dorma
Fixtures: Custom by architect, Kroin
Appliances and Equipment: Sub-Zero (refrigerator/freezer), Gaggenau (cooktop and oven)
Cost: Withheld at owner's request.

Site/Context

This apartment for a family of four is located on the top floors of a Mies van der Rohe steel and glass highrise building in Chicago.

Design

The clients desired a minimally furnished and dynamically detailed space that would reflect and extend the design Mies conceived for the building. The plans for the apartment are organized around a new stair element with an articulated floor opening that ties the upper and lower floors into a legible architectural volume. The informal living spaces—kitchen, dining room, study, and children's bedrooms—are located on the lower level and the formal spaces—living room, office, and master bedroom—are on the upper level.

The two levels' spatial continuum extends both horizontally and vertically. The layering of common elements and the inclusion of various materials—specified for their visual strength, durability, and ease of maintenance—affect the perception of light, space, and texture.

RIGHT: *View of living room*

LEFT: *View of apartment building*

Construction

The stair, the apartment's main architectural element, required some clever maneuvering on the part of the architects in order to be completed as specified. The treads cantilever out from a string with half-inch-thick steel walls that runs along one side and is welded to two barely perceptible columns. When it came time to weld the tube to the columns, the string warped from the heat. To solve the problem, the architects tracked down a retired bridge straightener from Indiana for help. Chains were first wrapped around the tube and secured around the building's exterior. The tube was then reheated and the chains winched to pull the string back in line.

Existing conditions

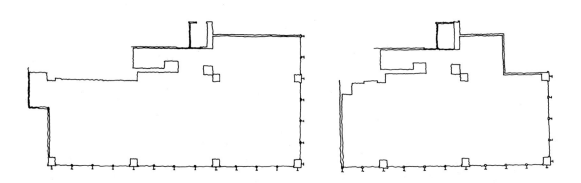

Preliminary sketch

Upper level floor plan

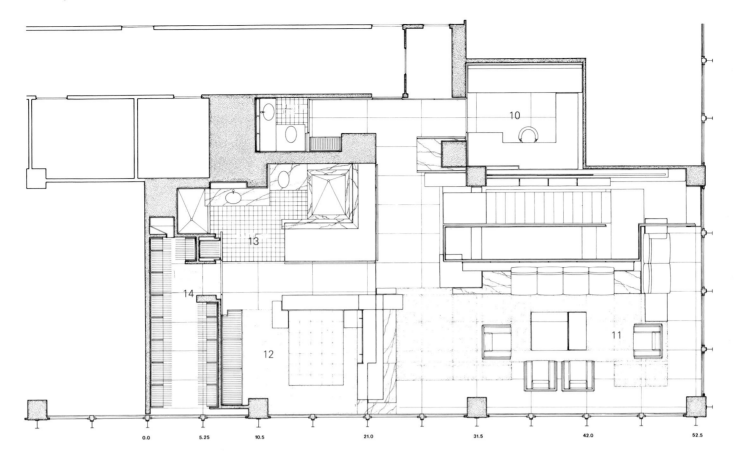

Lower level floor plan

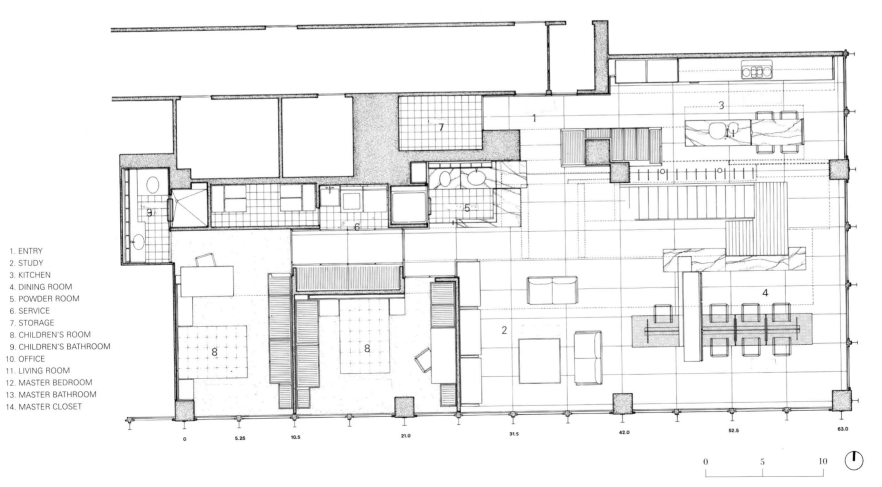

1. ENTRY
2. STUDY
3. KITCHEN
4. DINING ROOM
5. POWDER ROOM
6. SERVICE
7. STORAGE
8. CHILDREN'S ROOM
9. CHILDREN'S BATHROOM
10. OFFICE
11. LIVING ROOM
12. MASTER BEDROOM
13. MASTER BATHROOM
14. MASTER CLOSET

0   5   10

RIGHT: *Views of cantilevered stair*

Section with stair in elevation

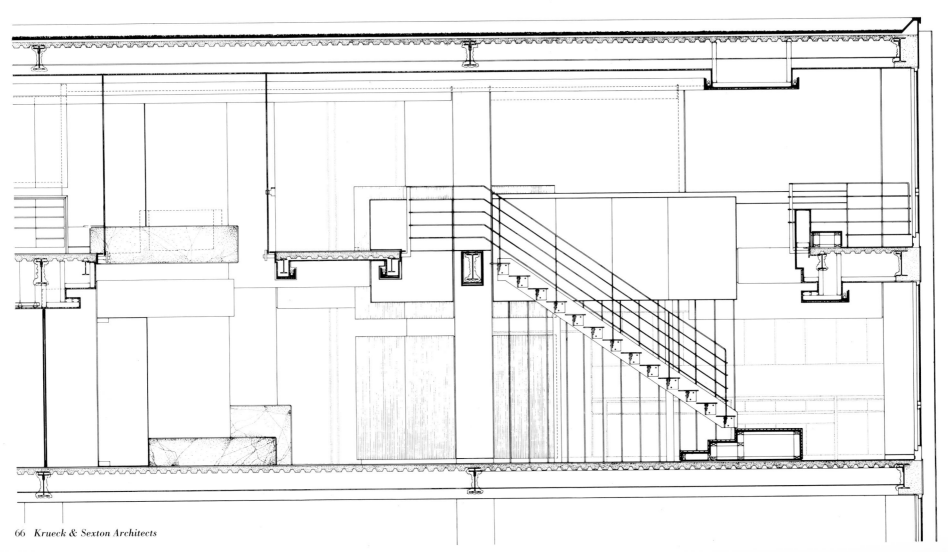

Rendering of stair details

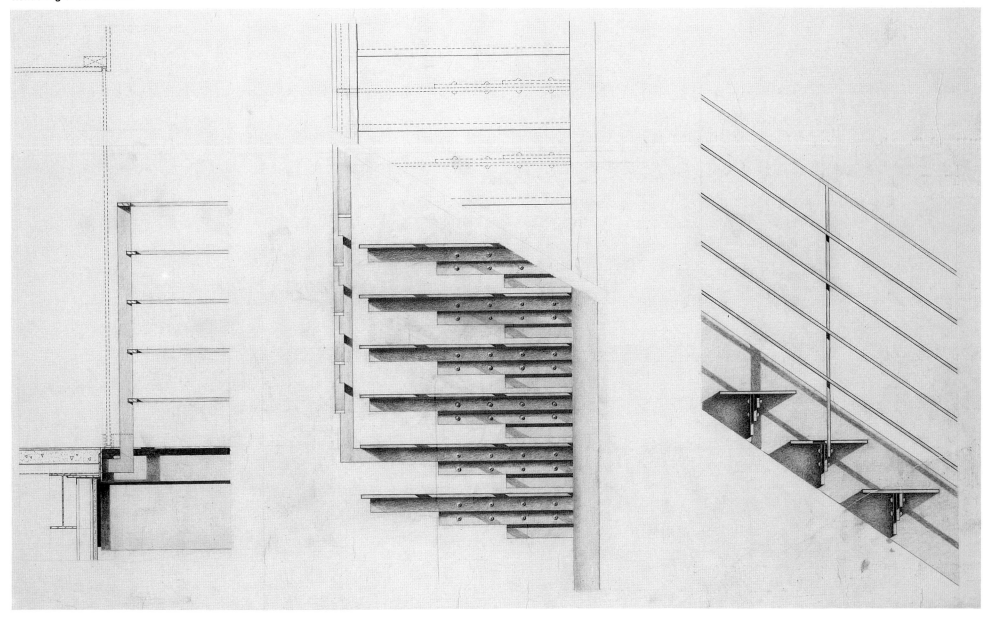

Jamb and dining room divider details

Soffit/fascia detail at master bathroom

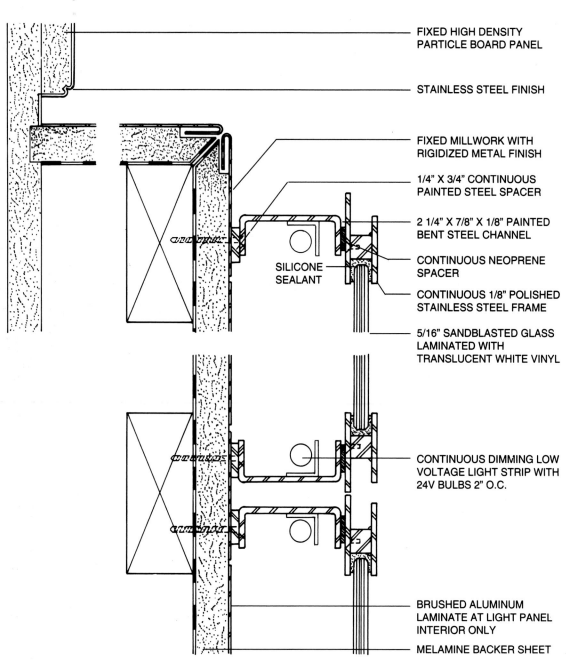

FIXED HIGH DENSITY
PARTICLE BOARD PANEL

STAINLESS STEEL FINISH

FIXED MILLWORK WITH
RIGIDIZED METAL FINISH

1/4" X 3/4" CONTINUOUS
PAINTED STEEL SPACER

2 1/4" X 7/8" X 1/8" PAINTED
BENT STEEL CHANNEL

SILICONE
SEALANT

CONTINUOUS NEOPRENE
SPACER

CONTINUOUS 1/8" POLISHED
STAINLESS STEEL FRAME

5/16" SANDBLASTED GLASS
LAMINATED WITH
TRANSLUCENT WHITE VINYL

CONTINUOUS DIMMING LOW
VOLTAGE LIGHT STRIP WITH
24V BULBS 2" O.C.

BRUSHED ALUMINUM
LAMINATE AT LIGHT PANEL
INTERIOR ONLY

MELAMINE BACKER SHEET

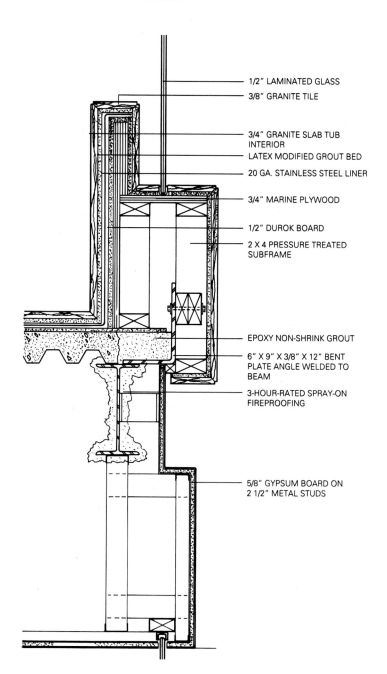

1/2" LAMINATED GLASS

3/8" GRANITE TILE

3/4" GRANITE SLAB TUB
INTERIOR

LATEX MODIFIED GROUT BED

20 GA. STAINLESS STEEL LINER

3/4" MARINE PLYWOOD

1/2" DUROK BOARD

2 X 4 PRESSURE TREATED
SUBFRAME

EPOXY NON-SHRINK GROUT

6" X 9" X 3/8" X 12" BENT
PLATE ANGLE WELDED TO
BEAM

3-HOUR-RATED SPRAY-ON
FIREPROOFING

5/8" GYPSUM BOARD ON
2 1/2" METAL STUDS

Soffit/fascia detail at entry bridge

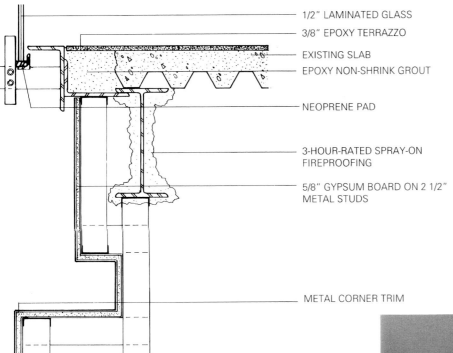

- 1/2" LAMINATED GLASS
- 3/8" EPOXY TERRAZZO
- EXISTING SLAB
- EPOXY NON-SHRINK GROUT
- NEOPRENE PAD
- 3-HOUR-RATED SPRAY-ON FIREPROOFING
- 5/8" GYPSUM BOARD ON 2 1/2" METAL STUDS
- METAL CORNER TRIM

Interior on Central Park West

1987-1988

AGREST & GANDELSONAS, ARCHITECTS

Owner: Name withheld at owner's request.
Architect: Agrest and Gandelsonas, Architects, New York, New York
Design Team: Diana Agrest, AIA, Mario Gandelsonas, AIA (designers); Kevin Kennon (associate); Jeff Inaba, Tom Van Der Bout (assistants).
Engineer: Robert Sillman (structural)
General Contractor: Clark Construction
Photography: Paul Warchol

Site: New York, New York
Program: Complete renovation including exterior walls of duplex apartment. Entry level: Double-height entry hall, living room, dining room, media room, kitchen, breakfast area, exercise room, guest room. Upstairs: Master bedroom suite open to living room, dressing area, master bathroom, 2 bedrooms with private bathrooms.
Square Footage: 5500
Structural System: Dry construction, metal studs, skin coated and painted gypsum board
Mechanical System: Central air conditioning
Major Interior Materials: Lace wood and Pomele veneers, stainless steel, hot rolled treated steel, steel mesh, White Oak floors , 12"x12" black ceramic tiles, green viridian antique marble, flamed granite, carpeting.
Furnishings and Storage: Custom by architect: Stainless steel and leather Cone chair and Cone stool, pearwood and leather mannequin chair and ottoman, stainless steel and mahogany Flamingo table, silk velvet settee, silk velvet chair, makerai and silk DIA daybed, crutch mahogany and hot-rolled steel Suspended Elliptical Table and Suspended Circular Table, stainless steel and glass coffee table, mahogany and hot-rolled steel side table.
Doors and Hardware: Custom by architect.
Windows: Custom by architect.
Fixtures: Custom by architect.
Appliances and Equipment: Traulsen (refrigerators, wine cooler), Thermador (cooktop), hood custom by architect.

Site/Context

This project involved the renovation—including exterior walls—of a Manhattan duplex on Central Park West.

Design

With particular emphasis on the urban works of Loos and Mies, the architects explored the intersection of architecture and the city in this Central Park West interior. The first floor is punctuated by a pinwheel plan and curved stair. The pinwheel plan alternately appears as a figure in a neutral modern space while it also organizes the apartment's separate spaces, thereby allowing for the kind of spatial flow found in the free plan. The blurring of oppositions is carried through to the detailing, where luxury and austerity go hand in hand. The sequence of spaces and openings unfold from front to back, as though the interior space was being pierced by the forces of the city.

RIGHT: *View of living room, bar, and stair to upper level*

LEFT:
View of apartment building

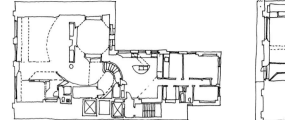

The apartment design subverts traditional notions of quality of materials and detailing and aims to deconstruct the separation between furniture and architecture. In this space, where materials, such as steel and wood abut each other while retaining their own characteristics. Further, the architects made use of complex sleight-of-hand detailing to achieve the desired effect of simplicity.

Doors are another important element. The portals cut into the fireplace wall between the living and dining rooms invoke the notion of continuous space. The waist-high steel plates on either side of the opening are flush against the wood wall, as if they were leaning against it, and the alabaster lintel above it is treated as a floating plane that is almost dematerialized. The thickness of the door that separates the living room from the media room creates a kind of transitional space, in this case the bar.

Construction

The architects reconfigured the entire space, as the existing apartment had been gutted prior to renovation. Dining room and kitchen window openings were modified, and new windows—custom by the architect—were installed. An elaborate sound system is centrally located, yet individual controls can be manipulated rom every room. A media center was also discreetly accommodated, set into the wall on the other side of the bar.

Upper level floor plan

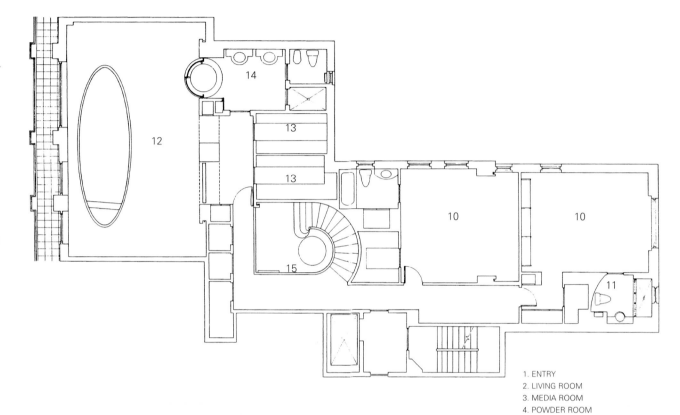

1. ENTRY
2. LIVING ROOM
3. MEDIA ROOM
4. POWDER ROOM
5. PRIVATE HALL
6. DINING ROOM
7. BREAKFAST ROOM
8. KITCHEN
9. GYM
10. BEDROOM
11. BATHROOM
12. MASTER BEDROOM
13. WALK-IN CLOSET
14. MASTER BATHROOM
15. HALL

Lower level floor plan

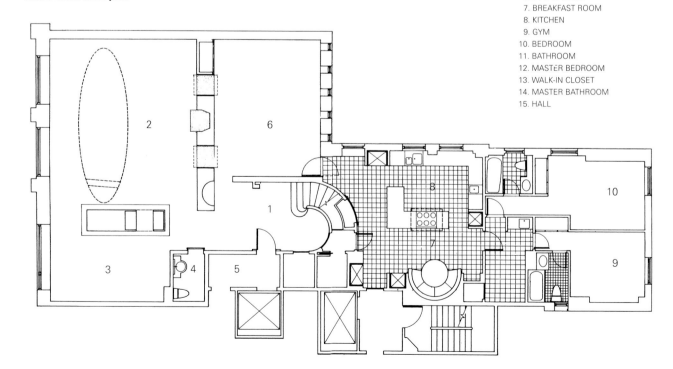

0   5   10

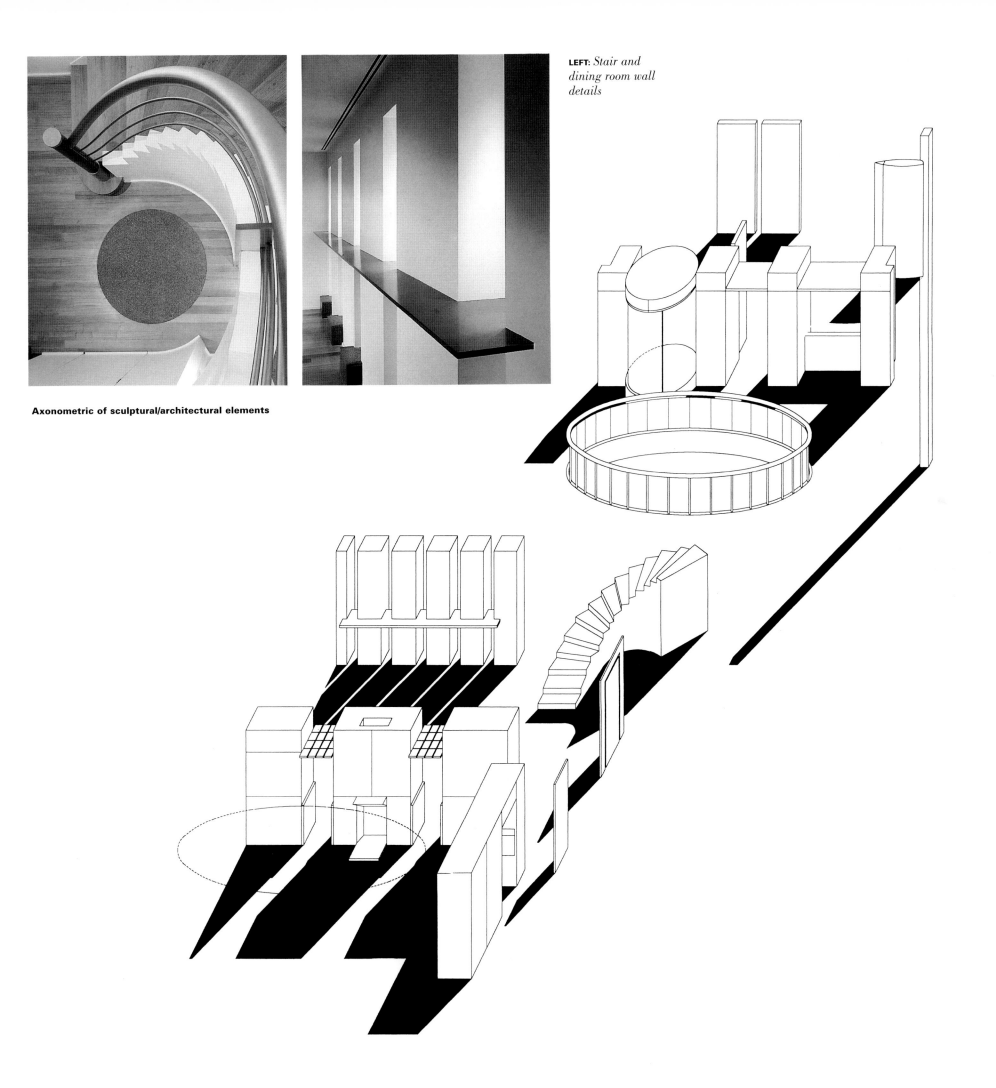

Axonometric of sculptural/architectural elements

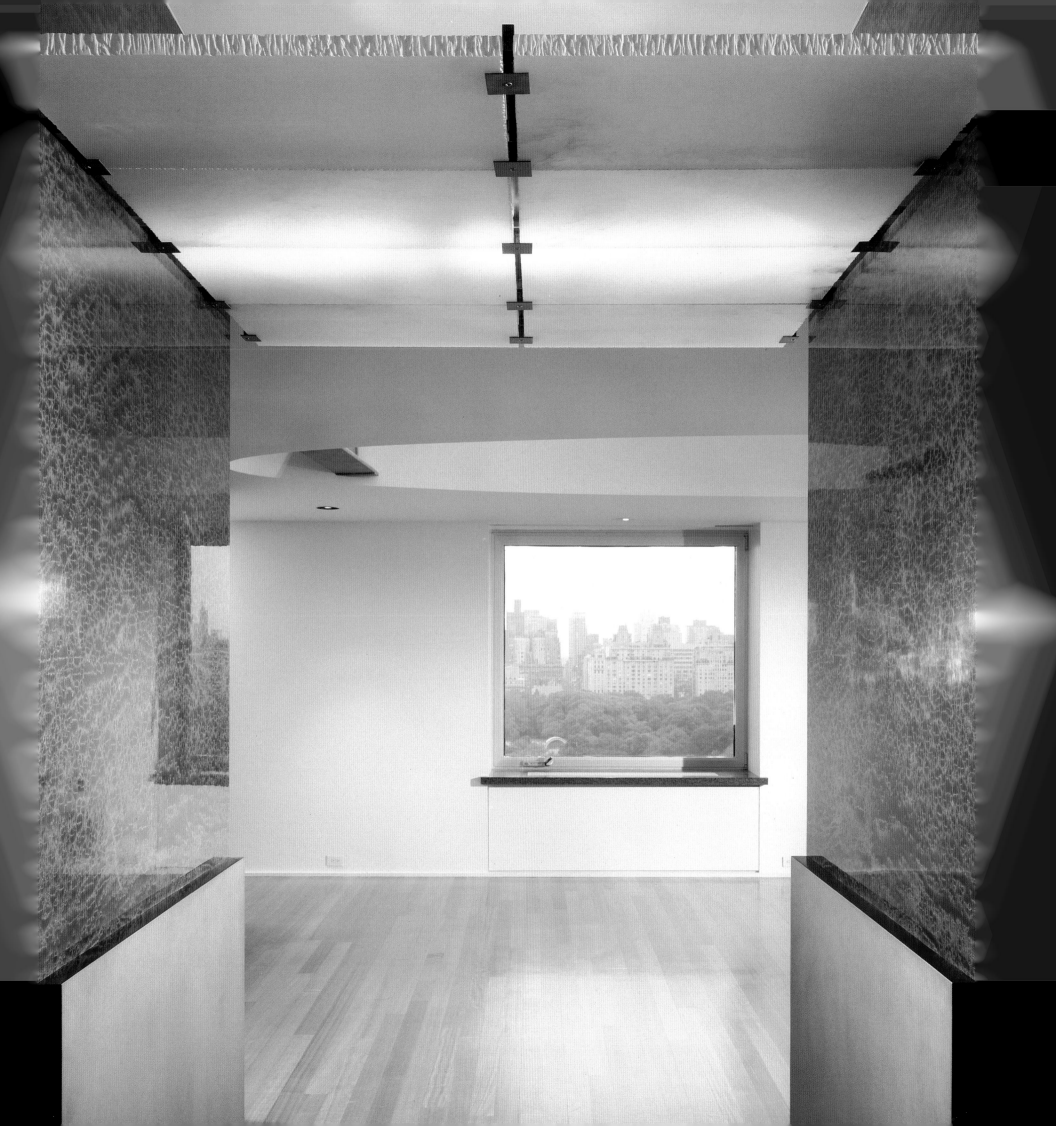

Whirlpool construction details

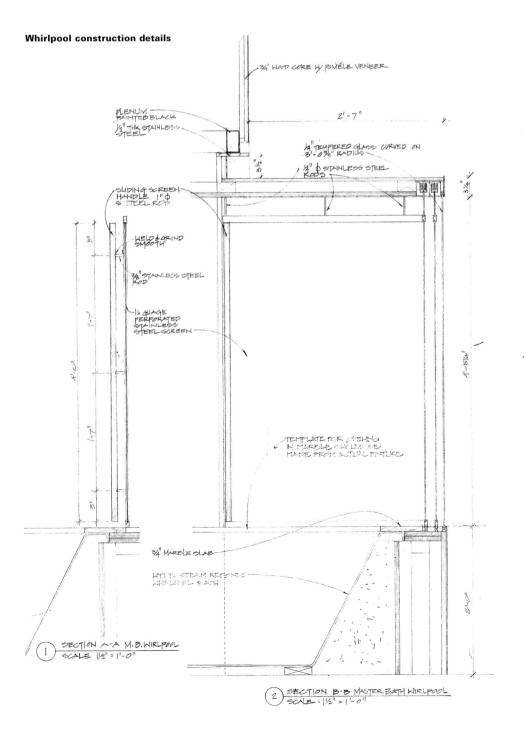

¾" WOOD CORE W/ POMELE VENEER

PLENUM PAINTED BLACK
⅛" THK STAINLESS STEEL

2'-7"

¼" TEMPERED GLASS CURVED ON 3'-0⅝" RADIUS

½" ⌀ STAINLESS STEEL RODS

SLIDING SCREEN HANDLE. 1" ⌀ ⌀ STEEL ROD

WELD & GRIND SMOOTH

⅜" STAINLESS STEEL ROD

16 GUAGE PERFORATED STAINLESS STEEL SCREEN

TEMPLATE FOR OPENING IN MARBLE TO BE MADE FROM ACTUAL FIXTURE

¾" MARBLE SLAB

HYDRO STEAM REGENCY WHIRLPOOL BATH

① SECTION A-A M.B. WHIRLPOOL
SCALE: 1½" = 1'-0"

② SECTION B-B MASTER BATH WHIRLPOOL
SCALE: 1½" = 1'-0"

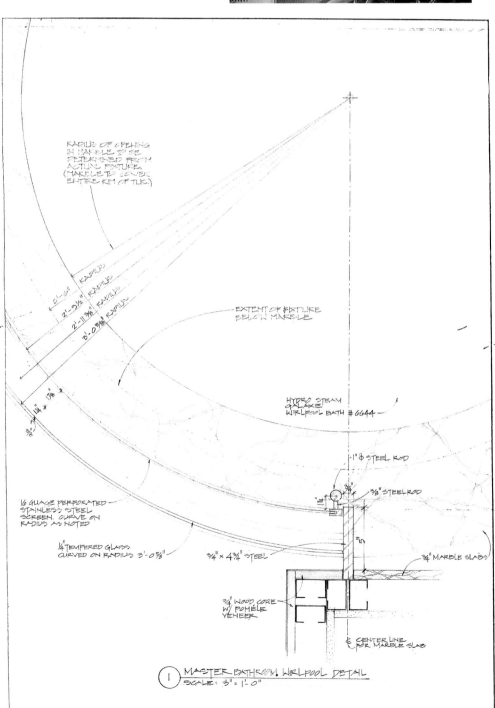

RADIUS OF OPENING IN MARBLE TO BE DETERMINED FROM ACTUAL FIXTURE. (MARBLE TO COVER ENTIRE RIM OF TUB)

2'-6" RADIUS
2'-9½" RADIUS
2'-11¾" RADIUS
3'-0⅝" RADIUS

EXTENT OF FIXTURE BELOW MARBLE

HYDRO STEAM GALAXIE WHIRLPOOL BATH # 6644

1" ⌀ STEEL ROD

⅜" STEEL ROD

16 GUAGE PERFORATED STAINLESS STEEL SCREEN. CURVE ON RADIUS AS NOTED

¼" TEMPERED GLASS CURVED ON RADIUS 3'-0⅝"

¾" x 4¾" STEEL

¾" MARBLE SLABS

¾" WOOD CORE W/ POMELE VENEER

℄ CENTER LINE FOR MARBLE SLAB

① MASTER BATHROOM WHIRLPOOL DETAIL
SCALE: 3" = 1'-0"

Steel sliding pantry door details

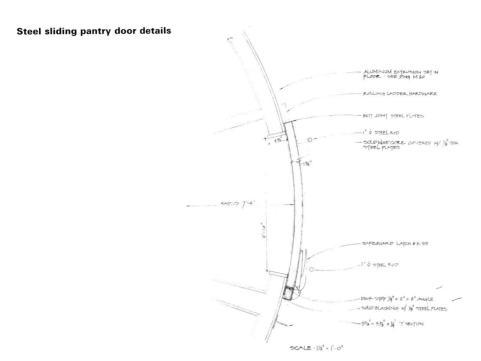

ALUMINUM EXTRUSION SET IN FLOOR · SEE DWG M-20

ROLLING LADDER HARDWARE

BUTT JOINT STEEL PLATES

1" Ø STEEL ROD

SOLID WOOD CORE COVERED W/ 1/8" THICK STEEL PLATES

RADIUS 7'-6"

SAFEGUARD LATCH # K-55

1" Ø STEEL ROD

DOOR STOP 1/4" × 2" × 2" ANGLE
SOLID BLOCKING W/ 1/8" STEEL PLATES
3 3/8" × 3 3/8" × 1/4" 'T' SECTION

SCALE · 1 1/2" = 1'-0"

RIGHT: *Curved steel door to pantry on library ladder tracks*

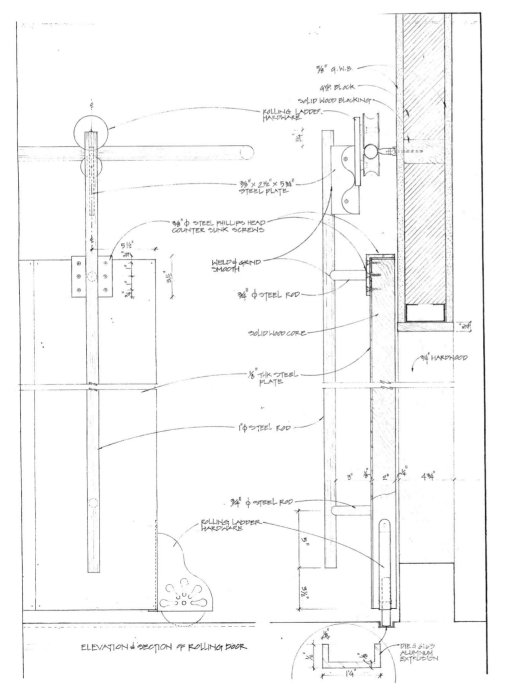

5/8" G.W.B.
GYP. BLOCK
SOLID WOOD BLOCKING
ROLLING LADDER HARDWARE

3/8" × 2 1/2" × 5 3/4" STEEL PLATE

3/8" Ø STEEL PHILLIPS HEAD COUNTER SUNK SCREWS

5 1/2"

WELD & GRIND SMOOTH

3/4" Ø STEEL ROD

SOLID WOOD CORE

1/8" THK STEEL PLATE

1" Ø STEEL ROD

3/4" HARDWOOD

3" 2" 4 3/4"

3/4" Ø STEEL ROD

ROLLING LADDER HARDWARE

ELEVATION & SECTION OF ROLLING DOOR

DIE # 6163 ALUMINUM EXTRUSION

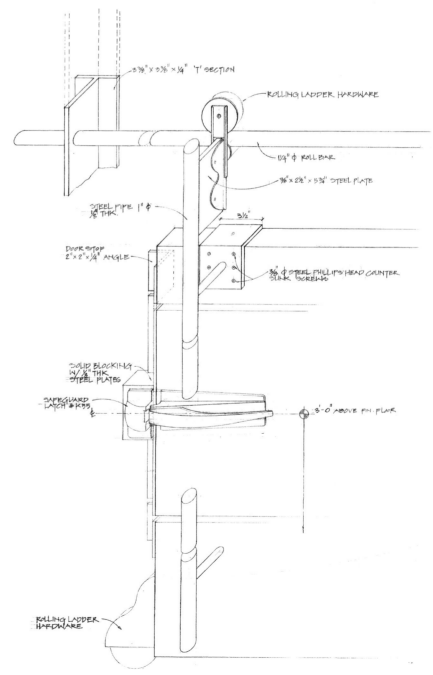

3 3/8" × 3 3/8" × 1/4" 'T' SECTION

ROLLING LADDER HARDWARE

1 1/4" Ø ROLL BAR

3/8" × 2 1/2" × 5 3/4" STEEL PLATE

STEEL PIPE 1" Ø 1/8" THK.

DOOR STOP 2" × 2" × 1/4" ANGLE

3 1/2"

3/8" Ø STEEL PHILLIPS HEAD COUNTER SUNK SCREWS

SOLID BLOCKING W/ 1/8" THK STEEL PLATES

SAFEGUARD LATCH # K-55

3'-0" ABOVE FIN. FLOOR

ROLLING LADDER HARDWARE

79

Back Bay Residence *1988-1991*
MACHADO AND SILVETTI
ASSOCIATES

Owner: Donald Brecher
Architect: Machado and Silvetti Associates, Inc., Boston, Massachusetts
Design Team: Rodolfo Machado, Jorge Silvetti, Adolfo Perez-Leiva, Douglas Dolezal, Barry Price.
General Contractor: Connaughton Brothers
Photography: Paul Warchol, Douglas Dolezal

Site: Back Bay, Boston, Massachusetts
Program: Renovation of townhouse duplex unit including living/dining room, kitchen, bedroom, library, dressing room, 2 bathrooms, powder room.
Square Footage: 2880
Structural System: Existing wood frame
Mechanical System: Forced-air heating and air conditioning
Major Interior Finishes: Lacewood, satinwood, pomelle mahogany, bird's-eye maple veneers, travertine, black granite, stainless steel, frosted glass.
Furnishings and Storage: Built-in by architects.
Fixtures: Capri, Halo, Lucifer
Appliances and Equipment: Sub-Zero, Gaggenau
Cost: Withheld at owner's request.

Site/Context

This renovated townhouse unit is located in Boston's historic Back Bay neighborhood, a section of the city characterized by gridded streets with a uniform urban fabric of nineteenth-century brick townhouses. On the top two floors of a typical five-story townhouse, the apartment is one of five units within the previously subdivided townhouse. The strict zoning regulations of the Back Bay did not permit exterior modifications, and interior alterations were limited by the existing conditions (such as the locations of load-bearing walls and the presence of mechanical systems shared with other apartments).

Design

Given these restrictions and the impossibility of substantially altering the spatial layout of the unit, the overall architectural strategy was to refine, modify, and formalize the existing spatial order through the introduction of new elements. Therefore, all the new work was articulated almost like individual pieces of furniture in order to provide architectural coherence within the apartment.

RIGHT: *View of living/dining room and stair to lower level*

LEFT: *View of townhouse*

Existing conditions

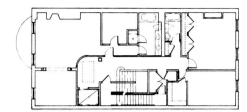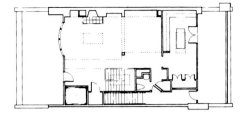

The design concentrated on materials, finishes, and details as a means to establish the character of the project. The architects chose a palette of materials with striking and unique natural qualities: strong, deep color and pattern in the wood paneling and stone, texture and opaqueness in the glass. The interventions were treated as veneers, panels, or planes that were applied to or set within the existing rooms. Visually stronger and richer materials were used on the vertical surfaces, such as the walls and cabinet faces (lacewood, satinwood, pomelle mahogany— all sustainable species— and gray/green travertine). These contrast with more neutral materials (black granite and plain maple) on the horizontal surfaces, such as the floors and countertops.

Larger elements such as fireplaces, the staircase, and cabinetry give complexity and richness to the existing building's shell. For example, in the living-dining room on the upper level, the visual play of materials centers on the fireplace—with the remainder of the room treated more neutrally—to establish an important focal point for the space. Symmetrical and objectlike, the fireplace is made of satinwood, steel, granite, and sandblasted glass. Two satinwood panels (detailed to display that they are veneers) open to show a slot of polished stainless steel that reveals the viewer's distorted image—a reinterpretation of the traditional mirror located over the mantel.

The design strategy for secondary spaces followed in a similar vein. Understood as occupiable objects in their own right, the bathrooms, dressing room, and kitchen were designed in a more encompassing manner, with materials and a level of detailing similar to those seen in the fireplace and staircase. In the private dressing room, wood cabinetry frames a green leather seat and encloses the intimate space. Just beyond, the master bathroom is defined by panels of veined travertine and frosted glass, while upstairs, the kitchen is clad in wood and glass on the vertical surfaces, with more muted stone countertops and floors.

Construction

Because of the fixed nature of the wood-framed and load-bearing masonry walls with spanning wood rafters, construction of the new elements followed an additive process. Veneers were fastened to wood strapping over the existing walls. Cabinets as well as 3/4-inch stone and one-inch wood panels were premanufactured in a shop, brought to the site, and then assembled in place.

Upper level floor plan

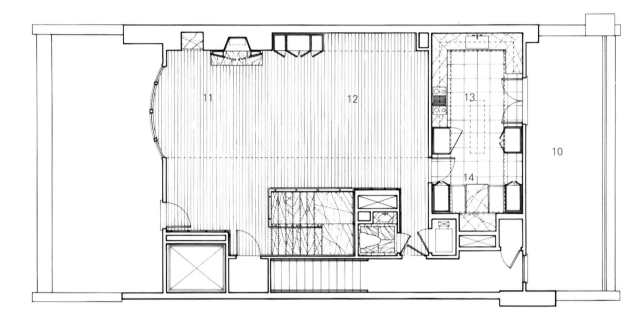

Lower level floor plan

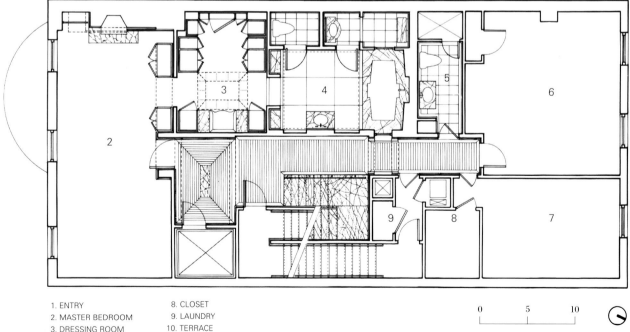

1. ENTRY
2. MASTER BEDROOM
3. DRESSING ROOM
4. MASTER BATHROOM
5. BATHROOM
6. FUTURE LIBRARY
7. GUEST BEDROOM
8. CLOSET
9. LAUNDRY
10. TERRACE
11. LIVING ROOM
12. DINING ROOM
13. KITCHEN
14. BREAKFAST ROOM

0   5   10

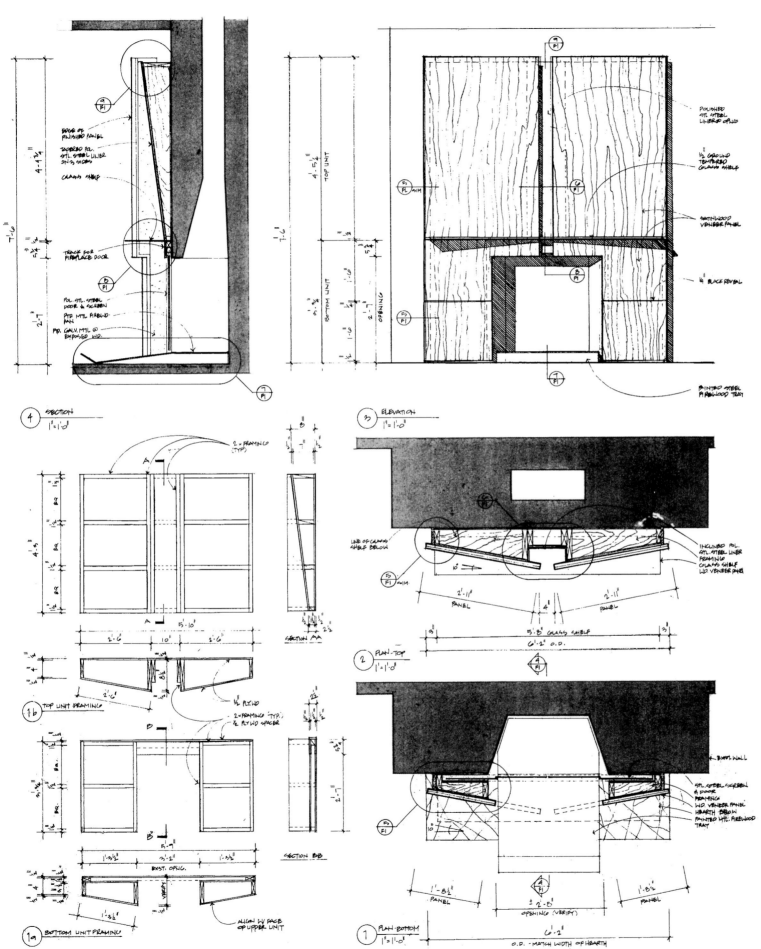

TOP: *View of dressing room*
BOTTOM: *Views of master bathroom*
FACING PAGE:
View of living/dining room with stair descending to lower level

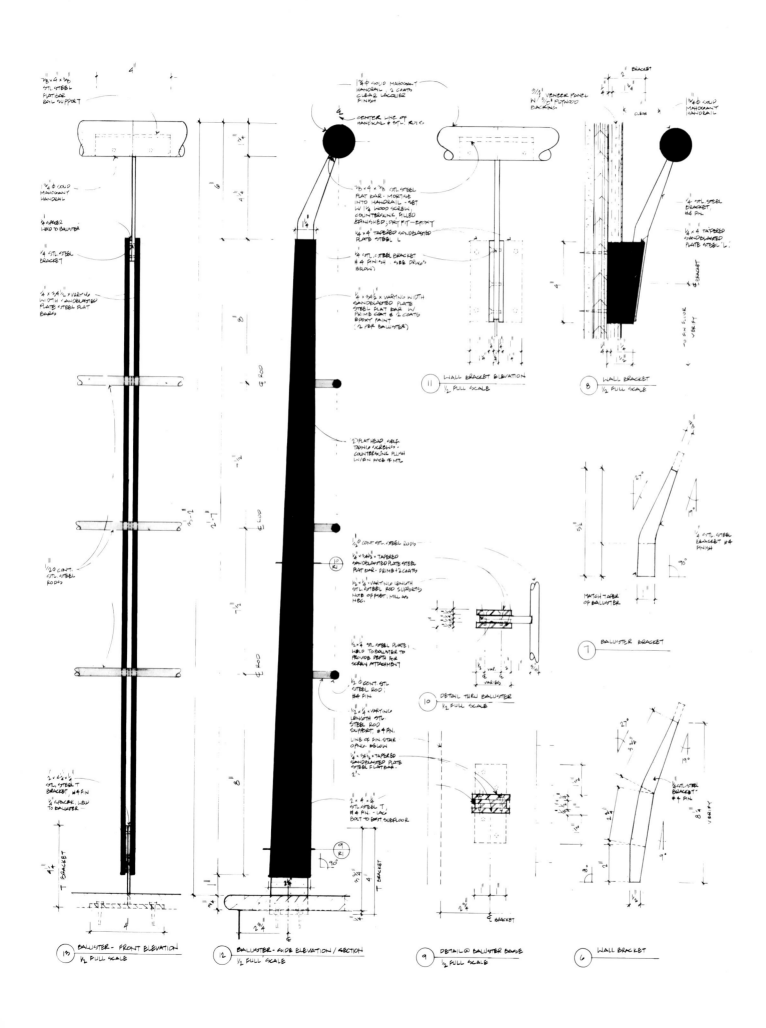

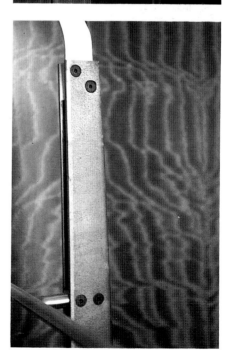

Cooper Bauer Apartment

1988-1989

DENISON/LUCHINI ARCHITECTS

Owner: Michael Cooper and Nancy Bauer
Architect: Denison/Luchini Architects, St. Louis, Missouri
Design Team: Dirk Denison and Adrian Luchini (project architects), Hunter Fleming, Mark Koeninger, Michael Moran.
General Contractor: Balance One Inc., Boston, Massachusetts
Photography: Jon Jensen, originally published in *Metropolitan Home* magazine, a publication of Hachette Filipacchi Magazines, Inc.; Adrian Luchini

Site: Boston, Massachusetts
Program: Single-family apartment including living room, dining room, kitchen, master bedroom, master bathroom, library, study rooms, music room.
Square Footage: 3800 in 3 floors
Structural System: Existing 12 x 12 wooden post and beam and 4 x 14 joists
Mechanical System: Forced air
Major Interior Materials: Laminated birch (walls), copper (walls, fireplace), maple (floors, doors), marble (bathrooms), gypsum board (walls), steel and bronze (stairs).
Furnishings and Storage: Built in by architect.
Doors and Hardware: Custom by architect.
Fixtures: Kohler, American Standard
Appliances and Equipment: Sub-Zero (refrigerator), "Ziggara" by Marco Zanuso (water closet)
Cost: $250,000

Site/Context

Located in the old "leather district" of the city of Boston, the apartment occupies three partial floors of an old warehouse building.

Design

The existing apartment's levels are interconnected by a three-story atrium space. Public spaces—the main entry, living room, dining room, kitchen, and music room—are on the fourth floor. Above, one finds the master bedroom suite (including dressing area, reading area, and master bedroom), along with a sitting area and two study rooms. The library, which also doubles as a guest room, is on the top floor.

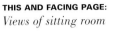

THIS AND FACING PAGE:
Views of sitting room

LEFT: *View of former warehouse building*

Two fundamental moves organize the spatial arrangement. A long wall clad in copper organizes the master bedroom suite and the study room on the second level. Further, a wall that splits between the first and second level divides the music room from the living area and the master bath/dressing zone from the sitting area. In this way, all the private spaces remain isolated from the public ones while maintaining spatial definition in the context of the plan.

Construction

Walls are finished in both birch veneer on plywood and in copper. The apartment's existing wood floors were refinished, and slate tiles installed in the master bathroom.

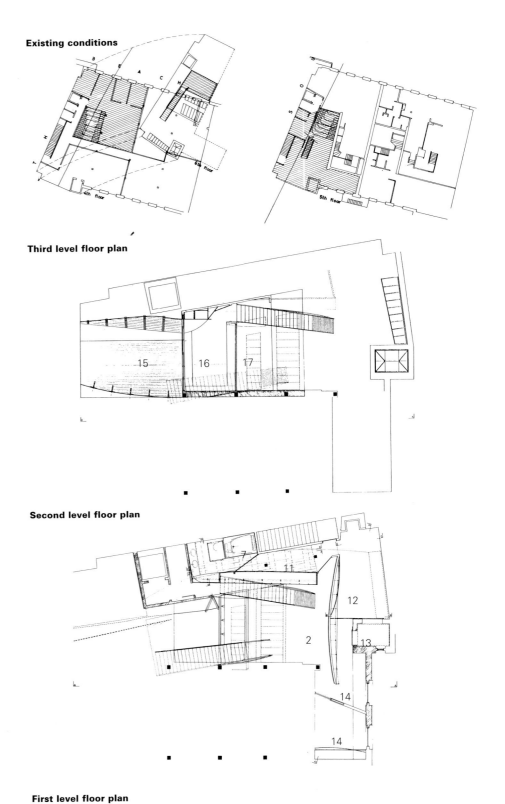

Existing conditions

Third level floor plan

Second level floor plan

First level floor plan

1. ENTRY
2. SITTING ROOM
3. DINING ROOM
4. KITCHEN
5. STORAGE
6. MECHANICAL ROOM
7. BATHROOM
8. LAUNDRY
9. MUSIC ROOM
10. BAR
11. DRESSING ROOM
12. MASTER BEDROOM
13. READING ROOM
14. STUDY
15. TERRACE
16. LIBRARY
17. OPEN

0   5   10

Composite drawing of stair and treated walls

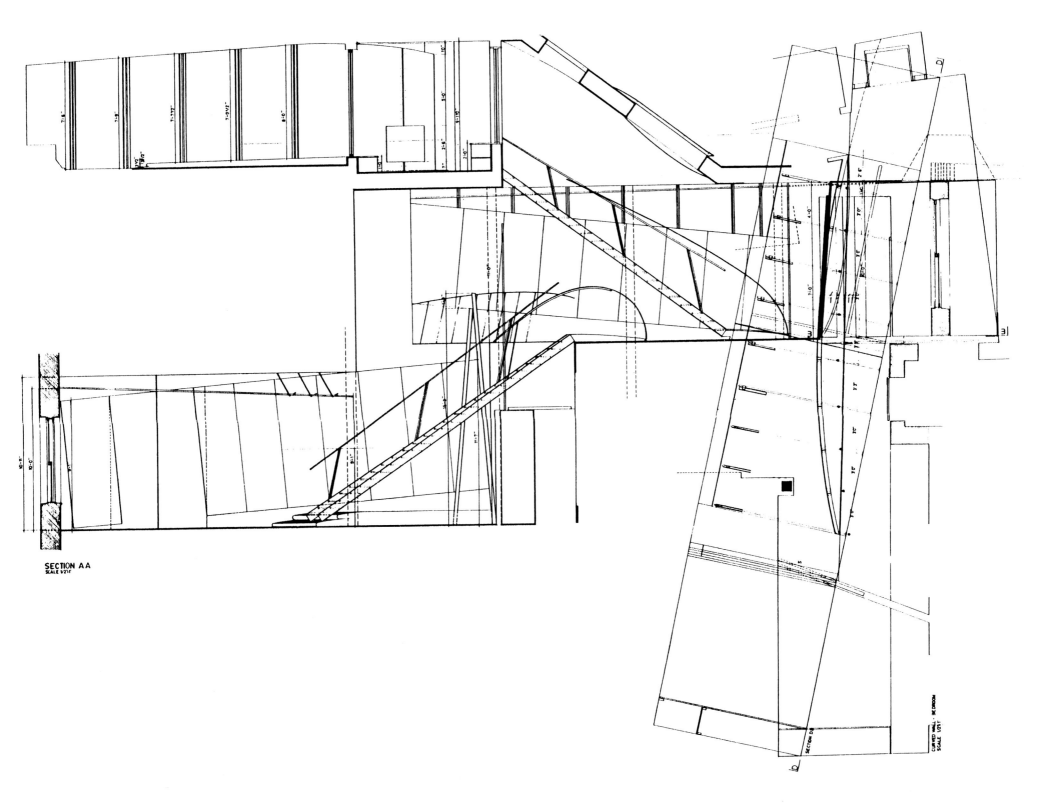

SECTION A A
SCALE 1/2"1'

Preliminary sketch

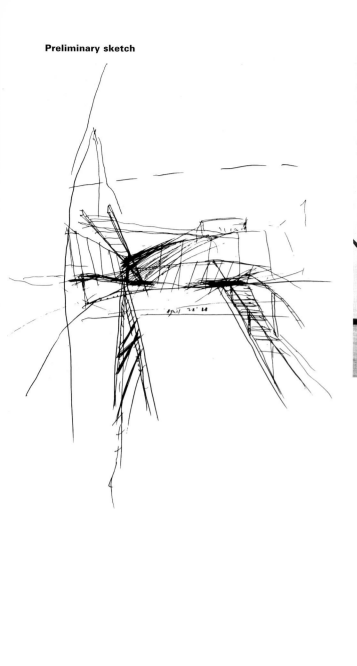

Stair details

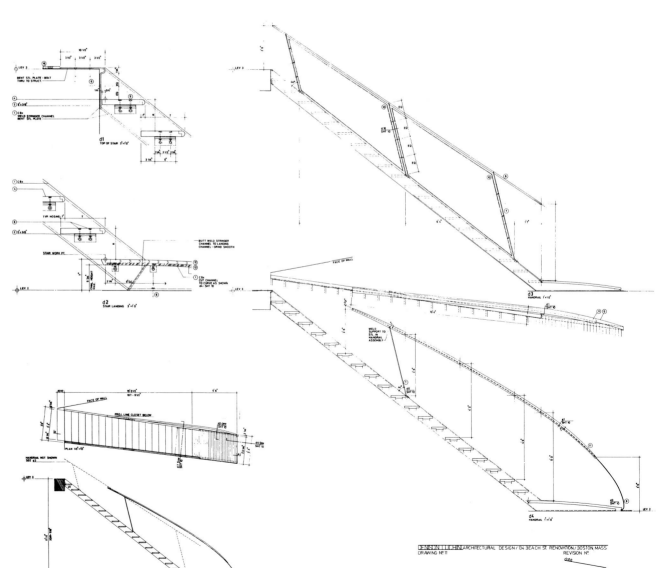

Wall assembly details

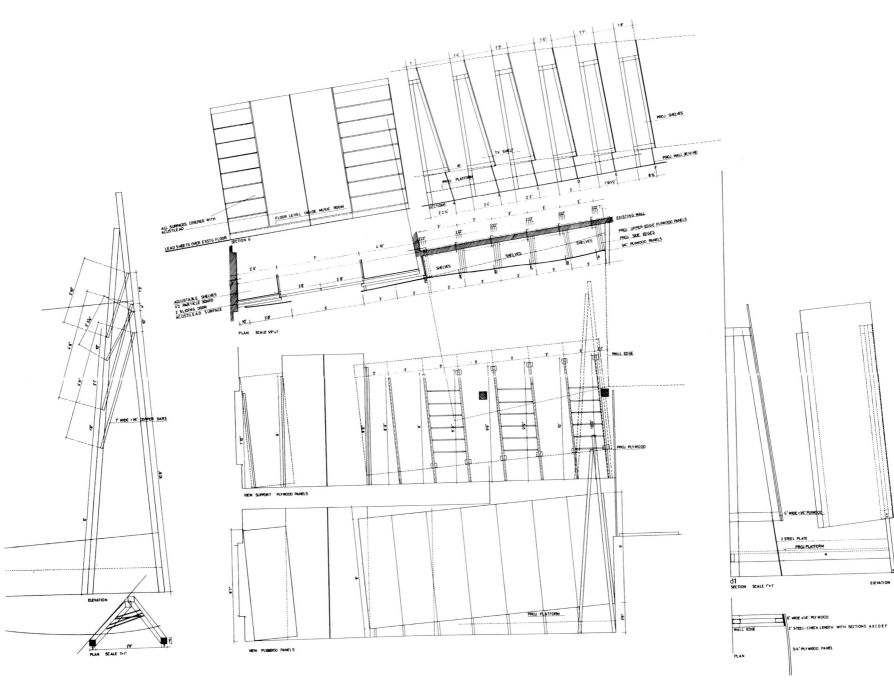
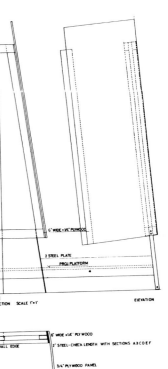

East Side Apartment *1988-1991*
JOSEPH GIOVANNINI & ASSOCIATES

Owner: Name withheld at owner's request.
Architect: Joseph Giovannini & Associates, New York, New York
Design Team: Edwardo Calma, David Kesler, Berj Malikian, Zoran Belog.
Engineer: Guy Nordensen (structural)
Photography: Michael Mundy, © Wayne N.T. Fujii, © Arch Photo, Inc. Edward Hueber

Site: New York, New York
Program: Foyer, living room, dining room, kitchen, maid's bedroom and bathroom, powder room, sitting room, master bedroom and bathroom, toilet, washroom, 2 bedrooms, bathroom.
Square Footage: 3350 in 2 floors
Structural System: Existing steel structure
Mechanical System: Remote-feed window air conditioners
Major Interior Materials: Tropical wood, frosted glass, anodized aluminum, steel.
Furnishings and Storage: Custom by architect.
Doors and Hardware: Custom by architect.
Fixtures: Custom by architect.
Appliances and Equipment: Sub-Zero (refrigerator)
Cost: Withheld at owner's request.

Site/Context

Located on the last two floors of a prewar brick-and-limestone building, the corner apartment enjoys south and west exposures and a view over a nearby Eastside park. While the building is not a designated historic monument, it is adjacent to a historic district and its occupants draw on the neighborhood's turn-of-the-century ethos for a sense of how to run the co-op and how to conceptualize the character of the building. They take great pride in its interiors, especially in such details as the moldings.

Design

The existing apartment's original character had been severely compromised in a 1931 renovation that left it with mixed moldings and a warren of small rooms on the second floor. The floor plan, which assumed both downstairs and upstairs maids, was also antiquated. The new owners favor a contemporary lifestyle and wanted to integrate the back rooms into the body of a reinvented plan. Governed by the rules of the building's co-op board, the architect kept most of the existing classical walls and moldings.

The design began without formal or organizational preconceptions in what Giovannini calls an "energy drawing." Allowing a "passive" pencil to sense moments of intensity, the architect created a drawing whose build-up yielded a conceptual strategy. The drawing revealed that the apartment's liveliness—the sun, view, fireplaces, and main living areas—was at the front of the apartment.

RIGHT: *View of living/dining space with custom furniture by architect*

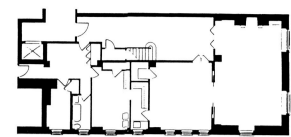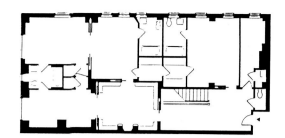

The new design had to distribute the advantages from the privileged front spaces to the underprivileged rear. The freehand sketch revealed a strong "desire line" running from the front of the apartment to the rear, breaking through an existing wall between the living room and dining room and thrusting toward the kitchen. Because the co-op board required keeping the apartment's right-angled geometry, the architect could not build the diagram in plan. The architect created a system of built-in, site-specific furniture—sculptures that establish a second architectural order to usher the light, view, and openness to the rear. Many elements of the program—cupboards, TV screen, light reflectors, counters, vanities, and bedboards—were accommodated as pieces of furniture. Some didn't even need to be drawn into the apartment's plan, as they were attached to walls and never touch the floors. In other words, they weren't "architecture," despite their architectural consequences, and so they didn't have to be approved by the board. The classical walls and moldings extended into what had been servant areas.

Rather than subordinate the old to the new or the new to the old, or fusing historical and contemporary styles into a transitional look, Giovannini used two contradictory design languages in the apartment. The energy diagram suggested the new furniture be conceived as debris caught in a storm moving through the apartment. The storm flows to the back of the first floor, rises through the second floor, and flows out to the front of the second floor, subsiding finally in front of the view that inspired it a floor below. The kitchen is the most intense moment in the apartment, where the storm swirls into a vortex that forces its way up through the ceiling into the hallway above, spinning out toward the front of the second floor via a series of balcony rails, benches, and desks. The storm creates a seating eddy on the landing, a desk area in the study, and a vanity in the master bath. The fragments—no more than a system of wood or metal built-ins—seem to penetrate walls and floors, establishing a feeling of movement within a masonry case that otherwise remains contained, static, and classical.

Construction

Construction materials for new walls were standard wood-stud construction with sheet rock. The surfaces, however, were intended to create a foggy, dematerialized environment, an impression achieved with frosted glass and exotic woods whose grains flicker when seen in movement. Reflective paint was used on certain surfaces.

Upper level floor plan

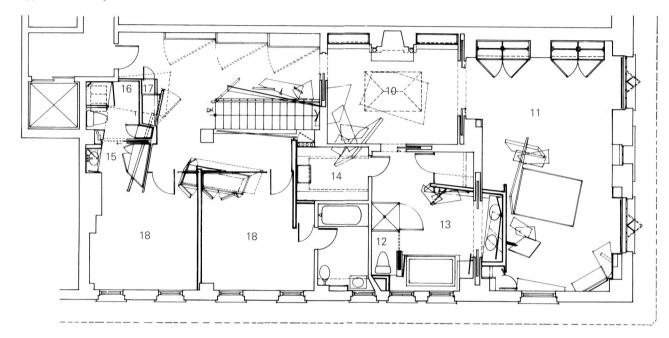

Lower level floor plan

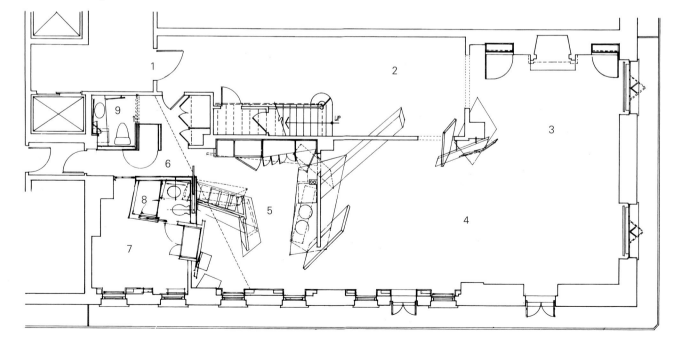

1. ENTRY	7. MAID'S ROOM	13. MASTER BATHROOM
2. FOYER	8. MAID'S BATHROOM	14. WALK-IN CLOSET
3. LIVING ROOM	9. POWDER ROOM	15. WASHROOM
4. DINING ROOM	10. SITTING ROOM	16. BATHROOM
5. KITCHEN	11. MASTER BEDROOM	17. CLOSET
6. CORRIDOR	12. TOILET	18. BEDROOM

0   5   10

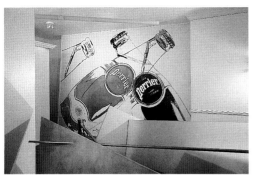

Axonometrics of plans and discrete elements

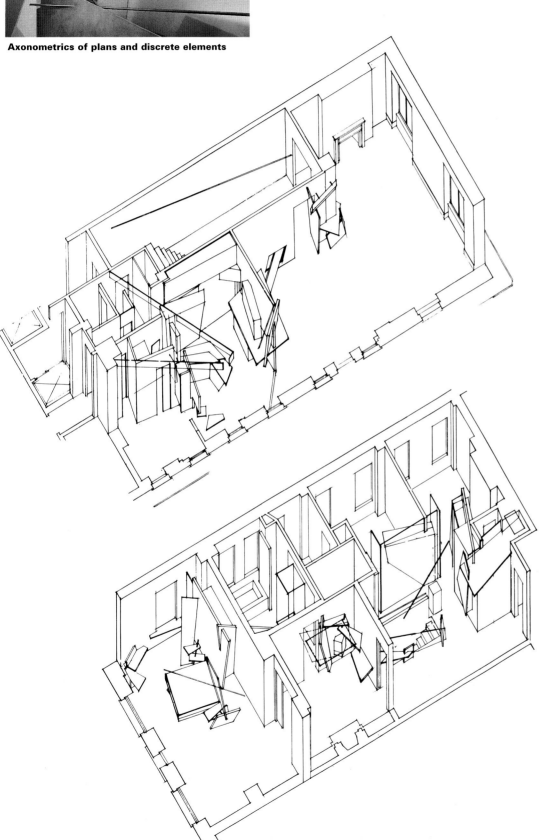

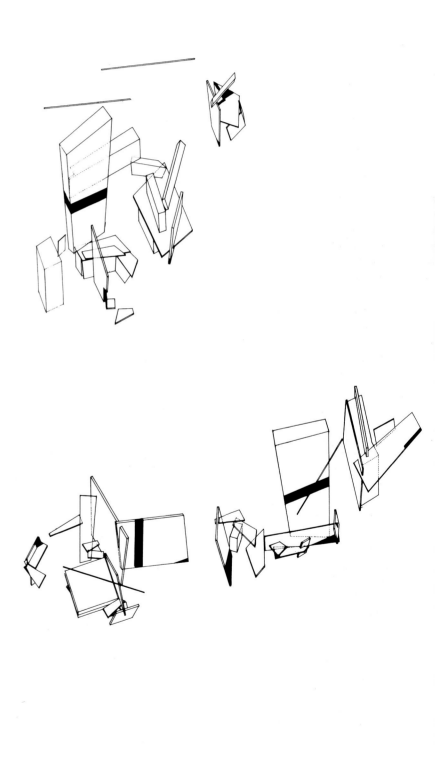

LEFT: *Living room*
MIDDLE: *Upper floor bedroom*
BOTTOM: *Upper floor bathroom*
FACING PAGE: *Glass parapet at top of stair*

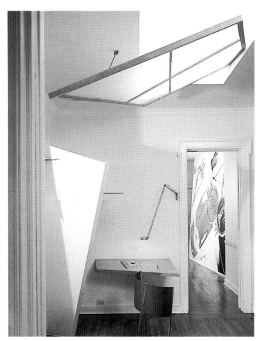

Glass parapet and stair details

Skylight details

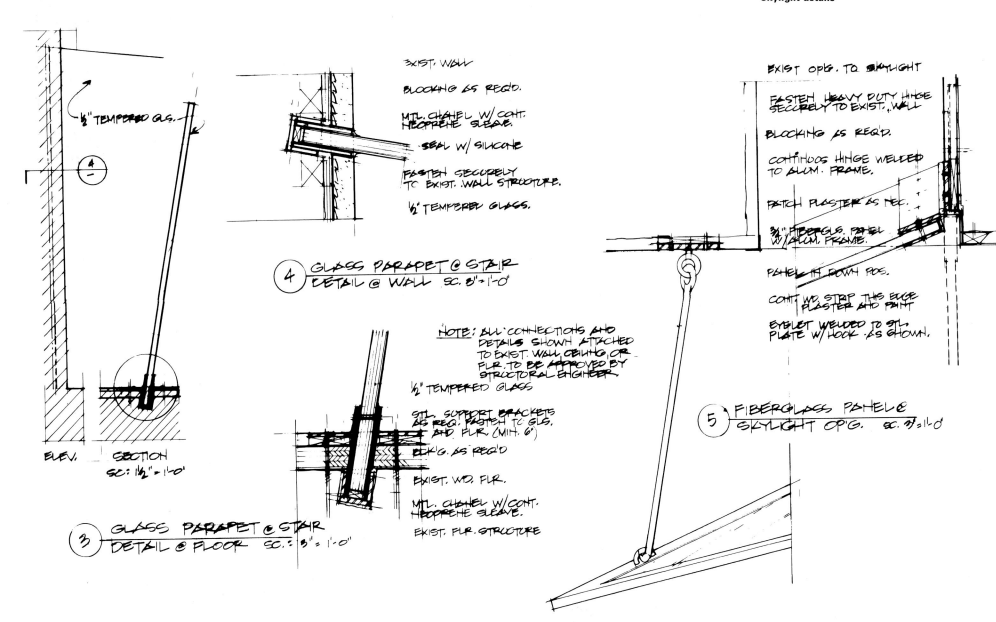

½" TEMPERED GLS.

④

ELEV.   SECTION
SC: 1½" = 1'-0"

③ GLASS PARAPET @ STAIR
DETAIL @ FLOOR SC.: 3" = 1'-0"

EXIST. WALL

BLOCKING AS REQ'D.

MTL. CHANEL W/ CONT.
NEOPRENE SLEEVE.

SEAL W/ SILICONE

FASTEN SECURELY
TO EXIST. WALL STRUCTURE.

½" TEMPERED GLASS.

④ GLASS PARAPET @ STAIR
DETAIL @ WALL SC. 3" = 1'-0"

NOTE: ALL CONNECTIONS AND
DETAILS SHOWN ATTACHED
TO EXIST. WALL, CEILING, OR
FLR. TO BE APPROVED BY
STRUCTURAL ENGINEER.

½" TEMPERED GLASS

STL. SUPPORT BRACKETS
AS REQ'D. FASTEN TO GLS.
AND FLR (MIN. 6")

BLK'G. AS REQ'D

EXIST. WD. FLR.

MTL. CHANEL W/ CONT.
NEOPRENE SLEEVE.

EXIST. FLR. STRUCTURE

EXIST OP'G. TO SKYLIGHT

FASTEN HEAVY DUTY HINGE
SECURELY TO EXIST. WALL

BLOCKING AS REQ'D.

CONTINOUS HINGE WELDED
TO ALUM. FRAME.

PATCH PLASTER AS NEC.

¾" FIBERGLS. PANEL
W/ ALUM. FRAME.

PANEL IN DOWN POS.

CONT. WD STRIP THIS EDGE
PLASTER AND PAINT

EYELET WELDED TO STL.
PLATE W/ HOOK AS SHOWN.

⑤ FIBERGLASS PANEL @
SKYLIGHT OP'G. SC. 3" = 1'-0"

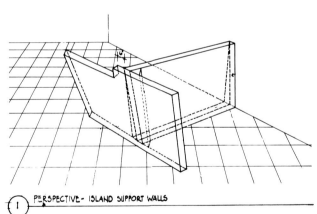

① PERSPECTIVE- ISLAND SUPPORT WALLS

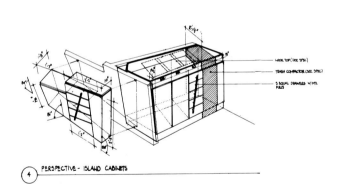

④ PERSPECTIVE- ISLAND CABINETS

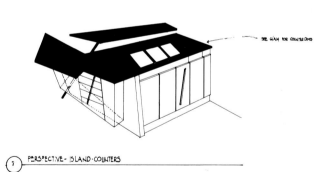

⑦ PERSPECTIVE- ISLAND- COUNTERS

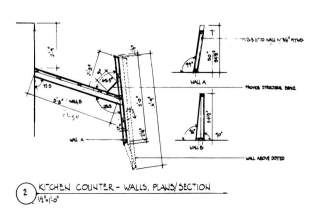

② KITCHEN COUNTER - WALLS, PLANS/SECTION
½"=1'-0"

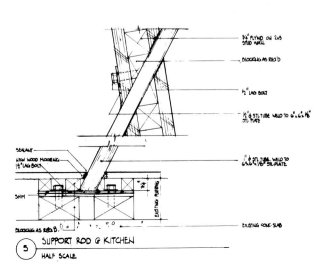

⑤ SUPPORT ROD @ KITCHEN
HALF SCALE

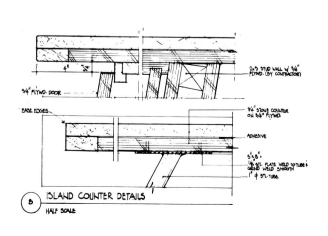

⑧ ISLAND COUNTER DETAILS
HALF SCALE

New York City Loft *1996*

SHELTON, MINDEL & ASSOCIATES ARCHITECTS

Owner: Lee F. Mindel, AIA
Architect: Shelton, Mindel & Associates Architects, New York, New York
Design Team: Lee F. Mindel, Peter L. Shelton, Reed Morrison (associate architect), Edwina Von Gall (landscape architect).
Engineer: The Office of James Ruderman (structural)
Consultant: Johnson Schwinghammer (lighting)
General Contractor: J & J Carpentry
Photography: Michael Moran

Site: New York, New York
Program: Master bedroom and bathroom, 2 bedrooms, 2 bathrooms, powder room, kitchen, living room, dining and seating area, outdoor garden room, penthouse conservatory.
Square Footage: 3800
Structural System: Steel columns and beams, concrete slabs
Mechanical System: Ducted hot and cool air with rooftop airhandling units, radiator steam heat
Major Exterior Materials: Aluminum, glass, stucco, concrete, cedar decking.
Major Interior Materials: Aluminum, white structural glass, stainless steel, wood, plaster.
Furnishings and Storage: Boffi (kitchen cabinets)
Doors and Hardware: Barwil (bathroom fittings)
Windows: Skyline Tilt and Turn (white framed), Studio Source (custom aluminum)
Fixtures: Kohler (bathtubs), American Standard (toilets), Pozzi Ginori (sinks)
Appliances and Equipment: Viking (cooktop), Best (hood), Sub-Zero (refrigerator), Miele (ovens and dishwasher).

Site/Context

The loft occupies the top floor of a flatiron manufacturing building in Manhattan.

Design

The architect sought to utilize all four potential exposures as well as the roof to create a series of spaces that form a relationship with the city. A central circular element inspired by the abundance of visible water towers is set into a double-sided vaulted rectangular glass cage. The combination of the solid form intersecting the glass vaults defines the public spaces—the living room to the south, and the dining area to the north. The service functions are tucked into an L-shaped band that contains kitchen, bathrooms, and storage, and separates the public areas from the bedrooms. There is also an angled service area to the west that masks the freight elevator, contains storage, and acts as a geometric foil to the rotunda.

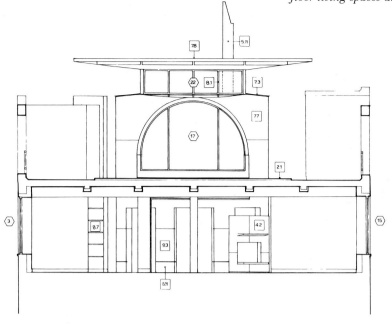

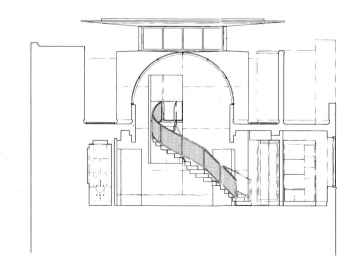

Existing conditions

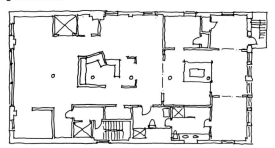

The double helix stainless steel stair in the glass vault provides the visual connection to the sky, north city views, and access to the conservatory and garden on the second level. The full expanse of the downtown view of Manhattan visible from the forty-foot window wall on the lower level is contrasted with the vista of uptown Manhattan through the glass vault on the second level. The roof plane appears to float freely as a clerestory of light separates the square cantilevered roof from the rotunda's round shape. The floating cantilevered roof is framed with an aluminum brise-soleil abstractly related to the crown of the Statue of Liberty.

Construction

The rotunda is asymmetrically cut open to create a visual continuum of cityscapes, reveal the shape of the stair, and provide light from all four exposures and the sky above. The southern exposure is the forty-foot expanse of window wall and convector cover/banquette made of stainless steel, white structural glass, and perforated metal. It acts as a view platform to all of downtown Manhattan—from the World Trade Center to the south, and from the East River to the Hudson River along the east-west axis.

The L-shaped storage and service band that separates the public areas from the private bedroom suites is contained by a series of sliding doors that enables various levels of enclosure. All of the service zones and the rectilinear glass vaulted space that contains the rotunda are delineated by the precast quartz floor.

The steel beam and concrete infill bay system are reflected by the alignment of the inlaid cherry borders in the white oak strip floor of the living spaces. A latex covered linen mat system further delineates seating areas throughout.

Roof plan

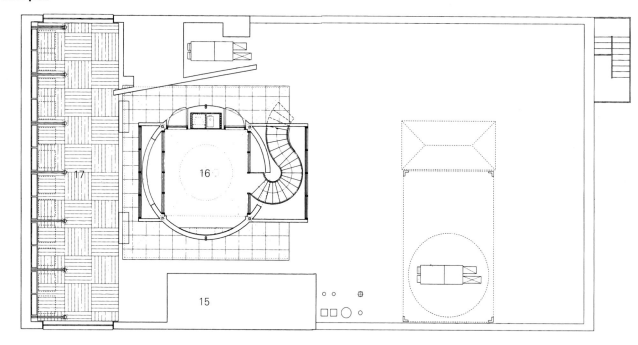

Lower level floor plan

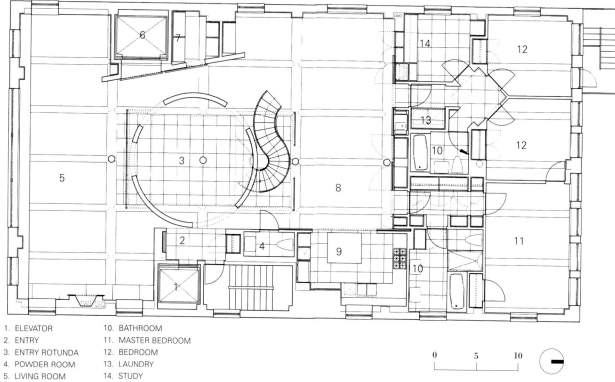

1. ELEVATOR
2. ENTRY
3. ENTRY ROTUNDA
4. POWDER ROOM
5. LIVING ROOM
6. FREIGHT ELEVATOR
7. STORAGE
8. DINING ROOM
9. KITCHEN
10. BATHROOM
11. MASTER BEDROOM
12. BEDROOM
13. LAUNDRY
14. STUDY
15. CONSERVATORY
16. ROOFTOP PAVILION
17. TERRACE

0   5   10

ABOVE: *Views of rotunda and stair; Ox chair by Hans Wagner, left, wood bench by Antonio Gaudí, center*

Longitudinal section

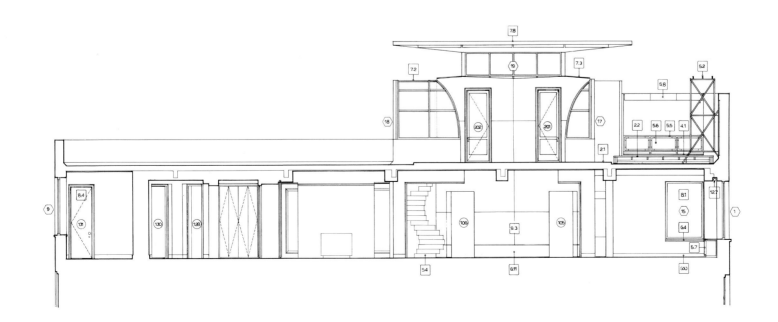

TOP: *Master bedroom*
BOTTOM: *Angled vestibule to bedrooms*
FACING PAGE: *Living room with round table by Jean Prouvé*

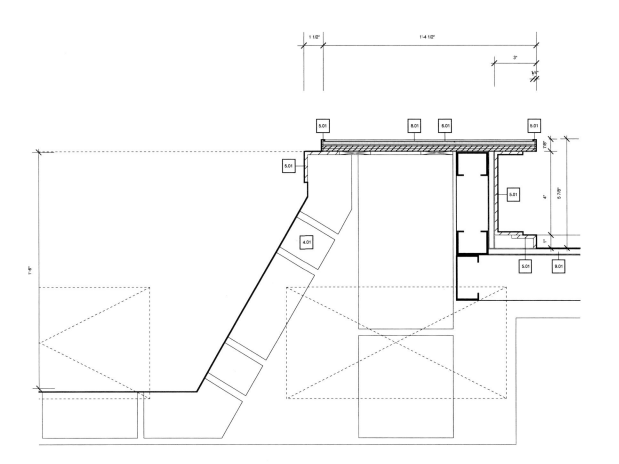

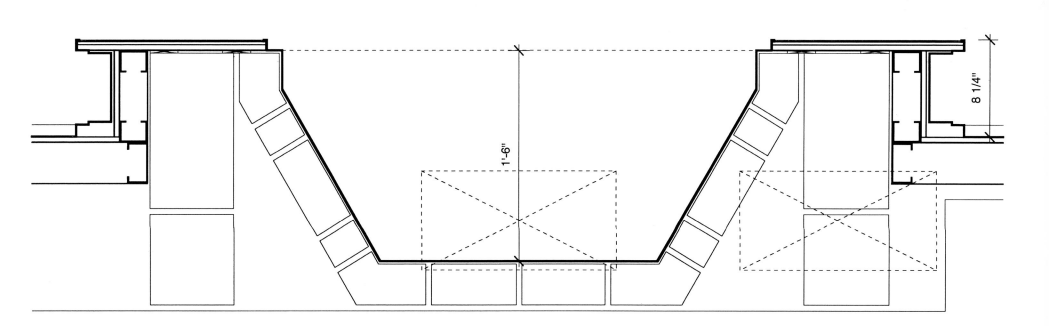

Buziak Penthouse *1989*

HARIRI & HARIRI

Owner: Robert Buziak
Architect: Hariri & Hariri, New York, New York
Design Team: Gisue Hariri and Mojgan Hariri (principals),
Kazem Naderi, Andre Bideau, Yves Habegger, Martha Skinner.
Fabricators: Dan George, Mark Gibian, and Scott R. Madison
(metalwork).
General Contractor: MJM Contracting Inc.
Photography: Paul Warchol, © Todd Eberle, John M. Hall

Site: New York, New York
Program: Entry, living/dining room, kitchen, master bedroom,
2 bathrooms, study.
Square Footage: 1200
Structural System: Steel column and beam
Mechanical System: Hot water radiant heat and central air
conditioning
Major Interior Materials: Plaster, stucco, flamed granite
(walls); bleached and stained wood boards, natural cleft slate,
marble tiles (floors); steel insulated glass (windows); steel, sand-
blasted glass (doors); stainless steel (mantel and lighting cove);
gypsum board (ceiling).
Furnishings and Storage: Le Corbusier (sofa, club chairs,
and chaise lounge), Noguchi (coffee table), custom by architect
(cabinets with stainless steel doors).
Doors and Hardware: A & S steel and sandblasted glass
Windows: A & S steel
Fixtures: Kohler, Grohe, Kroin, Speakman (bathrooms); Elkay,
LIM Form (sinks); custom by architect (medicine cabinets and
pendant light).
Appliances and Equipment: Sub-Zero (refrigerator),
Thermador (cooktop), Modern Maid (microwave and wall oven).
Cost: Withheld at owner's request.

Site/Context

From the top of its midtown-Manhattan building, this
apartment and wrap-around terrace command views of
the East River and nearby office towers. The unit is one
of two penthouses in a prewar, eighteen-story building.

Design

In this penthouse renovation the architects transformed
the rigid urban grid of the city into a different landscape, one in which a random play of volumes and
spaces counters the rhythms of the street below. To
achieve this, the design relies on the juxtaposition of
various tectonic elements.

RIGHT: *Fireplace mantel
and log box*
BOTTOM: *Lighting cove
above bar*
FACING PAGE: *View of
living/dining area*

LEFT: *View of apartment building*

Running through the apartment is a vertical steel and glass grid of doors and windows. This "rigid" organizational element is balanced by a series of architectural devices positioned throughout the apartment. For instance, in the living area are a lighting cove above the bar as well as a mantelpiece that curves in two directions. The existing corners are peeled away and articulated like setbacks of Manhattan towers at their tops. For this purpose the corner of a living room wall was removed and replaced with a grid of steel and glass to permit the entry of natural light and city views. The dining room corner steps back in a sculptural form and is finished with exterior rough stucco and composed with the shining steel lighting cove, reminding one of the "Chrysler building." The entry corner is treated similarly, this time carving a niche for umbrellas and a marble counter to leave keys on as one enters the apartment. This composition is completed with a steel and glass light fixture (Stasis Pendant).

The guest and master bathrooms focus on the experience of the naked body against different textures and tactile materials. The master bathroom is conceived as being quarry like, with its floor and bathtub made of natural cleft slate and walls of flamed granite. In contrast the wash basin is made of "spun" stainless steel and crowned with an eye-shaped cabinet. A device is designed and embedded in the corner articulation, facing the eye-shaped cabinet. This device holds jewelry and cosmetics in its pivoting compartments and also functions as a light fixture.

Construction

The larger framework of this project is its very own urban landscape, turned inside-out and captured within the shell of this penthouse; its walls, floors, and ceilings are white-washed monochromatically, creating an inviting space to celebrate this architectural phenomenon. Use of urban materials like steel, stone, and stucco reconnect the space to its city context.

Existing conditions

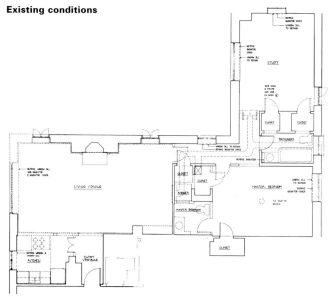

1. ENTRY
2. KITCHEN
3. BAR
4. DINING ROOM
5. LIVING ROOM
6. MASTER BEDROOM
7. CLOSET
8. MASTER BATHROOM
9. GUEST BATHROOM
10. STUDY
11. TERRACE

Floor plan

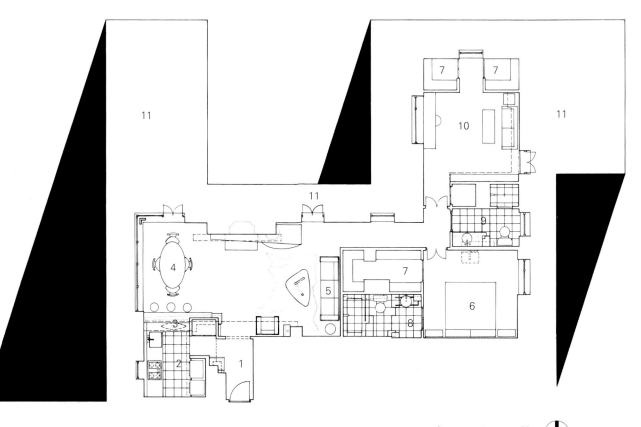

0   5   10

© *Todd Eberle*

ABOVE: *Dining area and corner living room wall*

East elevation

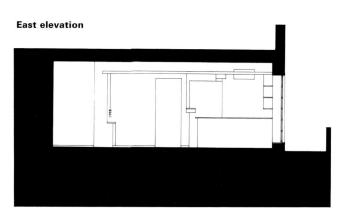

South elevation

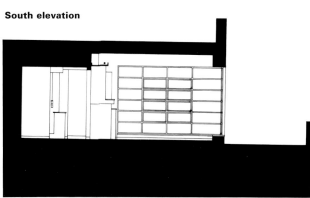

West elevation

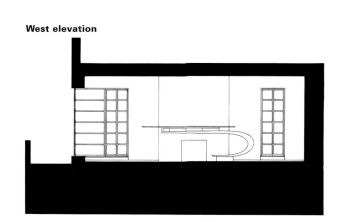

ABOVE AND BELOW: *Bar and lighting cove*

ABOVE AND BELOW: *Fireplace and log box*

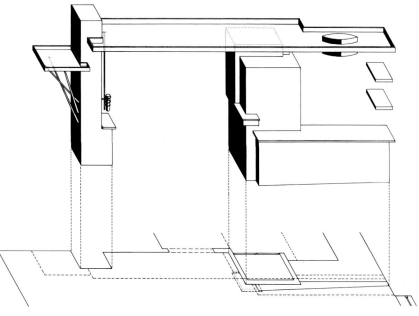

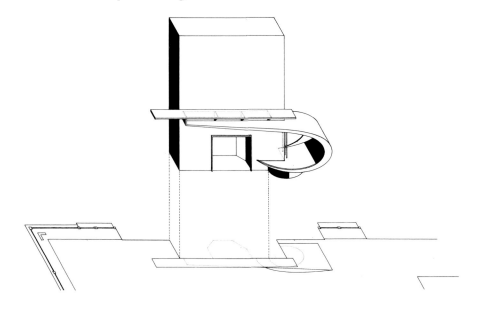

ABOVE AND BELOW: *Entry corner articulation*

ABOVE AND BELOW: *Guest bathroom detail*

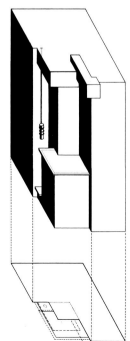

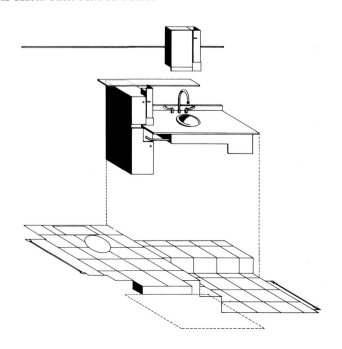

RIGHT: *Corner storage
unit and light*

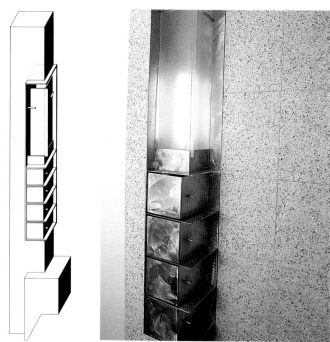

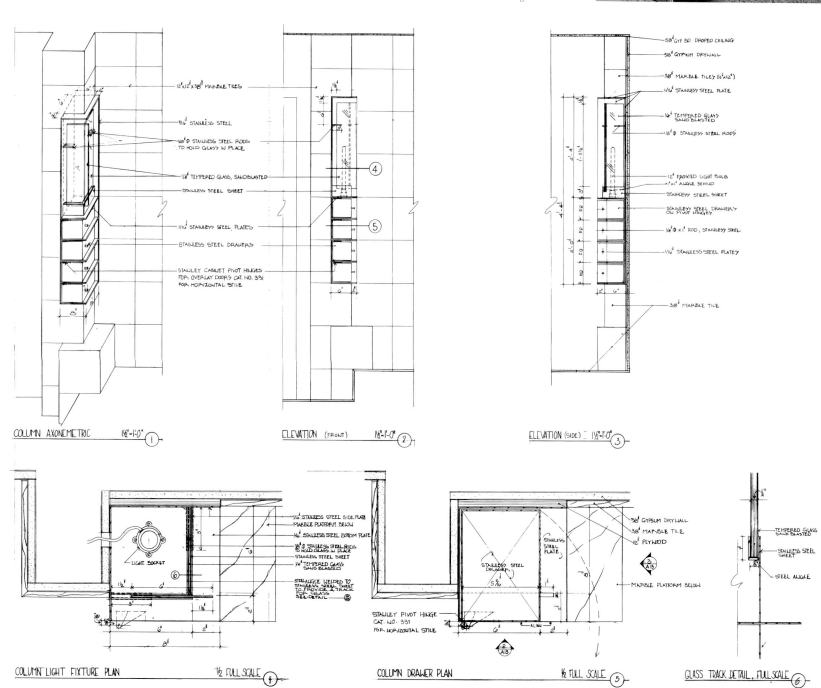

COLUMN AXONEMETRIC   1½"=1'-0" (1)

ELEVATION (FRONT)   1½"=1'-0" (2)

ELEVATION (SIDE) ⊑ 1½"-1'-0" (3)

COLUMN LIGHT FIXTURE PLAN   ½ FULL SCALE (4)

COLUMN DRAWER PLAN   ½ FULL SCALE (5)

GLASS TRACK DETAIL, FULL SCALE (6)

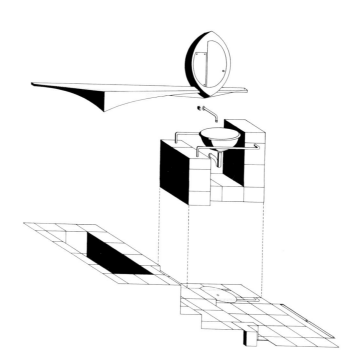

RIGHT: *Master bathroom sink and medicine cabinet*

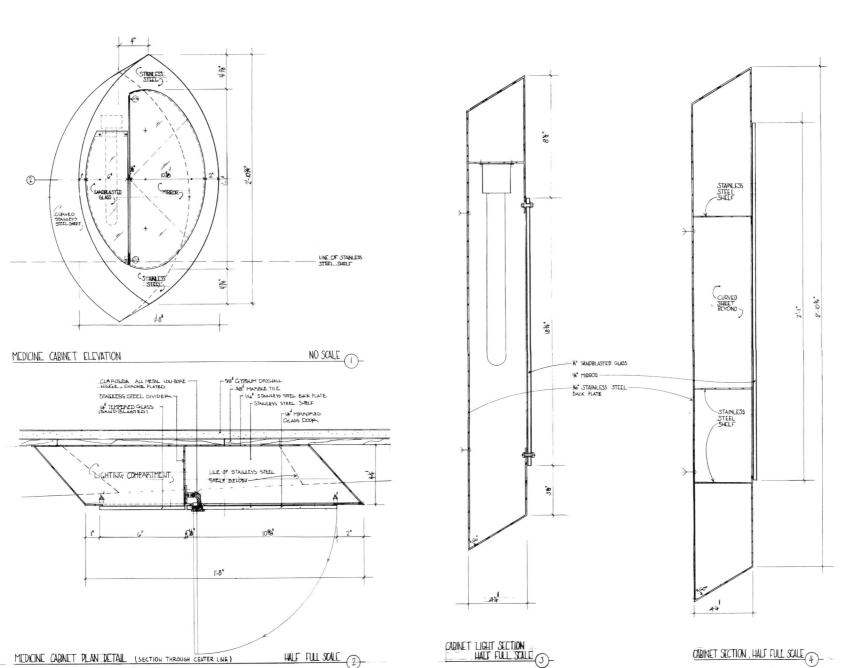

MEDICINE CABINET ELEVATION   NO SCALE ①

MEDICINE CABINET PLAN DETAIL (SECTION THROUGH CENTER LINE)   HALF FULL SCALE ②

CABINET LIGHT SECTION
HALF FULL SCALE ③

CABINET SECTION, HALF FULL SCALE ④

Art Collector's Apartment

1989

PASANELLA KLEIN STOLZMAN BERG ARCHITECTS

Owner: Name withheld at owner's request.
Architect: Pasanella Klein Stolzman Berg Architects,
New York, New York
Design Team: Henry Stolzman, AIA, Wayne Berg, FAIA, Lea
H. Cloud, AIA, Nancy Cooper, Harley Swedler, Tse-Yun Chu.
Engineer: Jack Green Associates (mechanical and electrical)
Consultants: Tse-Yun Chu Studio (materials and finishes),
Jerry Kugler Associates (lighting design)
General Contractor: Embassy Construction
Photography: Paul Warchol

Site: New York, New York
Program: Pied-à-terre and a showcase for owner's crafts collection with vestibule, gallery, living room, dining room, study,
terrace, bedroom, 2 bathrooms and kitchen.
Square Footage: 1800
Major Interior Materials: Oak with ebony borders (floors),
zinc (room entry "liners," cladding on cantilevered living room
display shelves), limestone (living room wall slabs), distressed
glass (dining room and living room wall panels), marble (terrace
floor), sandblasted steel (terrace doors), frosted glass (bedroom
and dining room pocket doors).
Furnishings and Storage: Custom by architect (bedroom/van-
ity night table, aluminum-framed bed, living room display
shelves, built-in cabinetry), Ward Bennet (terrace chair), Ben
Tre (terrace table), Gabriele Mucchi reproduction (bedroom
chair), Mario Botta (black living room occasional table and
chair), Philippe Starck (dining chairs), Stendig (living room
sofas), Mattia Bonetti and Elizabeth Garouste (living room
"Barbarian Chair" in bronze and cowhide).
Doors and Hardware: Custom by architect (terrace doors,
study and dining room pocket doors.)
Fixtures: P.E. Guerin
Cost: $340,000

Site/Context

This apartment is located in a beaux-arts building on
Manhattan's Fifth Avenue. Any period character the
interior once had had been erased in a 1950s "modern-
ization," but a spectacular view of Central Park
remained.

RIGHT: *View from living room
toward terrace*

Existing conditions

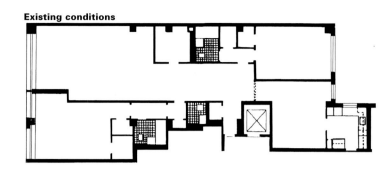

Design

The design team began by expanding the narrow interior with an open, fluid plan, while maintaining some sense of traditional room divisions. Another objective was to make the most of the park view. The process involved establishing a clear, consistent language of form and material, distilling essential design elements from superfluous details. It was critical that the interior architecture act as a setting for the client's art and craft objects, without competing with them for attention.

Toward the back of the apartment, thick zinc-lined portals divide the study and dining room and separate them from the entry vestibule. In the front the airy living room extends toward a glass-enclosed terrace, which acts as an "urban porch." Both the terrace and the bedroom adjacent to it are raised several inches, setting them apart from the rest of the interior. The terrace's steel-framed glass doors reveal Central Park and the skyline, and frame the collected pieces seen through them.

Construction

The apartment's materials—chosen for their richness, warmth, and solidity—are patinaed zinc, sandblasted steel, ebony, oak, and marble.

Floor plan

1. ELEVATOR
2. VESTIBULE
3. GALLERY
4. LIVING ROOM
5. BEDROOM
6. BATHROOM
7. TERRACE
8. STUDY
9. DINING ROOM
10. KITCHEN

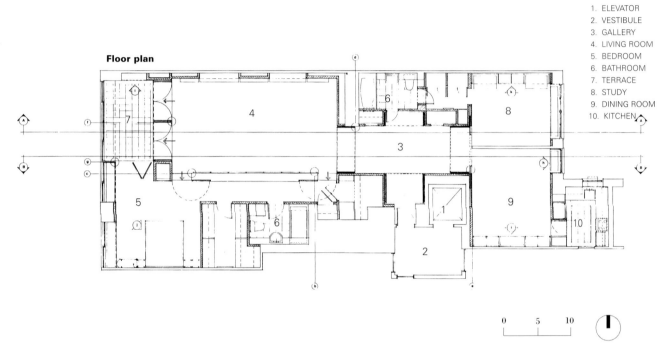

0   5   10

Longitudinal sections with interior elevations

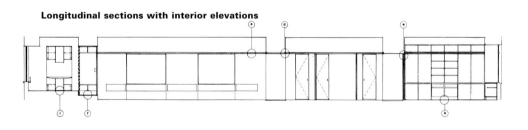

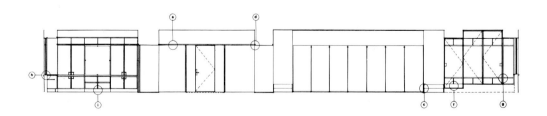

ABOVE: *View of living room*

Pencil studies for various furnishings and fixtures

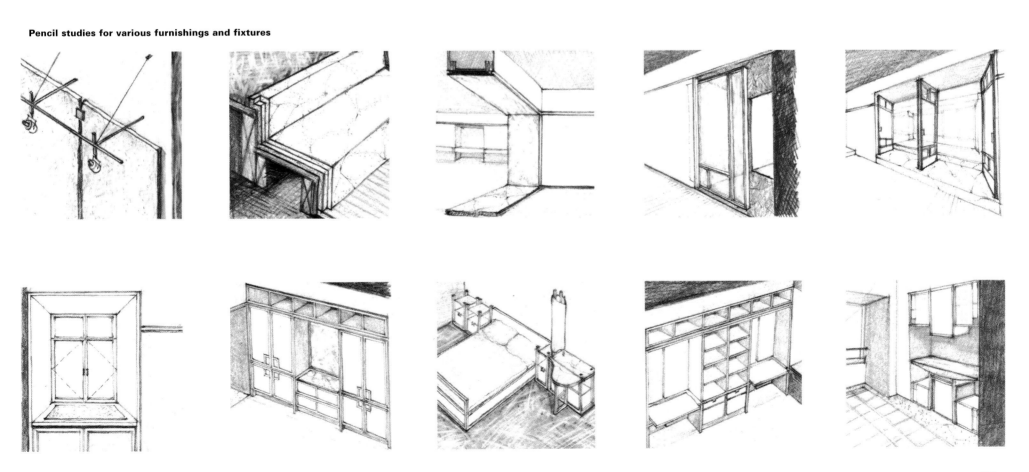

LEFT AND BOTTOM: *Steel frame terrace doors*
FACING PAGE: *View from gallery toward study and dining room*

Sketches and detail of custom vanity

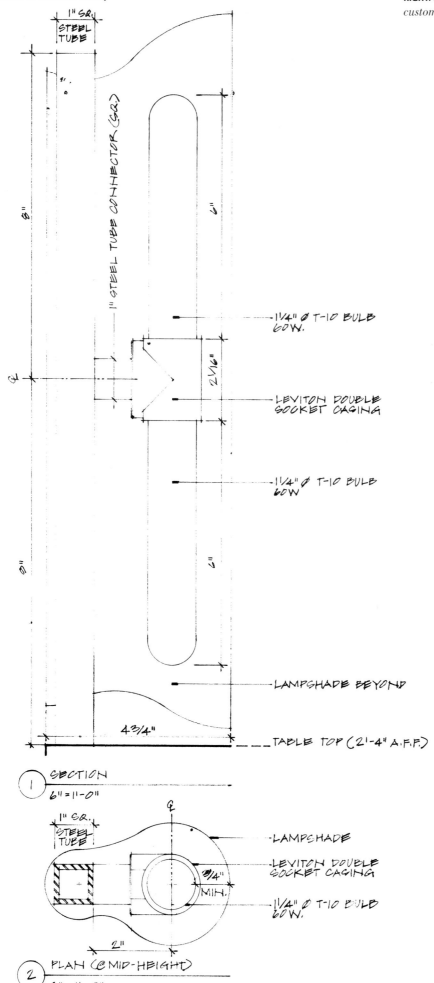

1" SQ. STEEL TUBE

1" STEEL TUBE CONNECTOR (SQ.)

1 1/4" ⌀ T-10 BULB 60 W.

LEVITON DOUBLE SOCKET CAGING

1 1/4" ⌀ T-10 BULB 60 W.

LAMPSHADE BEYOND

TABLE TOP (2'-4" A.F.F.)

(1) SECTION
6" = 1'-0"

1" SQ. STEEL TUBE

LAMPSHADE

LEVITON DOUBLE SOCKET CAGING

1 1/4" ⌀ T-10 BULB 60 W.

2"

(2) PLAN (@ MID-HEIGHT)
6" = 1'-0"

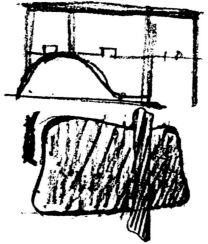

Steel door assembly details

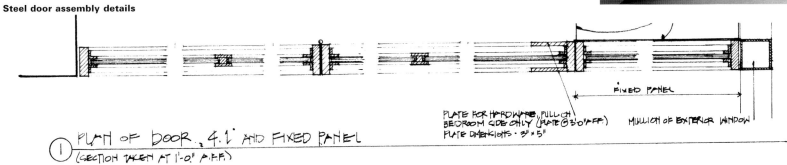

PLATE FOR HARDWARE, PULL (AT
BEDROOM SIDE ONLY (PLATE @ 3'0" A.F.F.)   MULLION OF EXTERIOR WINDOW
PLATE DIMENSIONS - 3" X 5"

FIXED PANEL

① PLAN OF DOOR, 4.1 AND FIXED PANEL
  (SECTION TAKEN AT 1'-0" A.F.F.)

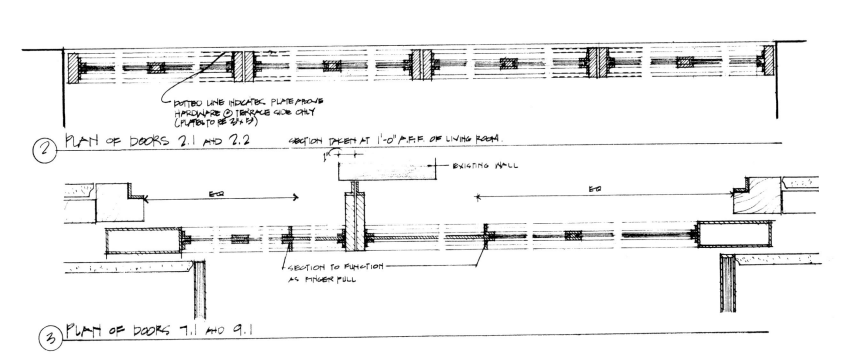

DOTTED LINE INDICATES PLATE ABOVE
HARDWARE @ TERRACE SIDE ONLY
(PLATES TO BE 3" X 5")

② PLAN OF DOORS 2.1 AND 2.2   SECTION TAKEN AT 1'-0" A.F.F. OF LIVING ROOM.

EXISTING WALL

EQ   EQ

SECTION TO FUNCTION
AS FINGER PULL

③ PLAN OF DOORS 7.1 AND 9.1

Quandt Loft *1988-1991*

TOD WILLIAMS BILLIE TSIEN AND ASSOCIATES

Owner: Colleen B. Rosenblat
Architect: Tod Williams Billie Tsien and Associates, New York, New York
Project Architect: David van Handel
Design Team: Marwan Al-Sayed, Kim DePole, Reenie Elliot, Brett Ettinger, Rick Gooding, Erika Hinrichs, Johannes Käferstein, Alexandra Yanacopoulos.
Engineers: Superstructures (structural), Ambrosino DePinto & Schmieder (mechanical)
Consultants: Edison Price, Inc. (lighting)
General Contractor: Clark Construction Corporation
Photography: Peter Paige

Site: Greenwich Village, New York, New York
Program: Entry, 4 bedrooms, dressing room, 3 bathrooms, powder room, kitchen, living room, dining room, library, study, studio, laundry, mechanical room.
Square Footage: 5000
Structural System: Existing steel and concrete
Mechanical System: Steam radiator heating with electric radiant floor warming; two-zoned forced air cooling; humidity control.
Major Interior Materials: Three-coat integrally colored plaster, skim-coated gypsum wall board, clear anodized and painted aluminum, satin finish stainless steel, pear wood, ebonized birch and painted birch millwork, masonite and barra board laminated millwork, stained oak strip (flooring), terrazzo, carved alberene stone, azul macaubus granite, emerald pearl granite, integrally colored fiberglass reinforced resin, cobalt blue laminated glass, opalescent laminated glass, translucent glass tiles, homasote, plastic laminate.
Furnishings and Storage: Custom by architect, Ligne Rosset (sofa), Gary Stephan (paintings).
Doors and Hardware: Modric, Rixson-Firemark
Windows: Skyline Windows
Fixtures: Speakman
Appliances and Equipment: Sub-Zero (refrigerator), Miele (dishwasher), Modern Maid (oven), Gaggenau (stove), Traulsen (wine cooler), Helo (sauna).
Cost: $1,200,000

Site/Context

The apartment inhabits the sixth floor of a building that was formerly used as a manufacturing plant and was later converted into residential units. The neighborhood is a combination of commercial and residential spaces. A restaurant occupies the building's ground floor.

Design

The design for this living and work space preserves and enhances the apartment's loft-like characteristics. A central terazzo-floored living area, framed by integrally colored plaster walls, is surrounded by the entrance, soldering studio, bathrooms, bedrooms, and kitchen. A series of sliding or rotating panels permits multiple uses and interpretations of the space, allowing the user to modify the architecture to suit various needs. For instance, the loft's spatial hierarchy is made clear from the moment of entry by a twelve-foot-long plywood partition that rotates around a metal pole. Pigmented-plaster walls suspended from the ceiling allow the master bedroom, dining room, and kitchen to be either open to or closed off from the apartment's central public space. Another such "open" divider in the form of a translucent glass and wood wall runs between the dining room and kitchen.

The architects also used color as a way of intensifying the sense of movement in the loft: natural light filters in through north and south, wall color alternates from mauve to beige, pearwood and aluminum happily coexist, and a cobalt vase set into a cantilevered metal arm stands guard in the foyer. While the design addresses complex programmatic requirements in a city that often feels like a battlefield, the orchestration and detailing of the architecture is such that the apartment always feels open and serene.

Construction

The architect paid close attention to all aspects of construction. The pivoting screen was first modeled at half scale to determine its center of gravity. Its construction came as a result of a collaboration between the metal fabricator, cabinetmaker, painter, and architects. Mounted at its center of gravity, the screen's thrust bearings absorb the lateral load and allow it to move quite freely. The plaster walls were created by a group of Brooklyn artists on site. Made of fiberglass reinforced resin, the living room table was fabricated by a California surf shop located near the project architect's alma mater; the stones on which it rests were carved by a Baltimore sculptor according to styrofoam models provided by the architects.

Existing conditions

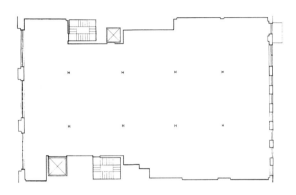

Floor plan

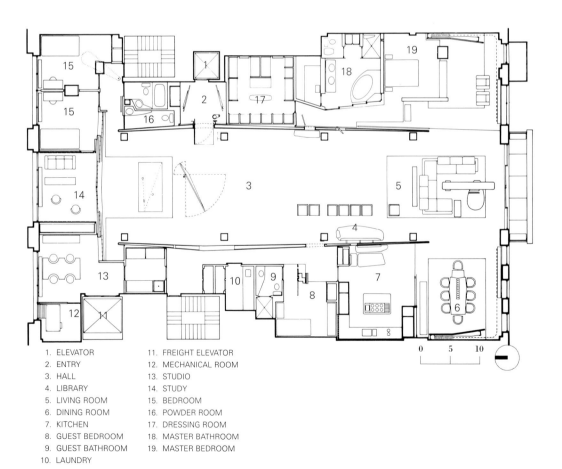

1. ELEVATOR	11. FREIGHT ELEVATOR
2. ENTRY	12. MECHANICAL ROOM
3. HALL	13. STUDIO
4. LIBRARY	14. STUDY
5. LIVING ROOM	15. BEDROOM
6. DINING ROOM	16. POWDER ROOM
7. KITCHEN	17. DRESSING ROOM
8. GUEST BEDROOM	18. MASTER BATHROOM
9. GUEST BATHROOM	19. MASTER BEDROOM
10. LAUNDRY	

LEFT: *Balcony*

Axonometric of space dividing devices

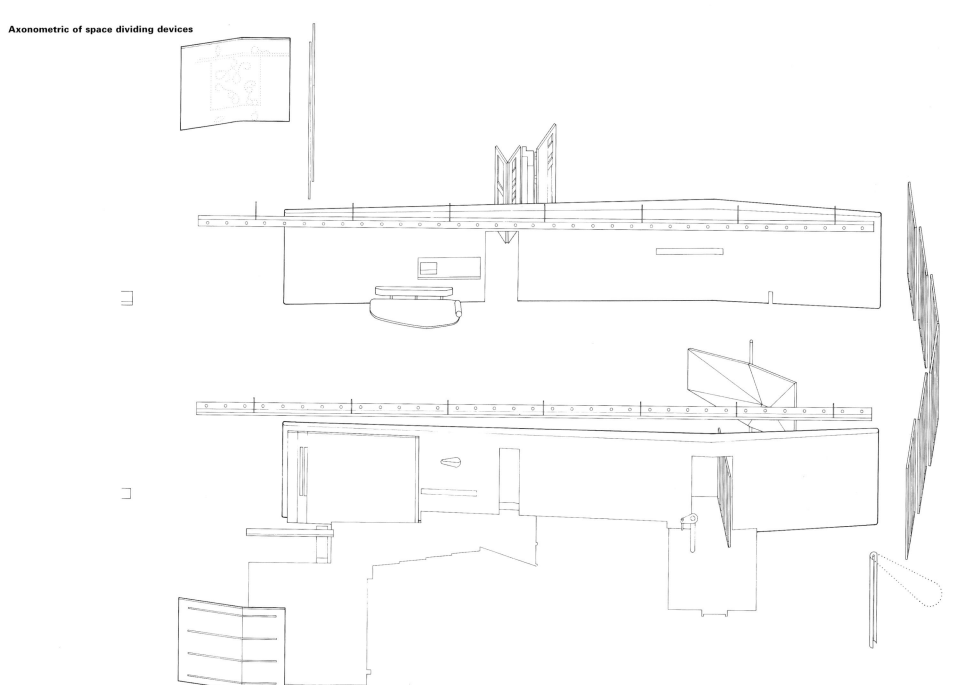

TOP LEFT: *Kitchen*
CENTER: *Various partitioning devices*
BOTTOM: *Various material applications and finishes*
FACING PAGE: *View of master bedroom suite with pigmented-plaster sliding partition at left*

RIGHT: *View of dining room and dining table details*

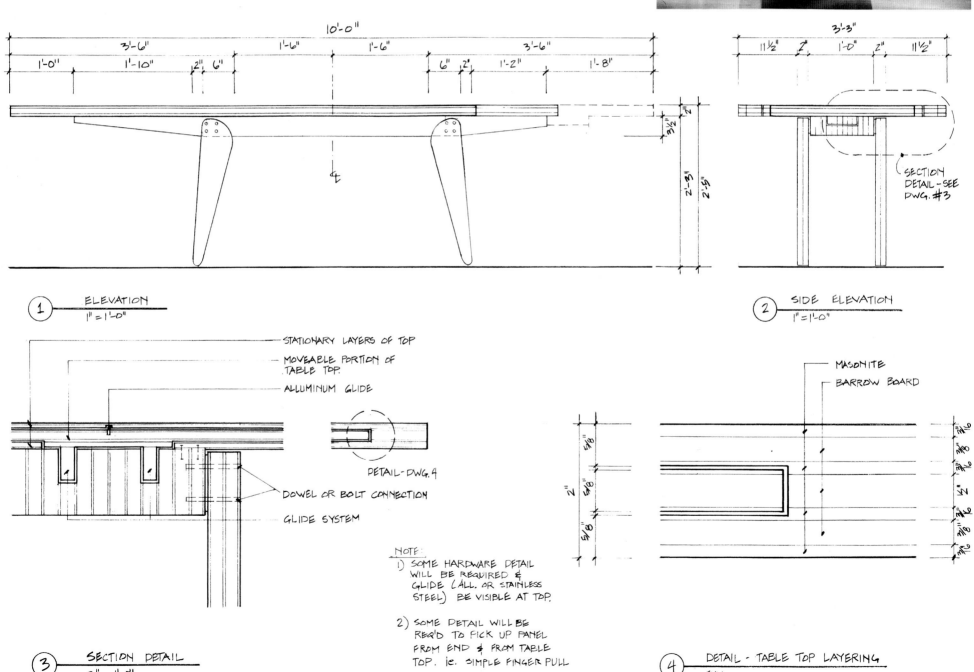

10'-0"

3'-6"   1'-6"   1'-6"   3'-6"

1'-0"   1'-10"   2" 6"   6" 2" 1'-2"   1'-8"

3 1/2" 2"

2'-3"
2'-5"

1) ── ELEVATION
      1" = 1'-0"

3'-3"

11 1/2" 2" 1'-0" 2" 11 1/2"

SECTION
DETAIL - SEE
DWG. #3

2) ── SIDE ELEVATION
      1" = 1'-0"

── STATIONARY LAYERS OF TOP

── MOVEABLE PORTION OF
   TABLE TOP.

── ALLUMINUM GLIDE

── MASONITE
── BARROW BOARD

DETAIL-DWG. 4

DOWEL OR BOLT CONNECTION

GLIDE SYSTEM

2"

5/8"

5/8"

NOTE:
1) SOME HARDWARE DETAIL
   WILL BE REQUIRED &
   GLIDE (ALL. OR STAINLESS
   STEEL) BE VISIBLE AT TOP.

2) SOME DETAIL WILL BE
   REQ'D TO PICK UP PANEL
   FROM END & FROM TABLE
   TOP. ie. SIMPLE FINGER PULL

3) ── SECTION DETAIL
      3" = 1'-0'

4) ── DETAIL - TABLE TOP LAYERING
      FULL

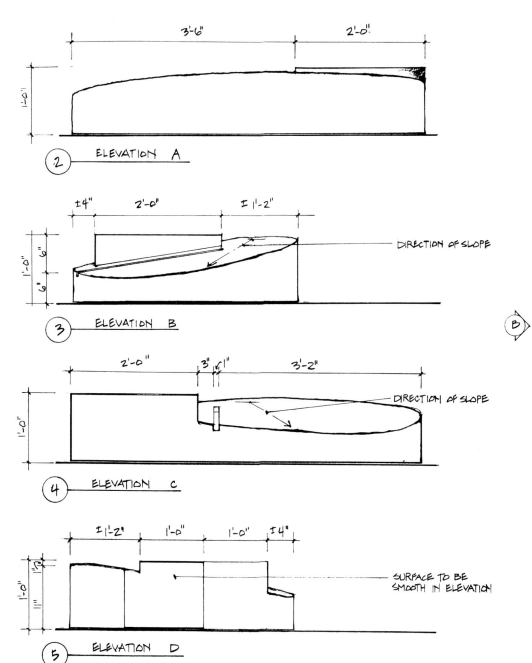

2 ELEVATION A

3 ELEVATION B — DIRECTION OF SLOPE

3'-6" 2'-0"

1'-0"

±4" 2'-0" ± 1'-2"

1'-0" 6" 6"

4 ELEVATION C — DIRECTION OF SLOPE

2'-0" 3" 1" 3'-2"

1'-0"

5 ELEVATION D — SURFACE TO BE SMOOTH IN ELEVATION

± 1'-2" 1'-0" 1'-0" ±4"

1'-0"

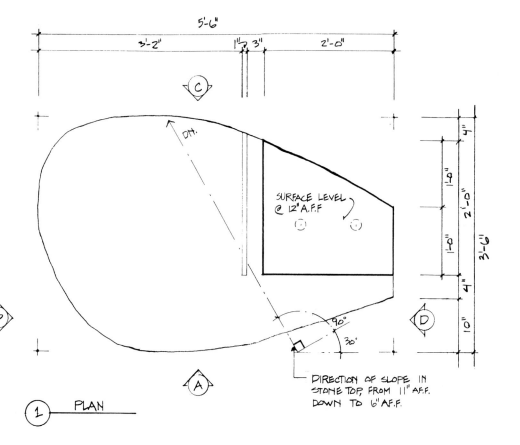

5'-6"

3'-2" 1" 3" 2'-0"

C

SURFACE LEVEL @ 12" A.F.F

ON.

90° 30°

B   A   D

4" 1'-9" 2'-0" 1'-0" 4" 1'-0" 3'-6"

DIRECTION OF SLOPE IN STONE TOP, FROM 11" A.F.F. DOWN TO 6" A.F.F.

1 PLAN

NOTES:

1) 2 STONES ARE TO BE CUT, 1 AS SHOWN IN DRAWING. THE OTHER TO BE 12' Ht. x 10"D. x 24" W.

2) ALL SURFACE TEXTURE TO BE DISCUSSED.

Holley Loft 1995
MEYERS HANRAHAN ARCHITECTS

Owner: Steve Holley
Architect: Meyers Hanrahan Architects, New York, New York
Interior Designer: Tse-Yun Chun
Design Team: Victoria Meyers, Thomas Hanrahan (project designers); Martha Coleman (project assistant).
Engineer: Manny Rubiano (mechanical)
General Contractor: J. Lauda Construction, Inc.
Photography: © Peter Aaron/Esto, Paul Warchol

Site: New York, New York
Program: Master bedroom and bathroom, living area, dining area, kitchen, music gallery, office, library, guest bathroom.
Square Footage: 3700
Structural System: Existing steel columns with concrete beams
Mechanical System: Steam heat with baseboard units and central air conditioning
Major Interior Materials: Glass, raw steel, maple, kirkstone, limestone tile, skim coated plaster gypsum wall board.
Furnishings and Storage: Custom by architect.
Fixtures: Kroin, Grohe
Appliances and Equipment: Sub-Zero (refrigerator/freezer), Miehle (oven, cooktop), Asko (dishwasher), Franke (kitchen sink and faucet), Thermador (compactor), Kohler (toilets, bathroom sinks, whirlpool bath), White Westinghouse (washer/dryer).
Cost: Withheld at owner's request.

Preliminary sketch

Site/Context

Because the loft is located in Manhattan, the architects sought to create "readings" of the city within the program. The interior space was considered an uninterrupted continuation of the exterior space. In the end, this residence captures the freedom but not the chaos of urban life.

Design

The design for the loft sprang from the very work the architects have explored in their practice: notions of transparency, light, reflectivity, and freedom in the plan. Following in the footsteps of Mies and Le Corbusier, the apartment is configured as a loose and relatively open grid of pure formal elements that float within a non-specific and unbounded context.

FAR LEFT: *View from living room toward entry*
LEFT: *View toward freight elevator entry*

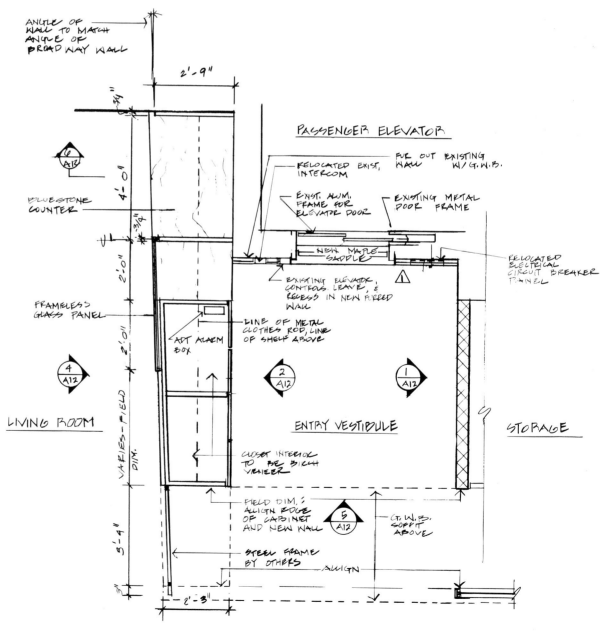

ANGLE OF WALL TO MATCH ANGLE OF BROADWAY WALL

2'-9"

PASSENGER ELEVATOR

RELOCATED EXIST. INTERCOM

FUR OUT EXISTING WALL W/ G.W.B.

BLUESTONE COUNTER

EXIST. ALUM. FRAME FOR ELEVATOR DOOR

EXISTING METAL DOOR FRAME

4'-0"

NEW MAPLE SADDLE

RELOCATED ELECTRICAL CIRCUIT BREAKER PANEL

EXISTING ELEVATOR, CONTROLS LEAVE, & RECESS IN NEW FURRED WALL

2'-0"

FRAMELESS GLASS PANEL

LINE OF METAL CLOTHES ROD, LINE OF SHELF ABOVE

ADT ALARM BOX

2'-0"

4 / A12

2 / A12

1 / A12

LIVING ROOM

ENTRY VESTIBULE

STORAGE

CLOSET INTERIOR TO BE BIRCH VENEER

VARIES-FIELD DIM.

FIELD DIM, & ALIGN EDGE OF CABINET AND NEW WALL

5 / A12

G.W.B. SOFFIT ABOVE

3'-4"

STEEL FRAME BY OTHERS

ALIGN

3"

2'-3"

③ / A12 PLAN DETAIL AT ENTRY VESTIBULE

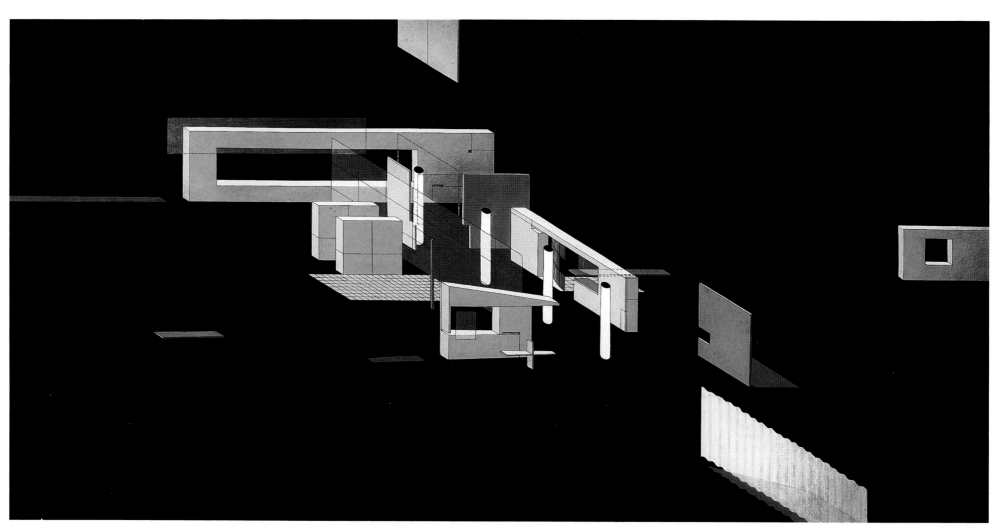

Axonometrics

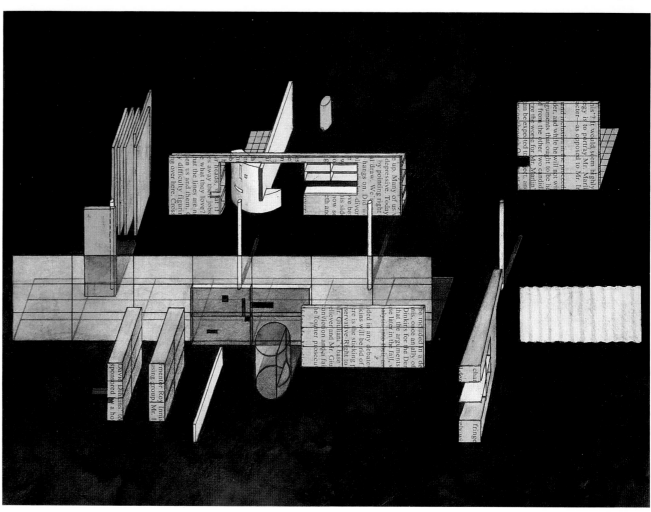

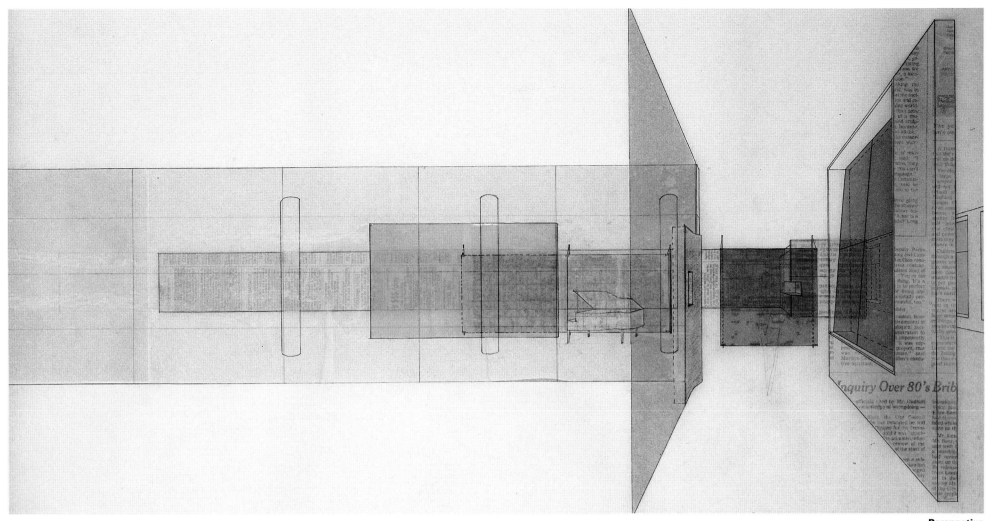

Axonometric

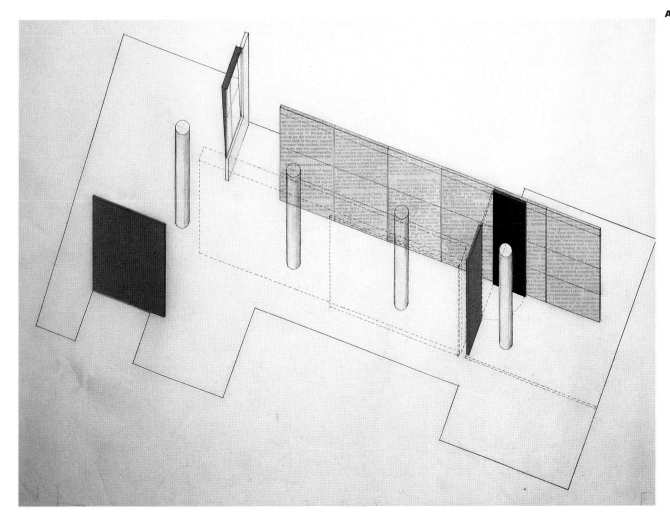

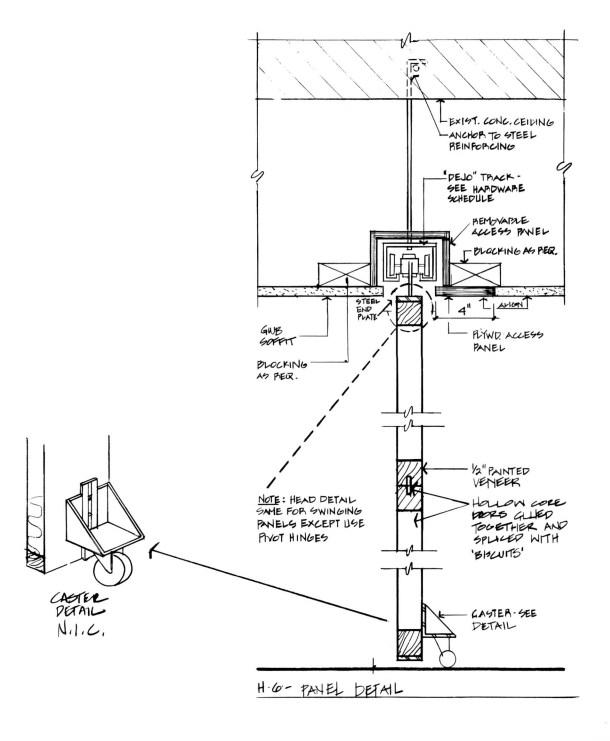

EXIST. CONC. CEILING
ANCHOR TO STEEL
REINFORCING

"DEJO" TRACK -
SEE HARDWARE
SCHEDULE

REMOVABLE
ACCESS PANEL

BLOCKING AS REQ.

STEEL
END
PLATE

4"

ALION

GWB
SOFFIT

PLYWD. ACCESS
PANEL

BLOCKING
AS REQ.

NOTE: HEAD DETAIL
SAME FOR SWINGING
PANELS EXCEPT USE
PIVOT HINGES

½" PAINTED
VENEER

HOLLOW CORE
DOORS GLUED
TOGETHER AND
SPLICED WITH
'BISCUITS'

CASTER - SEE
DETAIL

CASTER
DETAIL
N.I.C.

H·6· PANEL DETAIL

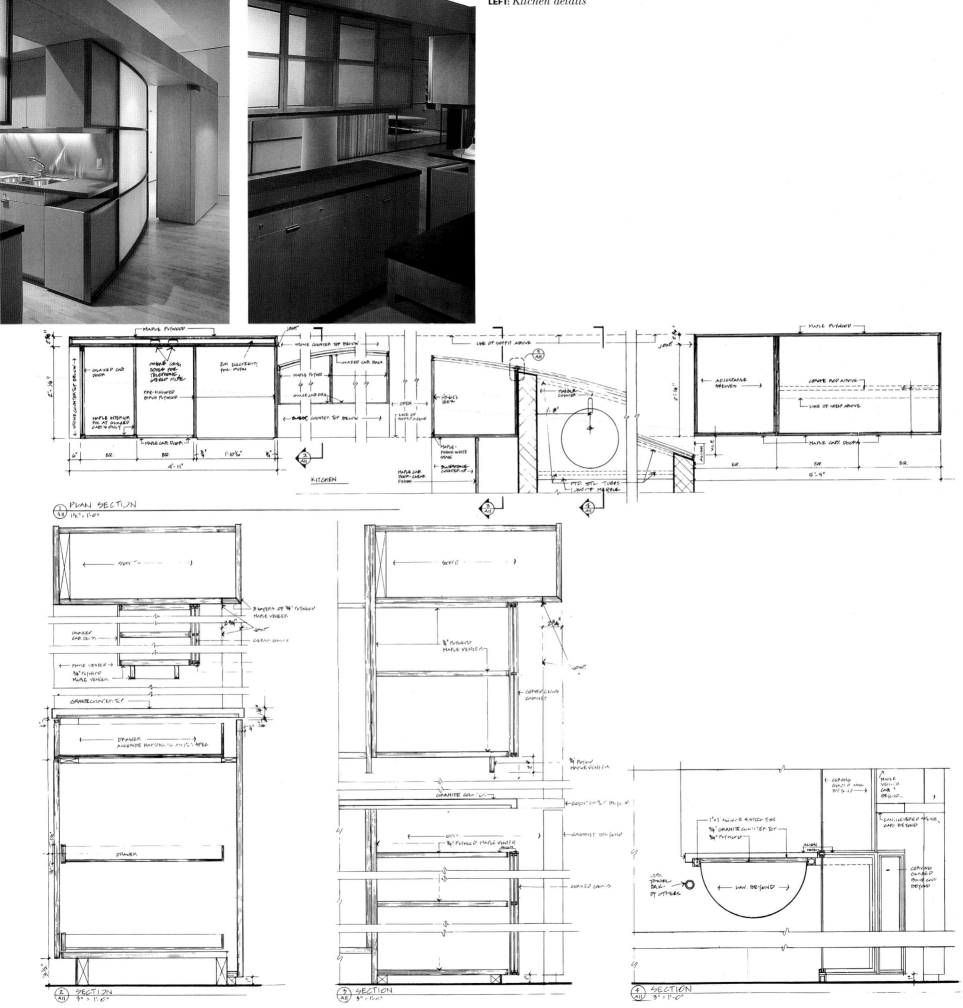

LEFT: *Kitchen details*

147

Model Apartment *1989*

SMITH-MILLER + HAWKINSON

Owner: Fourth Jeffersonian (client)
Architect: Smith-Miller + Hawkinson, New York, New York
Design Team: Laurie Hawkinson (principal-in-charge), Henry Smith-Miller, Ruri Yampolsky, Jennifer Stearns, Kit Yan.
Engineer: Severud and Associates
Consultants: Claude Engle Lighting Design; Philip Meskin, Stephen Iino (cabinetmakers); Metalforms (metalwork).
General Contractor: Martin Meyers
Photography: Paul Warchol

Site: New York, New York
Program: Model apartment in condominium development including kitchen, dining and living areas, bedroom, 2 bathrooms, powder room, study, and balcony.
Square Footage: 1200
Structural System: Existing poured-in-place concrete with steel frame
Mechanical System: Existing induction units
Major Interior Materials: Stainless steel, blackened miscellaneous steel, grey-stained maple plywood, sandblasted Plexiglass.
Furnishings and Storage: Custom by architect, Ron Arad ("Land Rover" seat), Walter Gropius (tube-and-rubber folding chairs).
Doors and Hardware: Custom by architect.
Fixtures: Custom by architect, Artemide ("Tolomeo" fixture with casters)
Appliances and Equipment: Existing
Cost: $86,000

Site/Context

The project involved the restructuring of an existing two-bedroom duplex in a speculative co-op building that had once been the headquarters of the New York City Police Department. The building occupies an entire city block in Lower Manhattan.

Design

The design of this apartment anticipates the future of the urban dwelling by addressing issues of "conversion" and the program required of living spaces. The urban site—a truncated trapezoid—informs the entire building as well as the configuration of the Model Apartment.

A new two-story cabinet/apparatus is inserted into the existing trapezoidal space and placed parallel to the exterior wall, thereby creating both an implied rectangular volume of the living/dining space as well as the trapezoidal passage from entry to corridor to study at the end of the apartment. This new oversized cabinet contains everything needed to live in the city: a bed, closets, bookshelves, and a "pegged wall" reminiscent of the Shaker way of storing objects off the floor.

RIGHT: *View of living area, oversized cabinet, and pivot door*

LEFT: *View of former Police Building*

A large translucent pivot door separates the living from the sleeping spaces, affording privacy when required. The pull down "Murphy Bed" resides together with books, pillows, and clothing, kept in storage areas within the new cabinetry. In the open position the door masks the bedroom apparatus and permits the living room to occupy space previously given over to the bedroom. An articulated canopy in the kitchen, cantilevered dining room table, and expanding seating create a dining space; these may be closed, rotated, and stored when not in use. A moving device allows the television to be viewed from all spaces—living, dining, bedroom, and balcony.

Construction

The majority of the elements were manufactured off-site and later installed. Movable pieces are either on casters, hinged, or operated by pulley; the television hangs from the ceiling and can be moved throughout the space mounted on a device photographers use to suspend lights. The architects cleverly masterminded the apartment's furnishings, among them a circular glass table propped on car jacks, an ashtray made from an engine cylinder head, and tube-and-canvas folding chairs used for "viewings" in funeral homes.

Existing Conditions

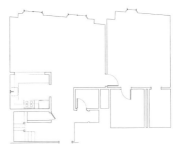

Upper level floor plan

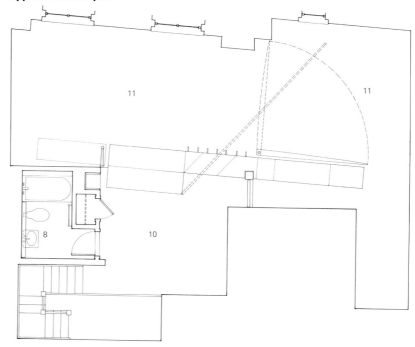

Lower level floor plan

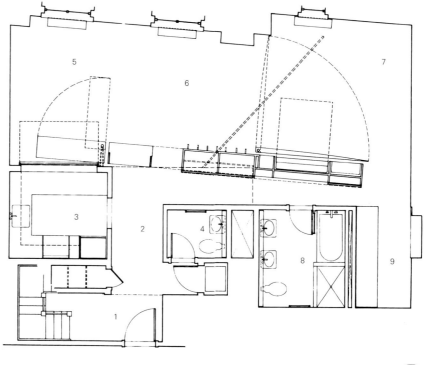

1. ENTRY
2. HALL
3. KITCHEN
4. POWDER ROOM
5. DINING ROOM
6. LIVING ROOM
7. BEDROOM
8. BATHROOM
9. STUDY
10. BALCONY
11. OPEN

0   5   10

Axonometric

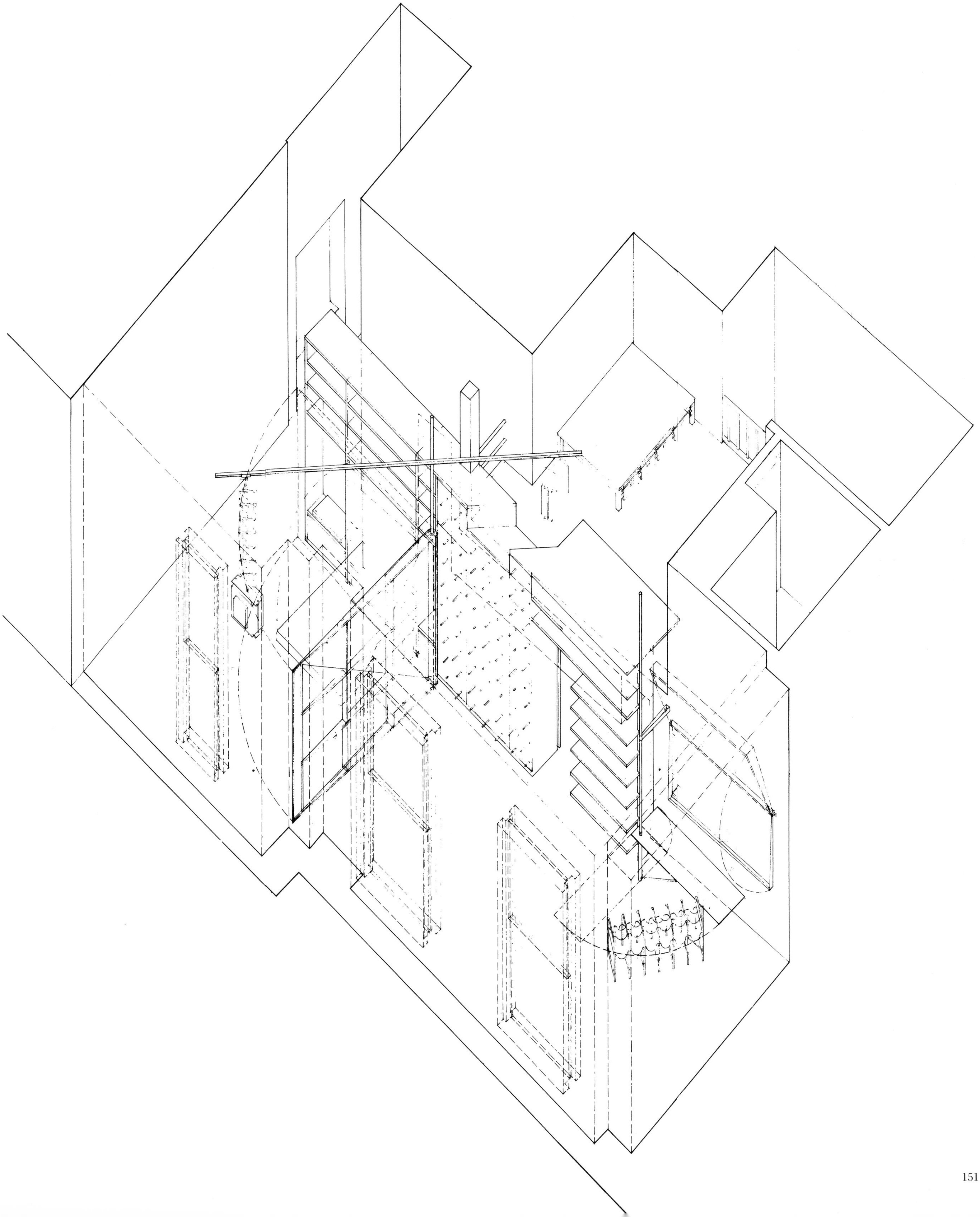

ABOVE: *Suspended television*
RIGHT: *View of living area with pegged wall*

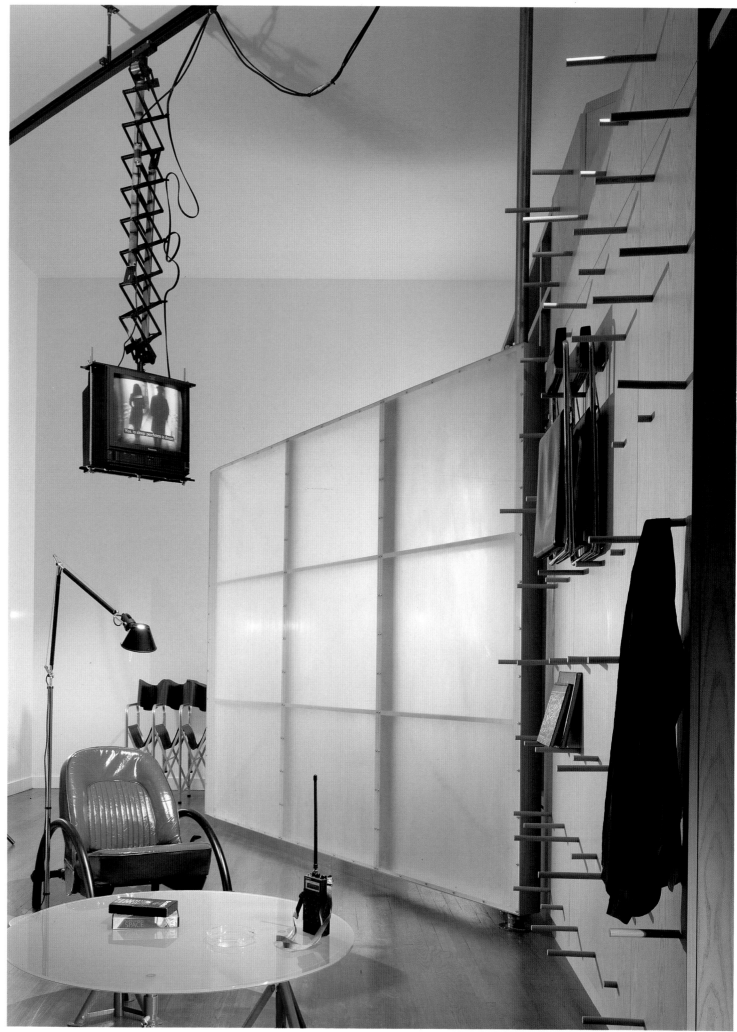

ABOVE AND LEFT: *Views of cantilevered dining table and screen*

153

LEFT: *View of "Murphy Bed" shelf, screen, and cantilevered dining table*

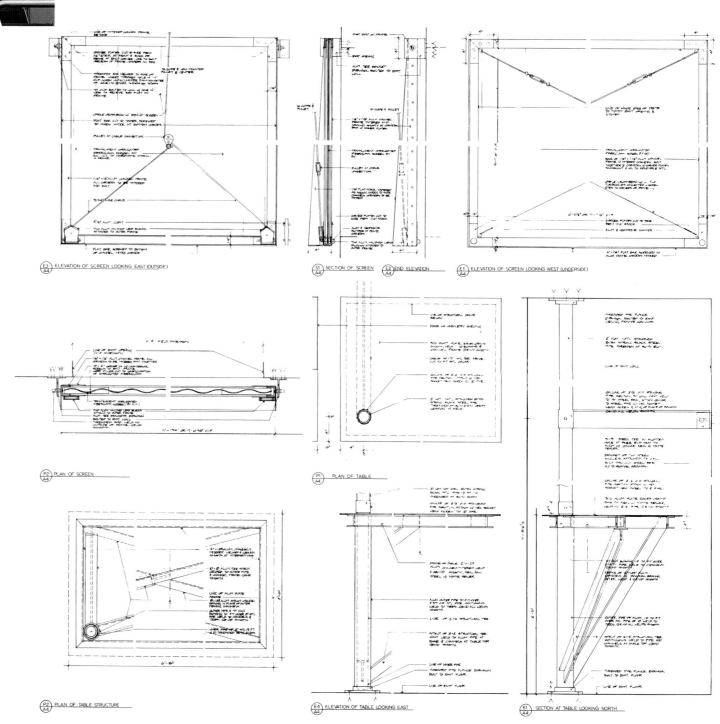

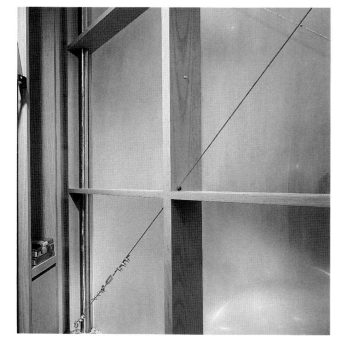

LEFT: *Pivot door detail*

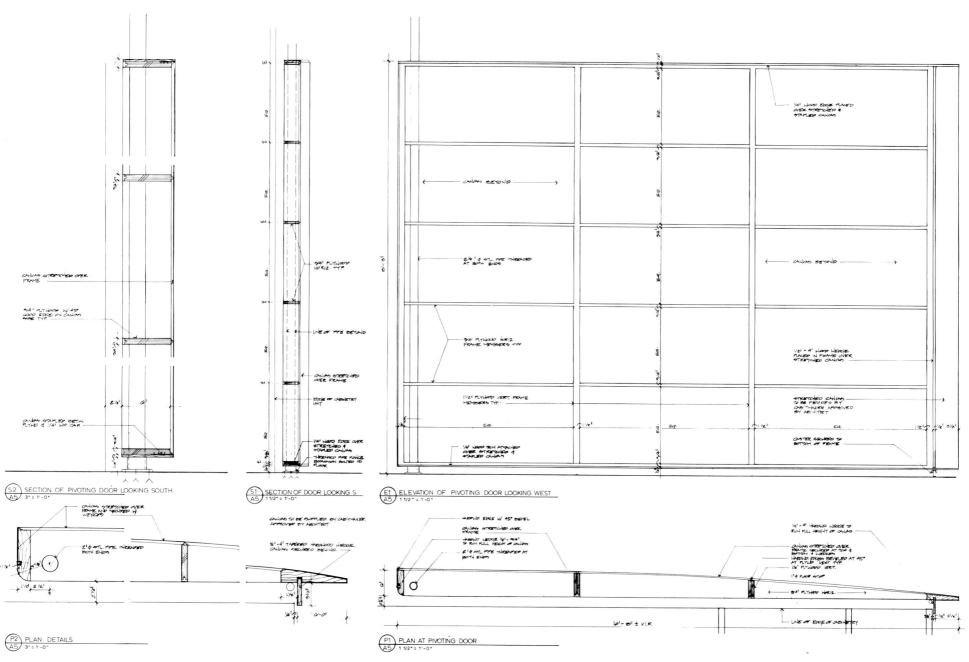

S2/A5 SECTION OF PIVOTING DOOR LOOKING SOUTH 3" = 1'-0"

S1/A5 SECTION OF DOOR LOOKING S. 1 1/2" = 1'-0"

E1/A5 ELEVATION OF PIVOTING DOOR LOOKING WEST 1 1/2" = 1'-0"

P2/A5 PLAN DETAILS 3" = 1'-0"

P1/A5 PLAN AT PIVOTING DOOR 1 1/2" = 1'-0"

Live/Work Dualities *1990*
DEAN/WOLF ARCHITECTS

Owners: Kathryn Dean and Charles Wolf
Architect: Dean/Wolf Architects, New York, New York
Design Team: Kathryn Dean and Charles Wolf
General Contractor: Dean/Wolf Architects
Photography: © Arch Photo, Inc. Edward Hueber

Site: Tribeca, New York, New York
Program: Dining/conference room, work area, work storage, kitchen, bedroom, bathroom.
Square Footage: 875
Structural System: Existing cast iron columns and heavy timber beam
Mechanical System: Existing hot water system
Major Interior Materials: Concrete, steel, heavy timber, plywood, fabric, woven aluminum.
Furnishings and Storage: Custom by architect.
Doors and Hardware: Custom by architect.
Windows: Custom by architect.
Fixtures: Custom by architect.
Appliances and Equipment: Custom by architect (cooktop and sink).
Cost: $18,000

Site/Context

The existing Tribeca loft's best feature was that it was filled with light from a wall of south-facing windows. However, its irregular shape was made even more problematic by two rooms at the rear that were small and dark.

Design

The open loft space was adapted to accommodate the dual functions of living and working in the same space. The first problem at hand was that two small, dark rear rooms not only interrupted the apartment's open plan, but they also failed to provide comfortable internal space. These partitions were removed to create a single volume into which the new program could be inserted. To preserve the newfound sense of openness, minimal furniture components that both define space and support specific functions were introduced.

The overall design strategy is one of the loft as an "operable collage," a system of movable components and a visual set of connections that expand both real and perceived spatial dimensions. The three primary dualities created are workroom/wall, bedroom/table, and bathroom/ladder.

The workroom/wall is the boundary and view connection between the work area and dining room. It contains the clutter of the office both behind its surface and literally on the tackable wool felt on the office side. Sliced at the eye level of a seated person, the aperture provides a visual connection between work area and dining room.

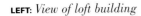

LEFT: *View of loft building*

Existing conditions

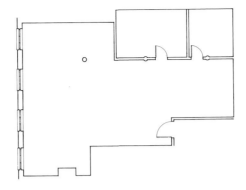

The two-sided woven metal surround, which occupies a corner position, contains the bedroom/table. An operable panel within the screen assembly hinges down to provide a visual connection as well as a table for breakfast in bed.

The screen with the highest degree of operability is the canvas and steel bathroom door/ladder. Open both physically and visually, the canvas enclosure brings in light during the day and emits light at night. Its steel frame acts as a ladder, giving access to the guest loft above.

Construction

The shell of the loft space was left intact; the cast iron columns, wood floor, and plaster walls were refurbished and painted to create a neutral ground against which the constructed elements are positioned. Concrete, steel, and heavy timber are the structural components of each piece, and allude to the tectonic of the existing building shell. Juxtaposed with these rugged materials are the delicate fabric infills of each piece—canvas, cotton, wool, and woven aluminum—that lend the pieces an air of domesticity.

Longitudinal section

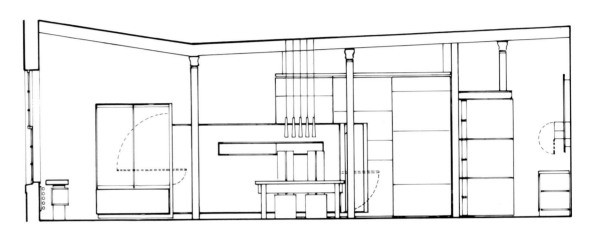

Floor plan

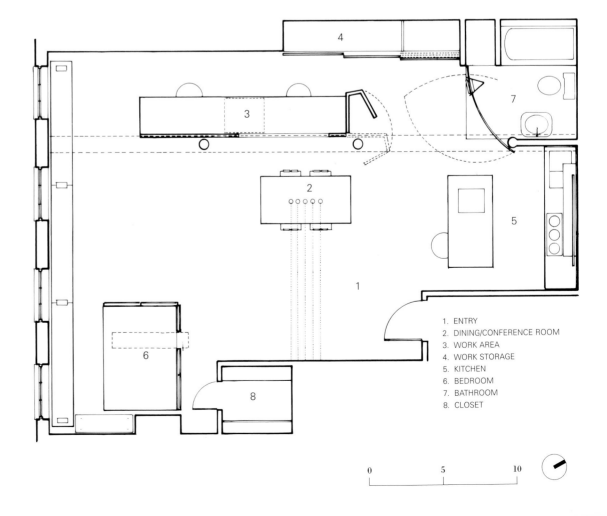

1. ENTRY
2. DINING/CONFERENCE ROOM
3. WORK AREA
4. WORK STORAGE
5. KITCHEN
6. BEDROOM
7. BATHROOM
8. CLOSET

0   5   10

159

TOP AND BELOW LEFT: *Views of workroom wall with horizontal aperture*
BELOW RIGHT: *Dining area with bathroom door in background*
FACING PAGE: *View from bathroom to living area with canvas and steel bathroom door in foreground*

LEFT TOP AND BOTTOM:
Bathroom door/ladder details
FACING PAGE: *Bathroom door
and kitchen*

Exploded axonometric of bathroom door/ladder

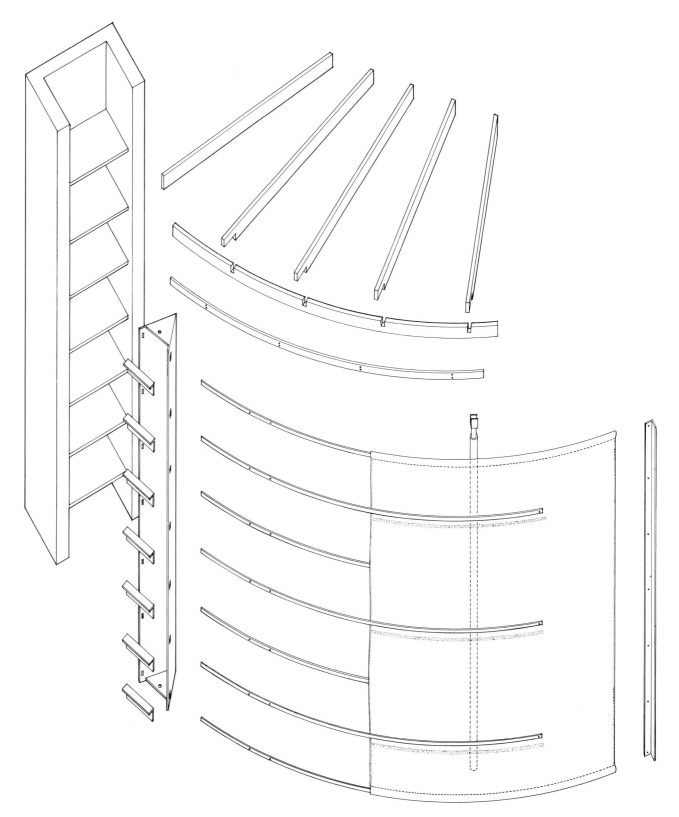

Levy Loft *1993*

M. ALI TAYAR

PARALLEL DESIGN PARTNERSHIP

Owner: Ellen Levy
Architect: M. Ali Tayar, Parallel Design Partnership, New York, New York
Interior Designers: Parallel Design Partnership, Gayle Camden
Engineer: Attila Rona (structural)
General Contractor: Richard Baronio and Associates
Photography: John M.Hall, David Sundberg

Site: West Village, New York, New York
Program: Cooperative residential loft renovation. Open plan first floor with entry, livingroom, diningroom, kitchen, study, den/guestroom areas, guest bathroom, second floor master bedroom, master bathroom, dressing area with surrounding terrace.
Square Footage: 1900 in 2 floors
Structural System: Existing reinforced concrete with non-load bearing brick facade.
Mechanical System: Existing central air and steam heat
Major Interior Materials: Cherry hardwood/veneer (kitchen cabinets, paneling, window ledges, sliding wall, baseboards, bookshelves, bathroom door), cork (floor), slate (countertops), skim coat plastered gypsum board (outer walls and ceiling).
Furnishings and Storage: Woodwork by Lance Schoenhuber, Thomas Garcia, and Miles Jackson.
Doors and Hardware: Sugatsune door and cabinet pulls (bathrooms, kitchen, closets), Parallel Design shelf bracket system (bookshelves, prototype for "Ellen's brackets"), Putnam library ladder.
Appliances and Equipment: SubZero (refrigerator)
Cost: $350,000.00

Site/Context

This penthouse in an eight-story former warehouse is located on an oddly-angled corner of the West Village, surrounded by blocks largely made up of buildings of six stories or less. The loft's five 7' x 16' windows thus command unusual panoramic views of the Manhattan Bridge through the midtown skyline to the Hudson River. The architect's design both frames these views and allows them to be seen from every corner of the apartment.

Design

The loft was designed around a tightly defined core containing the kitchen, guest bathroom, and washer/dryer unit. In order to permit privacy and flexibility of function, the den/guestroom areas feature one fixed, half-height room divider and two sliding, ceiling-mounted, full-length room dividers. The surfaces of the loft core change according to the function of the facing area but are unified by a system of prefabricated panels, based on the geometric ordering principles of the tartan grid analogous to a curtain wall. The same construction is applied to both deployable walls which, when extended along their ceiling track, provide privacy for the guestroom/study. The only intervention along the exterior wall is a two-foot-deep wood sill structure, which frames the steel-framed grid of the loft's industrial windows, a grid reflected in turn by the paneling system.

Construction

The omnipresent cherrywood and cork flooring were chosen to bring a feeling of warmth and intimacy to this space wrapped in glass and hard-edged urban vistas. The woodwork was designed with prefabricated systems in mind, to be constructed off-site while basic renovations went on, then installed within a few days at the project's end. Details of the highly finished woodwork include blueprint- and slip-matched half-sawn veneer panels, 1/16-inch reveals between panels, dovetailed corners, and mechanical-free drawers fitted to openings. The panels of the sliding walls are connected by wood knuckle joints to create a folded plate in full extension. The aluminum shelf brackets and standards make innovative use of the extrusion process; they have since gone into production.

Existing conditions / Demolition Plan

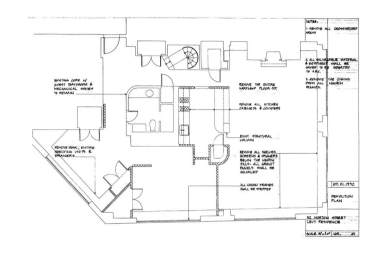

1. ENTRY
2. STUDY/GUEST BEDROOM
3. GUEST BATHROOM
4. CLOSET
5. KITCHEN
6. PANTRY
7. LIVING ROOM
8. DINING ROOM

Lower level floor plan

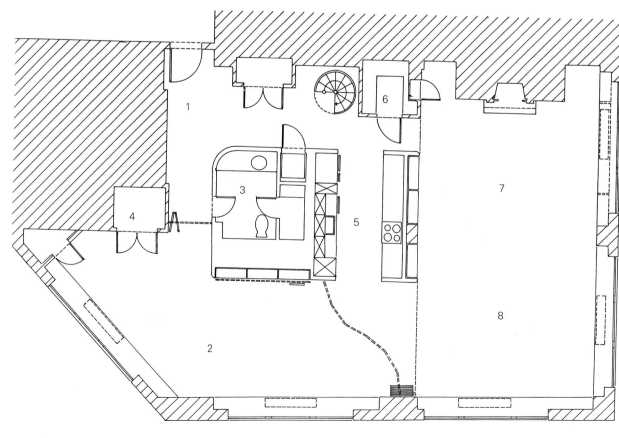

0   5   10

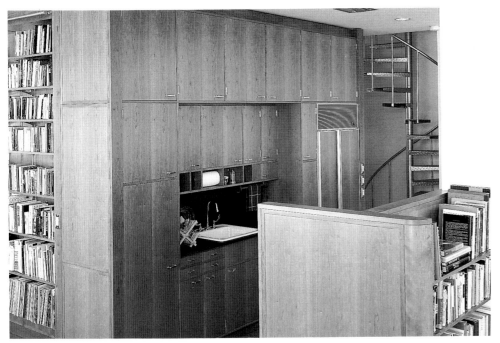

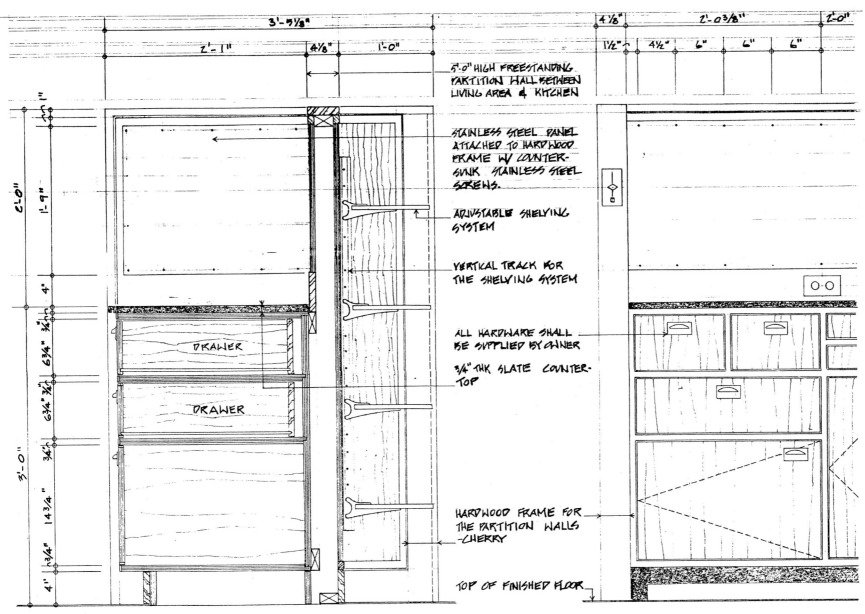

5'-0" HIGH FREESTANDING PARTITION WALL BETWEEN LIVING AREA & KITCHEN

STAINLESS STEEL PANEL ATTACHED TO HARDWOOD FRAME W/ COUNTERSUNK STAINLESS STEEL SCREWS.

ADJUSTABLE SHELVING SYSTEM

VERTICAL TRACK FOR THE SHELVING SYSTEM

ALL HARDWARE SHALL BE SUPPLIED BY OWNER

3/4" THK SLATE COUNTERTOP

HARDWOOD FRAME FOR THE PARTITION WALLS -CHERRY

TOP OF FINISHED FLOOR

DRAWER

DRAWER

1 / 14   VERTICAL SECTION

2 / 14   ELEVATION

LEFT TOP: *View of living and dining areas*
BOTTOM: *View of den/guest area with wood folding wall in foreground*

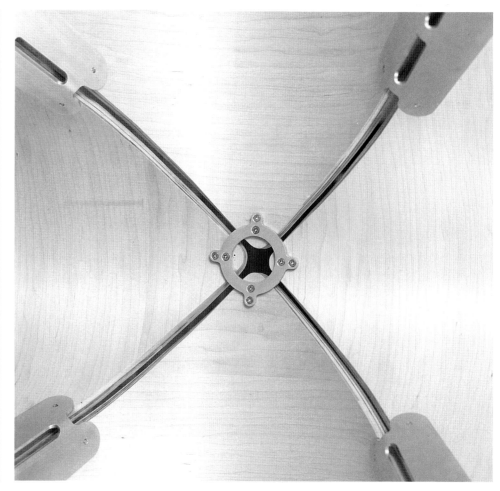

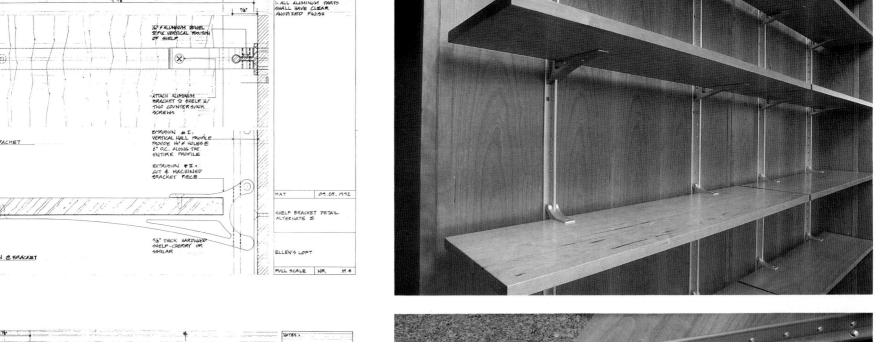

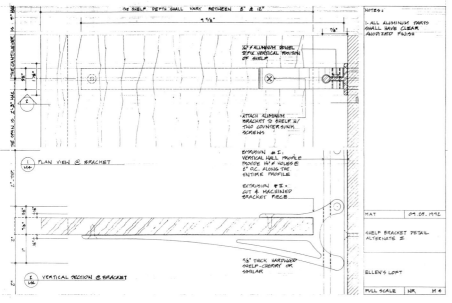

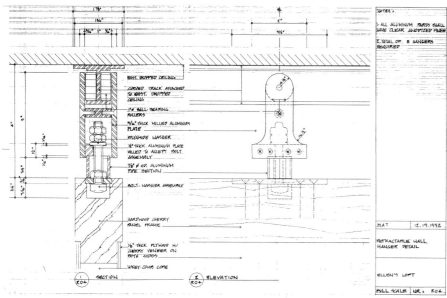

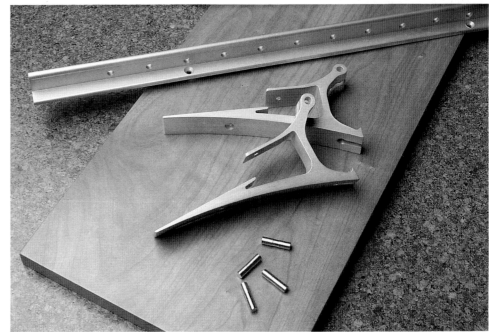

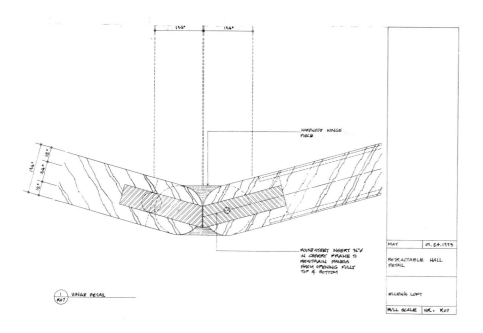

Apartment Renovation *1991*
FRANÇOIS DE MENIL, ARCHITECT

Owner: Name withheld at owner's request.
Architect: François de Menil, Architect, New York, New York
Design Team: Phillip Turino, Sandra Forman, Pamela Belyea,
Jill Wheeler, Jack Pascarosa.
Engineer: Atkinson, Koven, Feinberg (mechanical)
Consultants: Petersen Geller Inc. (millwork),
Fayston Iron & Metal Works (metalwork)
General Contractor: FM Designs, Inc.
Photography: Paul Warchol

Site: New York, New York
Program: Foyer, dining room, living room, library/study,
powder room, 2 maid's rooms, kitchen, master bedroom, master
bathroom, study, 2 bedrooms, 2 bathrooms, laundry room.
Square Footage: 3900
Structural System: Existing steel and concrete
Mechanical System: Steam heat and through-the-wall
air conditioning
Major Interior Materials: Mahogany, White Oak, Virginia
Serpentine stone, Virginia Alberene stone, English kirkstone,
Vermont slate, glass, stainless steel, solid Birch, Makore veneer.
Furnishings and Storage: Cabinetry custom by architect.
Doors and Hardware: Custom by Petersen Geller Inc. (doors)
Windows: Zeluck Inc.
Fixtures: Speakman
Appliances and Equipment: Sub-Zero (refrigerators),
Modern Maid (ovens), Gaggenau (cooktops), Miele (dishwashers).
Cost: Withheld at owner's request.

Site/Context
The apartment is located in a typical Manhattan prewar
building on Park Avenue.

Design
Because the program called for leaving the basic plan
intact, the architect limited himself to two major spatial
interventions. First, the entrance foyer and staircase
were reorganized to create a double-height volume and
better express the linkage between the apartment's two
floors. The new space made the experience of entering
the apartment more free, and also helped define the
circulation corridor which repeats on the floor above.

Further liberation of the apartment was achieved by
removing the wall between the living room and the
library. The resulting larger open plan space now
accommodates the library in a freestanding elliptical
book cabinet and adjacent passageway element.

TOP: *Stair to upper level*
BOTTOM: *Interior window*
FACING PAGE: *View of living room*

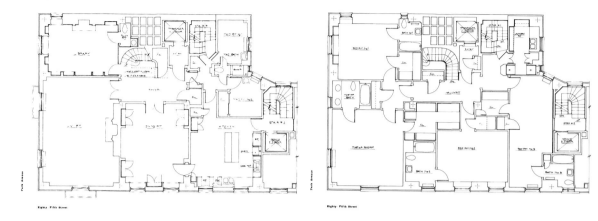

LEFT: *View of apartment building*

The unifying element throughout the apartment is the simple geometry of the square. The square geometry of the doors and interior windows was carried through to the cabinets and flush doors as cut-out pulls. This geometry, coupled with the strong tactility, consistency, and sensuousness of the materials used, results in an architecture that is both receptive and complementary to the furniture and artworks. The architect designed a number of pieces of furniture to complement the period pieces and overall scheme. These include beds, side tables, tables, and a chaise.

Construction

The apartment was demolished to the perimeter walls. New walls were placed six to eight inches in from the building walls to create both a uniform skin and a deep return at the windows. The rest of the design issues centered around surface texture, materials, and details.

Upper level floor plan

Lower level floor plan

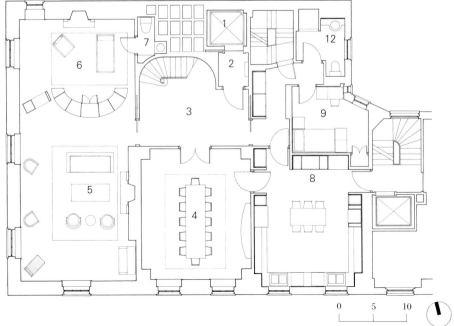

1. ELEVATOR
2. ELEVATOR VESTIBULE
3. FOYER
4. DINING ROOM
5. LIVING ROOM
6. LIBRARY/STUDY
7. POWDER ROOM
8. KITCHEN
9. MAID'S ROOM
10. HALL
11. BEDROOM
12. BATHROOM
13. MASTER BEDROOM
14. MASTER BATHROOM
15. MASTER CLOSET
16. STUDY
17. LAUNDRY

0   5   10

RIGHT: *Custom furnishing details*

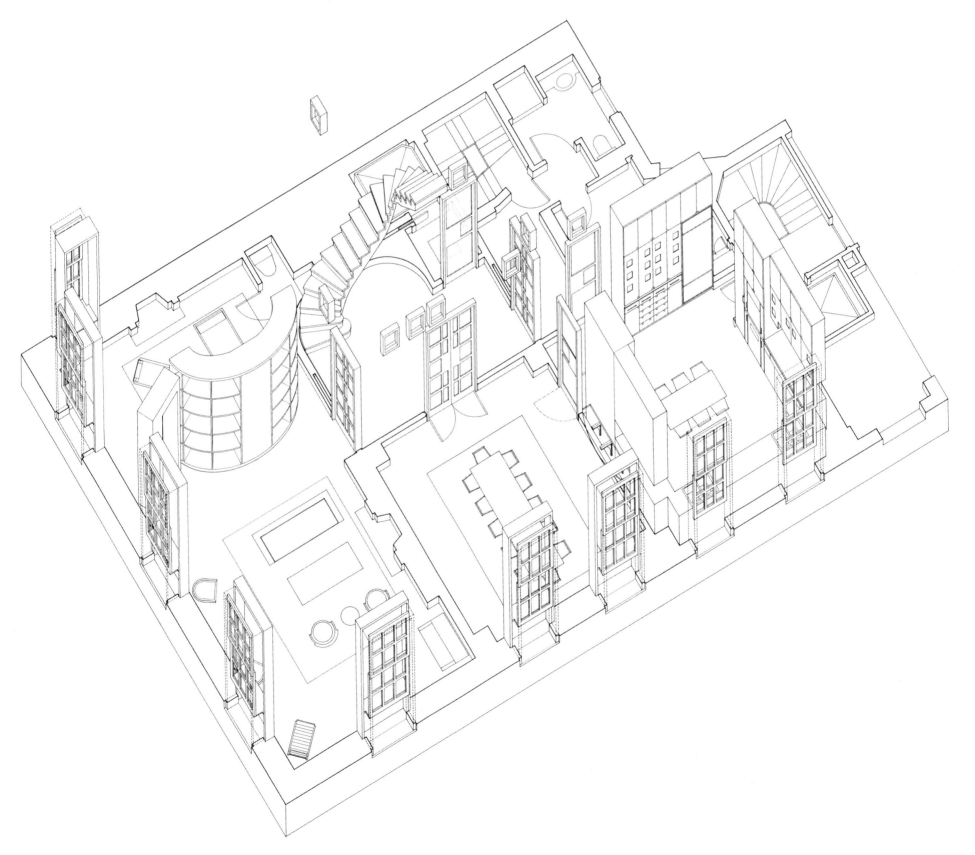

ABOVE AND BELOW: *Dining room shelf*

ABOVE AND BELOW: *Fireplace and chaise*

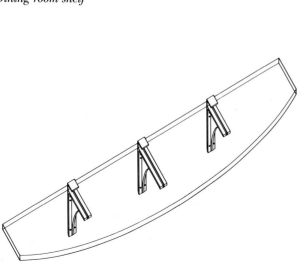

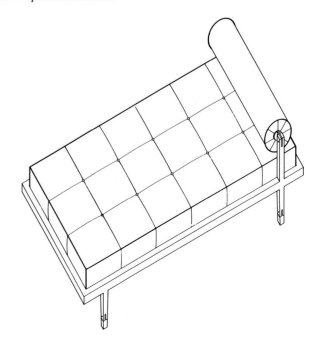

ABOVE AND BELOW: *Glass top desk*

ABOVE AND BELOW: *Bedroom and sidetables*

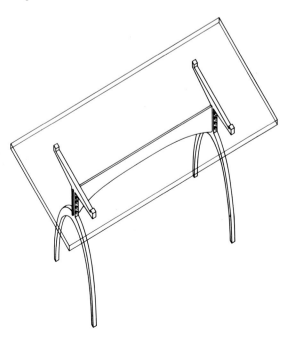

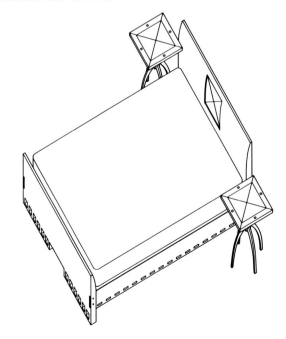

177

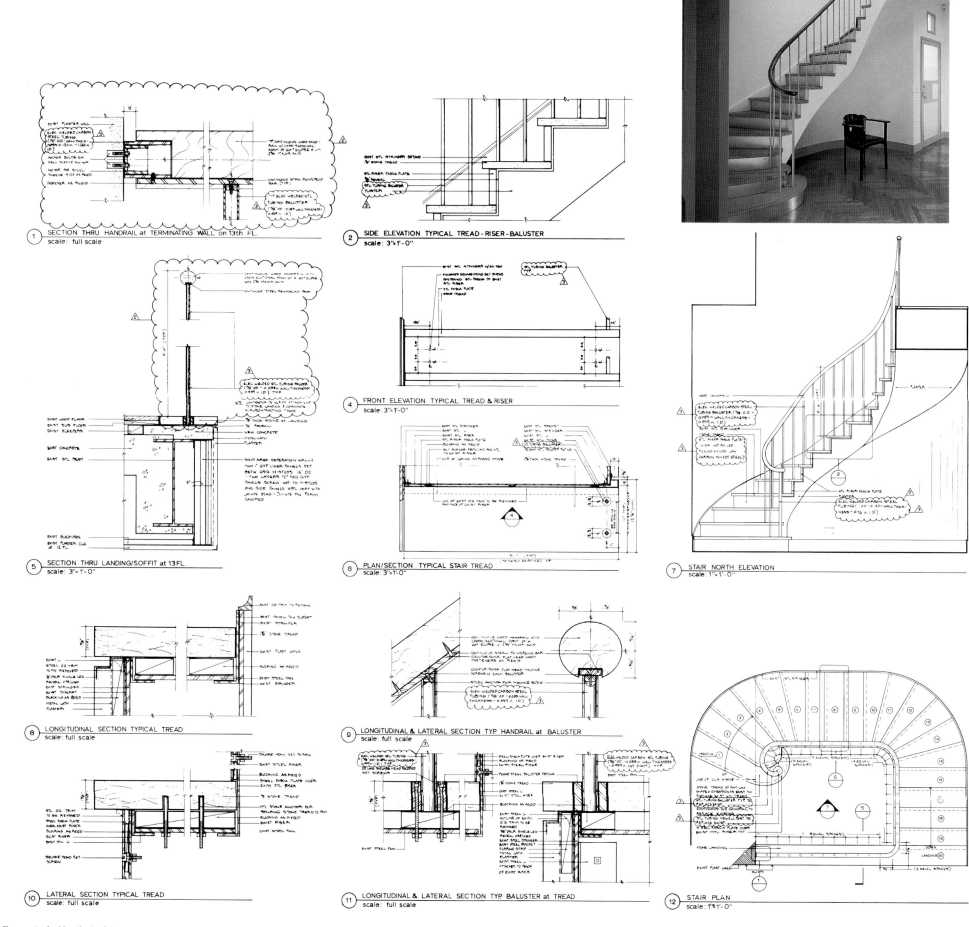

1. SECTION THRU HANDRAIL at TERMINATING WALL on 13th FL.
   scale: full scale

2. SIDE ELEVATION TYPICAL TREAD-RISER-BALUSTER
   scale: 3"=1'-0"

4. FRONT ELEVATION TYPICAL TREAD & RISER
   scale: 3"=1'-0"

5. SECTION THRU LANDING/SOFFIT at 13 FL.
   scale: 3"=1'-0"

6. PLAN/SECTION TYPICAL STAIR TREAD
   scale: 3"=1'-0"

7. STAIR NORTH ELEVATION
   scale: 1"=1'-0"

8. LONGITUDINAL SECTION TYPICAL TREAD
   scale: full scale

9. LONGITUDINAL & LATERAL SECTION TYP HANDRAIL at BALUSTER
   scale: full scale

10. LATERAL SECTION TYPICAL TREAD
    scale: full scale

11. LONGITUDINAL & LATERAL SECTION TYP BALUSTER at TREAD
    scale: full scale

12. STAIR PLAN
    scale: 1½"=1'-0"

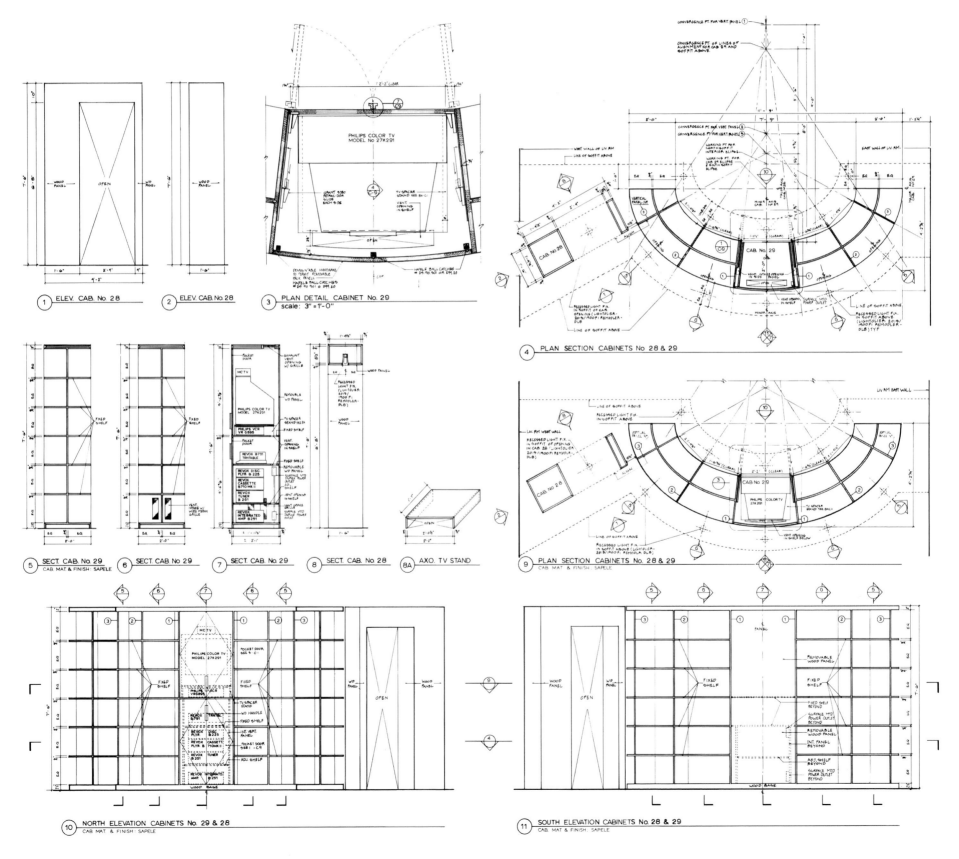

(1) ELEV. CAB. No 28

(2) ELEV. CAB. No 28

(3) PLAN DETAIL CABINET No 29
scale: 3" = 1'-0"

PHILIPS COLOR TV
MODEL No. 27K291

(4) PLAN SECTION CABINETS No 28 & 29

(5) SECT. CAB. No 29
CAB. MAT. & FINISH: SAPELE

(6) SECT. CAB. No 29

(7) SECT. CAB. No 29

(8) SECT. CAB. No 28

(8A) AXO. TV STAND

(9) PLAN SECTION CABINETS No. 28 & 29
CAB. MAT. & FINISH: SAPELE

(10) NORTH ELEVATION CABINETS No. 29 & 28
CAB. MAT. & FINISH: SAPELE

(11) SOUTH ELEVATION CABINETS No. 28 & 29
CAB. MAT. & FINISH: SAPELE

Central Park West
Apartment *1995*
TSAO & McKOWN ARCHITECTS

Owner: Calvin Tsao
Architect: Tsao & McKown Architects
Interior Designer: Tsao & McKown Architects, New York, New York
Design Team: Ted Kruger (project architect), Werner Franz, Linda Kohlman, Gary Morgenroth, Trish McKinney, Adam Rolston, Ross Wimer.
Engineers: Michael Guilfoyle of Stanley Goldstein, PC (structural)
Consultants: T. Kondos Associates and William Armstrong Lighting Design (lighting), Michael Curtin of Advanced Electric Design (electrical/audio), AWL Industries (metalwork), Bennett Cabinet (woodwork).
General Contractor: Giovannitti
Photography: Richard Bryant/Arcaid, Jen Fong (exterior)

Site: New York, New York
Program: Foyer, living room, dining room, kitchen, utility, 3 bathrooms, 2 bedrooms, dressing room, study.
Square Footage: 3500
Structural System: Concrete-encased steel frame with concrete floor slabs.
Mechanical System: Cast iron radiators, hot water from building's boiler, air conditioning from through-the-wall packaged units.
Major Interior Materials: Stainless steel, Pietra Serena limestone, Jatoba (Brazillian cherry), bluestone, soapstone, palladium, painted aluminum.
Furnishings and Storage: Giovannitti (sofa and table)
Doors and Hardware: Custom by architect, Urban Archeology (antique nickel-plated knobs).
Fixtures: Custom by architect, Urban Archeology (round light fixtures in powder room).
Appliances and Equipment: Sub-Zero (pantry refrigerator), AEG (kitchen refrigerator), 5-Star (oven, cooktop), Miele (dishwasher), custom by architect (bathtub).
Cost: Withheld at owner's request.

Site/Context
Located in a 1930s building that embodies the historic and cultural vibrancy of Manhattan's Upper West Side, this two-story unit, offering spectacular views of Central Park and the New York skyline, was originally a dark and fragmented space that housed disparate styles from several eras.

Design
A strong interest in the spirit and aesthetic values of minimalism led the architects to choose for their own apartment a strategy that would increase and liberate the existing space.

RIGHT: *View of living and dining room with stair to upper level*

LEFT: *View of apartment building*

Upper level floor plan

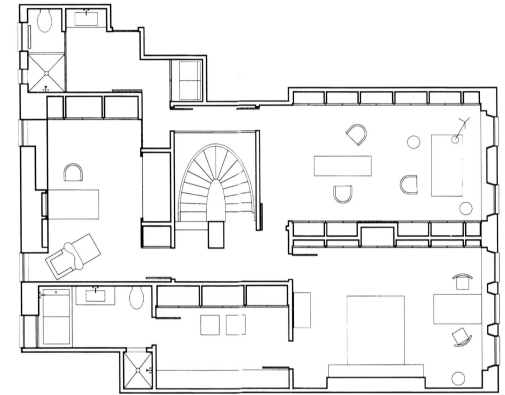

The design's central element was created by replacing the existing staircase and opening a two-story space in which the new staircase, transcending its functional role of separating public from private space, becomes the apartment's visual centerpiece. Approached as a plastic form, the steel structure with lime-putty and plaster finish is offset by a ribbon of Brazilian cherry wood that cascades down the steps. Its smooth, curving form is an elegant counterpoint to the straight lines that dominate the rest of the composition.

The architects expanded the first floor by demolishing most of the existing walls, placing services including a bathroom and pantry in perimetral positions. Windows line the living and dining room to further "open" the space, while a series of palladium-leafed panels on the living room's west wall accommodate storage. These rectangular forms, hovering inches above the floor, also introduce outdoor reflections to the interior.

The more private second-floor rooms unfold from the central stair hall. The simplicity of the bedrooms serves as the perfect backdrop for displaying the architects' carefully chosen collection of art and objects from their travels.

Harmony was achieved throughout by balancing color and materials. The staircase's cherry floors continue throughout the apartment to provide compositional continuity and contrast with the space's predominantly white palette, silver palladium leaf panels above the fireplace, and stainless steel kitchen and bathrooms.

Construction

A program was developed to establish the dimensions of the new stair within the building's concrete-encased steel frame structure. Portions of the existing concrete floor slabs were removed to provide a new slab at the "bridge" of the future staircase. Shop fabricated, then disassembled and brought on site to be rebuilt and welded into place, the steel-plate stair structure was attached directly to the existing steel beams.

Other aspects, including custom lighting, were site-built to address unique requirements. Most fixtures and furnishings were custom designed, while others—like antique fluorescent lamps from a subway train—were culled from the owners' private collection. Functions of blinds, sound system, and HVAC were centrally integrated on a computer system for convenience.

Lower level floor plan

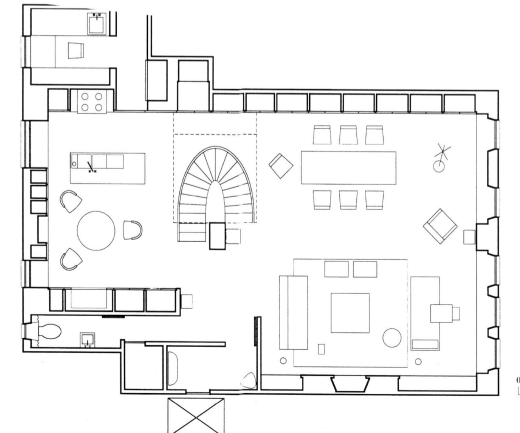

1. ENTRY
2. LIVING ROOM
3. DINING ROOM
4. UTILITY
5. KITCHEN
6. MASTER BATHROOM
7. MASTER BEDROOM
8. DRESSING ROOM
9. STUDY

0   5   10

CLOCKWISE FROM TOP LEFT:
*Master bathroom; powder
room; guest bathroom sink*
FACING PAGE: *Kitchen*

LEFT AND BELOW:
Stair details

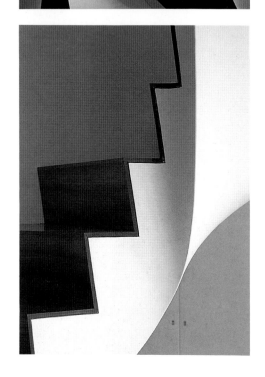

Cross section

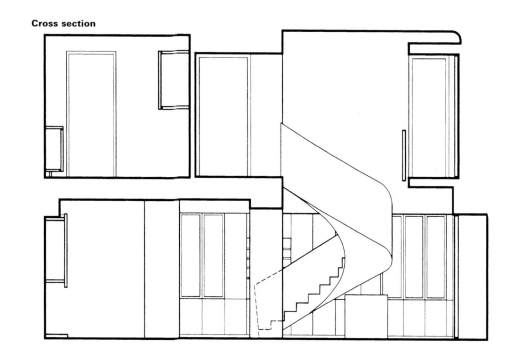

Longitudinal section

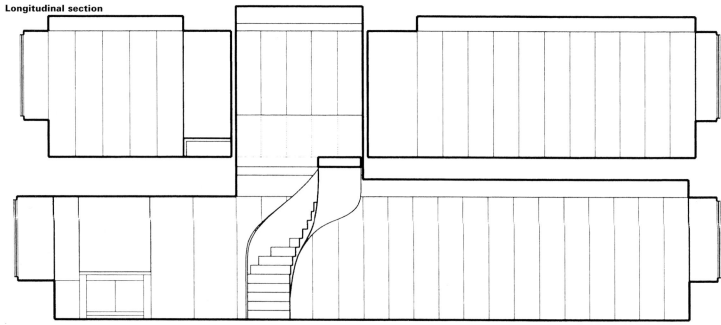

LEFT AND BELOW: *Master bedroom with custom night table*
FACING PAGE: *Dressing room toward master bedroom*

RIGHT AND BELOW: *Study with built-in seat*
FACING PAGE: *Guest bedroom*

K-Loft *1995*
GEORGE RANALLI

Owner: Jacque Metheny and Robert Kirschbaum
Architect: George Ranalli, New York, New York
Design Team: George Ranalli (principal and designer);
John Butterworth (project architect); Stephania Rinaldi
Kutscher, Nathaniel Worden (assistants).
Engineers: Robert Silman & Associates (structural),
ACM Engineering (mechanical)
Consultants: Stephen Falk, Falk Associates (specifications),
Joseph DiBernardo (lighting)
General Contractor: Lauda Construction, John Lauda,
President
Photography: Paul Warchol, George Ranalli

Site: Chelsea, New York, New York
Program: New interior for a family including 2 bedrooms,
2 bathrooms, living room, dining room, kitchen, studio,
laundry room, and entry.
Square Footage: 2100
Structural System: Walls are metal frame, gypsum board,
and plaster; platform is steel frame and metal deck.
Mechanical System: Existing steam heat, sleeve
air conditioners
Major Interior Materials: Skim coat gypsum board, laminate
glass, Finnish plywood, Russian plywood, Surell, ceramic tile,
walnut trim, acid etched glass.
Furnishings and Storage: Custom by architect
Doors and Hardware: Doors custom by architect, J. Lauda
(fabricator); Schlage hardware
Fixtures: American Standard, Kroin (bathroom);
Surell (kitchen sink)
Appliances and Equipment:: GE Monogram series
(refrigerator/freezer), GE (stove, oven, washer, dryer),
Bosch (dishwasher), Thermasol (steam shower), J. Depp Inc.
(laminate glass).
Cost: Withheld at owner's request.

Site/Context

The apartment is located in an industrial building in the
Chelsea section of Manhattan. Built almost ninety years
ago as part of the turn-of-the-century construction in lower
Manhattan, the building's interior has windows only on the
front and back. The loft is located on a lower floor of the
building, so the amount of natural light is very limited.

The architect found the existing space compelling: a
brick room with exposed brick bearing walls running the
length of the space, and a brick ceiling with a series of
vaults spanning steel sections from the front to the back
of the loft.

Design

The interior organization had to take into account the
requirement of natural light and ventilation in habitable
rooms as well as the programmatic desires of the owners,
who went from being a single couple to a family. The
existing mechanical risers, elevator, and stair helped to

LEFT: *View of former industrial building*

arrange the apartment layout, which is designed to maximize the passage of light from one space to another.

The owner's programmatic requirements are contained in a series of new forms, or volumes, inserted by the architect. Not only do these volumes contain two bedrooms, a master bathroom, and kitchen, but the original loft's open, airy quality is preserved.

As built, the solution features a series of volumes that allow the space of the room to remain continuous. Each volume takes a key position in the apartment, so that it contains space as well as produces space between the forms. First constructed of plaster, the volumes are then fixed with translucent glass set into the blocks. These glass openings permit the passage of light from one room to another. The corners are protected with large panels of birch plywood which are cut in irregular profiles to help establish a second range of scale to the rooms. These panels are affixed to the plaster walls with a pattern of screw fasteners. All doors, lamps, cabinets, and other decorative objects are custom designed as part of the project.

Among the owner's criteria was that the project be completed within an acceptable budget—and it was.

Construction

The project was designed and built in high-finish materials to accent, and contrast with the rough container of the existing brick shell. The main structure and surface of the new elements is frame and skimcoat gypsum board. This gives a smooth, durable finish to the new shapes. The corners of these blocks are covered with sheets of Russian plywood. This protects the plaster corners from damage as the spaces are used, and also provides a second level of detail and design.

Surell was used in the kitchen and bath because it is an impervious material that can be worked like wood, and also because it can be joined without seams. Detailed as a wall surface in the master bathroom, the material then repeats in the sink block, vanity counter, and radiator covers. In the kitchen Surell was used for the counter, backsplash, and to protect the low counter at the end of the kitchen. The architect's investigations of material joinery led to the interlocking of both wood and Surell panels. The alteration of panel size and shape explores the possibilities of design, pattern, and decoration in contemporary sheet stock material.

Existing conditions

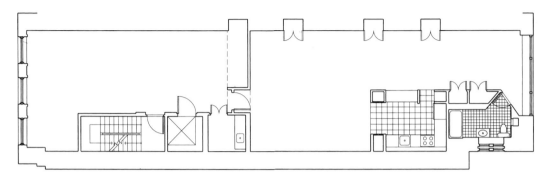

Floor plan

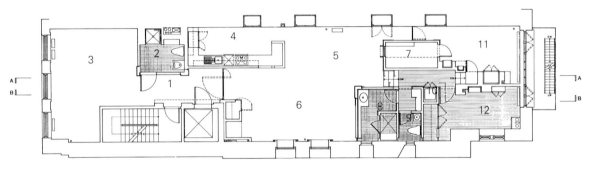

1. ENTRY
2. BATHROOM
3. STUDIO/GALLERY
4. KITCHEN
5. DINING ROOM
6. LIVING ROOM
7. MASTER DRESSING ROOM
8. MASTER BATHING ROOM
9. TOILET
10. LAUNDRY
11. MASTER BEDROOM
12. CHILD'S ROOM

0   5   10

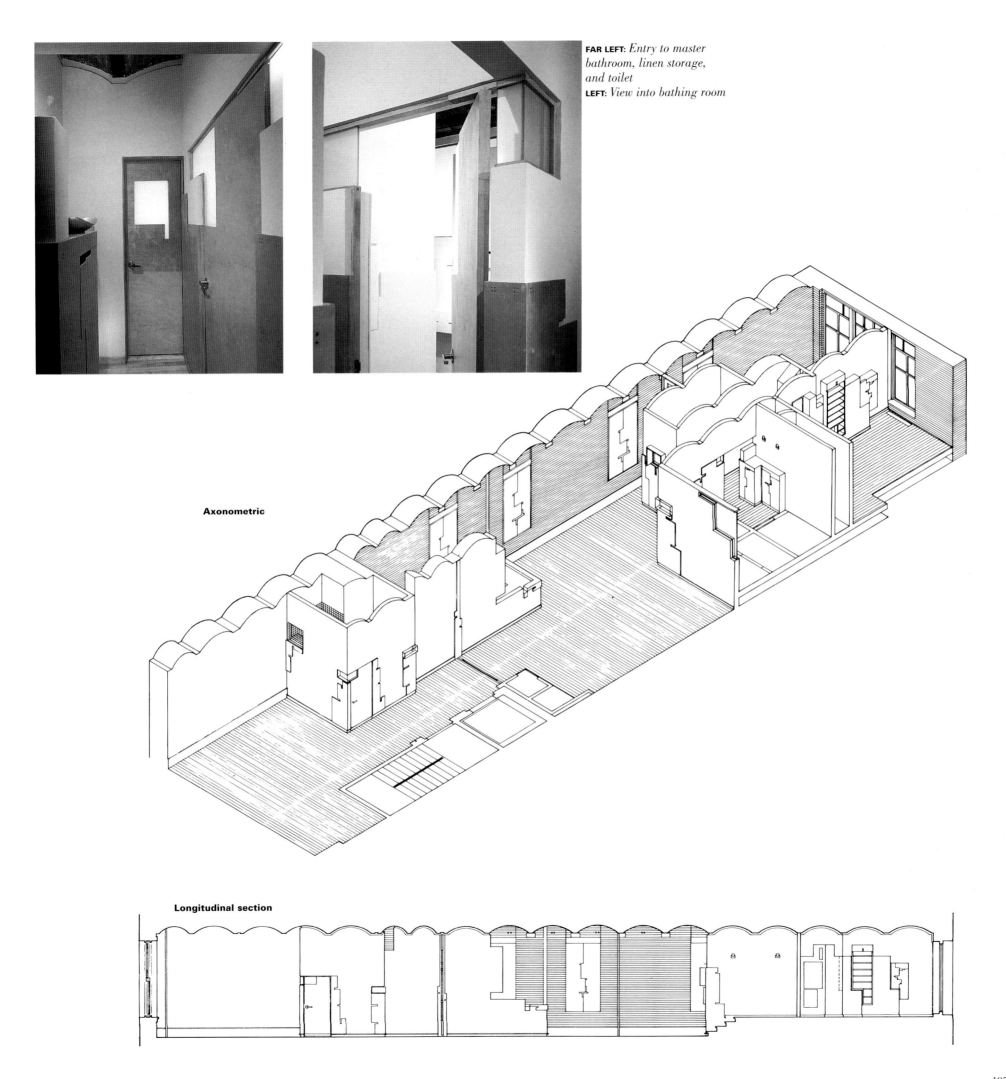

FAR LEFT: *Entry to master bathroom, linen storage, and toilet*

LEFT: *View into bathing room*

Axonometric

Longitudinal section

CLOCKWISE FROM TOP LEFT:
*Entry to master bedroom
and child's bedroom;
bathing room; detail of
kitchen wall with cupboard
beyond; inlaid walnut stair
treads; master bedroom*
FACING PAGE: *Kitchen*

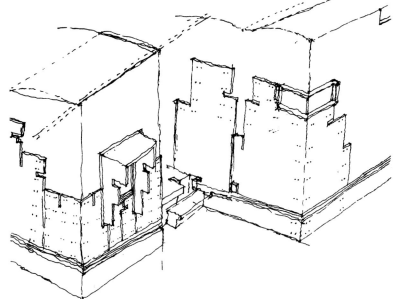

LEFT: *Volumes with glass panels*

Volume construction drawings

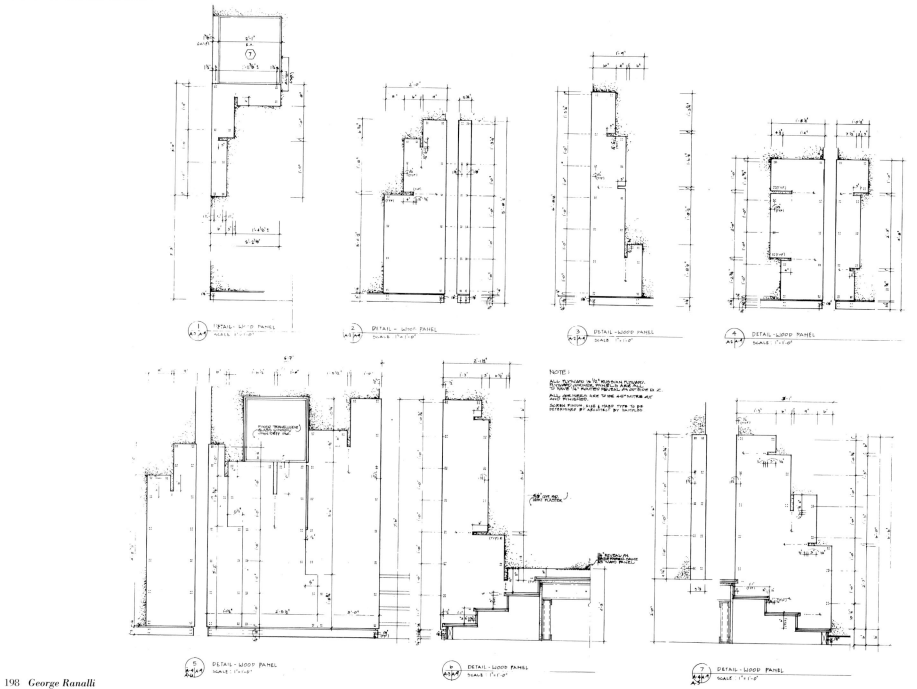

Axonometric of master bedroom

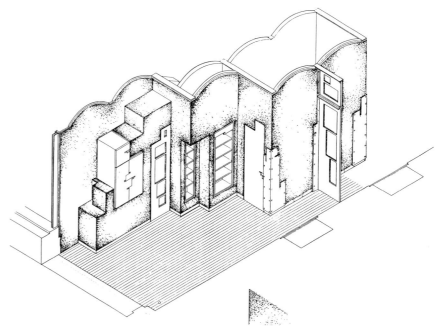

Master bedroom entry door details

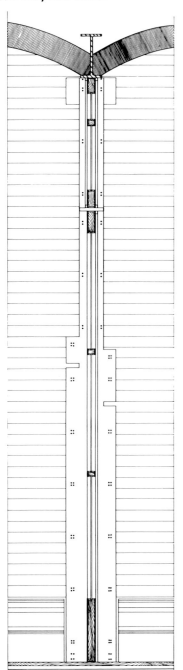

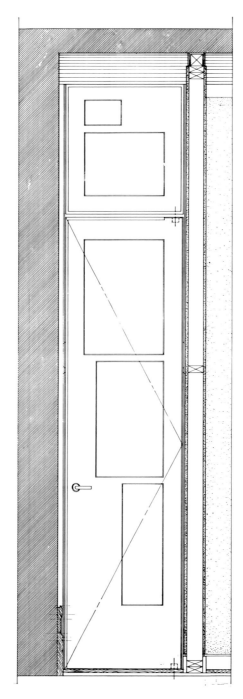

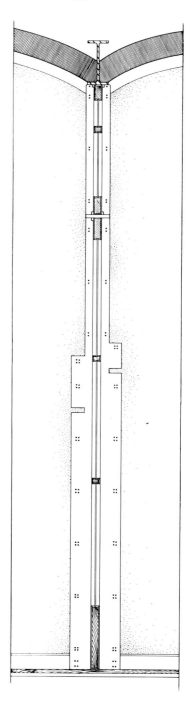

Chelsea Loft

1993-1994

SCOTT MARBLE &
KAREN FAIRBANKS ARCHITECTS

Owner: Name withheld at owner's request.
Architect: Scott Marble & Karen Fairbanks Architects,
New York, New York
Design Team: Karen Fairbanks, Scott Marble, Jay Berman,
Pete Cornell.
General Contractor: Up-Rite Construction
Photography: Peter Paige, © Arch Photo Inc., Eduard Hueber

Site: New York, New York
Program: Residential loft for family of four. Living room,
dining room, family room, kitchen with utility area, breakfast
room, study, 4 bedrooms, 3 bathrooms.
Square Footage: 4500
Structural System: Existing concrete beams and columns
Mechanical System: Central air conditioning
Major Interior Materials: Dyed ash (kitchen cabinets),
black granite (countertop), cork and linoleum, maple, walnut
(floors), fiberboard, translucent glass.
Furnishings and Storage: Purchased by owner; kitchen
cabinets custom by architect.
Doors and Hardware: Custom by architect, fabricated
by Sub Urban Building Studio, Inc.
Fixtures: American Standard
Appliances and Equipment: Sub-Zero (refrigerator)

Site/Context

Urban dwellers are more commonly turning to industrial
lofts as a residential alternative due to their generous
size and openness. This loft is located in an early-
twentieth-century industrial building in Chelsea that,
like many buildings of this type in New York, has
evolved into a residential cooperative. The neighborhood
is both residential and commercial, with a new influx of
art galleries relocating from Soho. Given the typical lot
within the Manhattan grid, this building is unusual for
its longitudinal orientation parallel to the street and its
southern exposure with numerous large windows.

Design

The building's orientation and resulting light and shadows cast by the window bays inspired the design of the
apartment's main feature, a series of sliding fiberboard
and glass screens and pivoting glass and aluminum
doors. Although areas are designated for specific domestic functions, four large sliding screens and three pivoting doors transform individual areas into an uninterrupted space, thereby allowing activities to freely mingle. At
certain times of day, shadows cross the floor and bend
up the face of the panels, combining with the diagonal
lines to form a collage of light and pattern and a perspectival illusion of a continuous space.

RIGHT: *View of main living/
dining space with wall of
windows*

Floor patterns, materials, and ceiling elements run between adjacent rooms to reinforce specific connections between related activities. For instance, a cork floor and low ceiling in the study continue into the parent's bedroom, making a link that is regulated by the pivot doors. The kitchen and breakfast alcove are linked by a low circular soffit overhead.

Construction

The architects achieved a minimalist effect by allowing the materials to be understood as surfaces without emphasizing their joints and connections. They collaborated closely with the fabricator of the sliding screens and pivoting doors, detailing them to support this notion.

The sliding screens are fiberboard and translucent glass. Each screen is uniquely configured, making its visual composition and physical weight distribution different. The glass in the screens slips between the fiberboard panels to become the structural connection from one section of fiberboard to another. The pivoting doors are fiberboard, translucent glass, and aluminum, designed to form a three-dimensional parallelogram. The aluminum panels contain two circular cutouts that allow light to pass through the doors while simultaneously providing structure for the asymmetrical pivot.

Floor plan

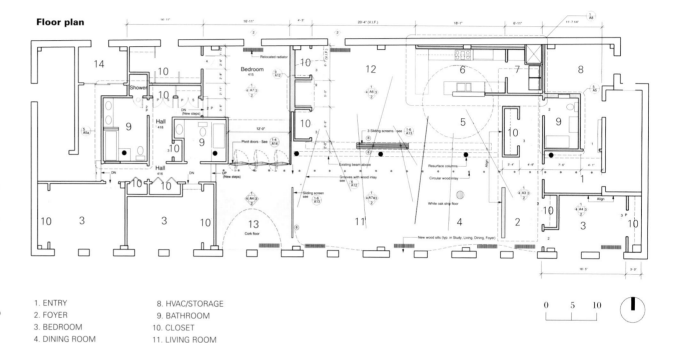

1. ENTRY
2. FOYER
3. BEDROOM
4. DINING ROOM
5. BREAKFAST ALCOVE
6. KITCHEN
7. UTILITY
8. HVAC/STORAGE
9. BATHROOM
10. CLOSET
11. LIVING ROOM
12. FAMILY ROOM
13. STUDY
14. HVAC

0   5   10

Sliding screens and pivoting doors in plan and elevation

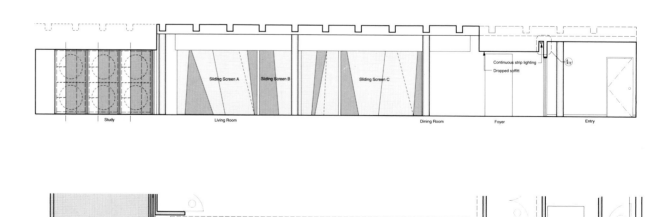

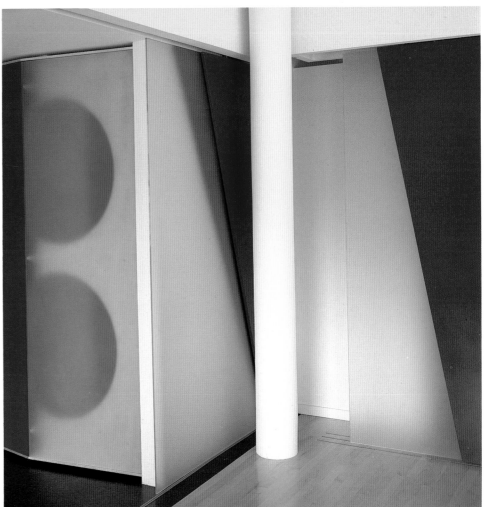

LEFT TOP AND BOTTOM: *Views of pivoting doors to bedroom*
FACING PAGE: *Selected details of door and screen construction*

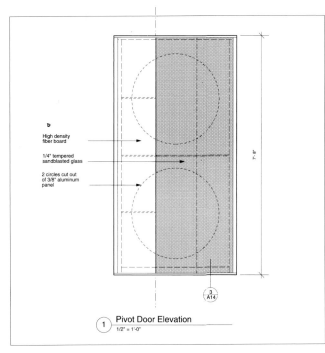

High density
fiber board

1/4" tempered
sandblasted glass

2 circles cut out
of 3/8" aluminum
panel

7'- 8"

3
A14

① Pivot Door Elevation
1/2" = 1'-0"

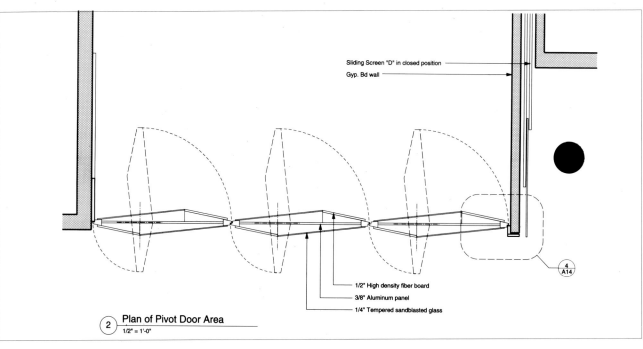

Sliding Screen "D" in closed position

Gyp. Bd wall

4
A14

1/2" High density fiber board

3/8" Aluminum panel

1/4" Tempered sandblasted glass

② Plan of Pivot Door Area
1/2" = 1'-0"

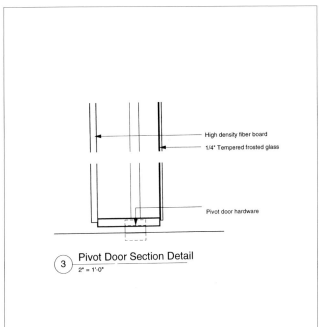

High density fiber board

1/4" Tempered frosted glass

Pivot door hardware

③ Pivot Door Section Detail
2" = 1'-0"

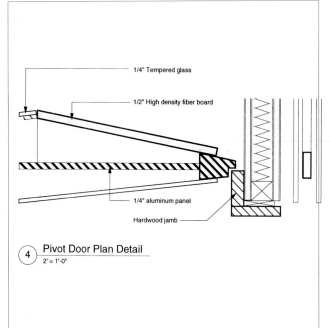

1/4" Tempered glass

1/2" High density fiber board

1/4" aluminum panel

Hardwood jamb

④ Pivot Door Plan Detail
2' = 1'-0"

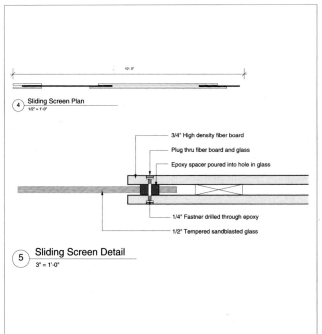

10'- 0"

④ Sliding Screen Plan
1/2" = 1'-0"

3/4" High density fiber board

Plug thru fiber board and glass

Epoxy spacer poured into hole in glass

1/4" Fastner drilled through epoxy

1/2" Tempered sandblasted glass

⑤ Sliding Screen Detail
3" = 1'-0"

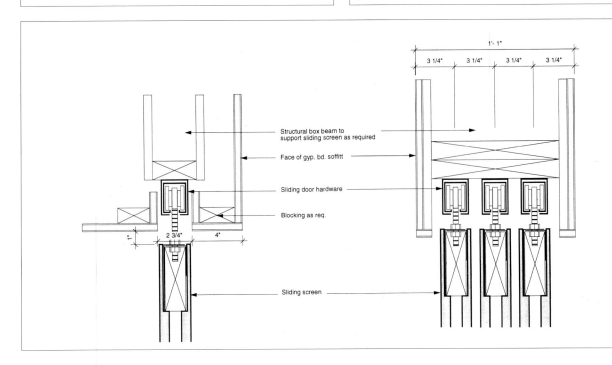

Structural box beam to
support sliding screen as required

Face of gyp. bd. soffitt

Sliding door hardware

Blocking as req.

Sliding screen

2 3/4"   4"

1'- 1"

3 1/4"   3 1/4"   3 1/4"   3 1/4"

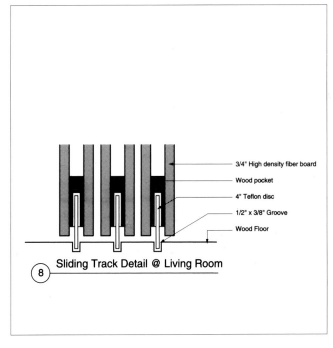

3/4" High density fiber board

Wood pocket

4" Teflon disc

1/2" x 3/8" Groove

Wood Floor

⑧ Sliding Track Detail @ Living Room

Private Residence with 13 Cabinets *1991-1994*
WESLEY WEI ARCHITECTS

Owner: Name withheld at owner's request.
Architect: Wesley Wei Architects, Philadelphia, Pennsylvania
Design Team: Wesley Wei AIA (principal-in-charge), Andrew Phillips, Barry Ginder, Suzanne Brandt, Hua Tran, Patrick McGranahan, Alice Chun, Christopher Dardis.
Addition: Daniel Magno, Douglas Patt, Michael Graff.
General Contractor: M. Kowalchick & Associates
Photography:© Catherine Bogert 1995

Site: Rittenhouse Square, Philadelphia, Pennsylvania
Program: Conversion of two contiguous apartments into one. Living/dining room, kitchen, master bedroom, master bathroom, study, laundry. Addition: study/dressing, bath annex.
Square Footage: 3000; Addition: 1300
Structural System: Existing steel frame, concrete slab
Mechanical System: Existing radiant water system
Major Interior Materials: Oak hardwood, polished concrete and marble (floors), painted plaster (ceilings and walls), marble tile (baths), aluminum and textured glass (window-walls), plate steel lintels, maple/bird's-eye maple (pivot doors).
Furnishings and Storage: Built-ins by architect; cabinet interiors fabrication by Daniel Magno, Steven Turk, Andrew Phillips, Wesley Wei.
Doors and Hardware: Hager, Rixson-Firemark, Schlage hinges.
Fixtures: Chicago, Grohe
Appliances and Equipment: Gaggenau (cooktop, extractor, dishwasher), Sub-Zero (refrigerator)
Cost: Withheld at owner's request.

Site/Context
The apartment occupies a sixth-floor corner unit in a 1950s Moderne building on Rittenhouse Square, one of the five original squares in the William Penn plan of the city. The program was to convert two contiguous units to one 3000-square-foot residence. The existing conditions were an accretion of additions and alterations made during the last thirty-five years, resulting in a cacophony of senseless spaces. The ceiling height (8'-2") defined a wafer-like space.

Design
The primary theme was developed in response to the oppressive quality of the existing space. The "weight" of the building was countered with the use of interstitial columns. Derived from utilitarian and poetic intentions, these twelve columns established the order of the project. Some of them appropriated existing structure and mechanical chases while acting together to provide a framework for further interventions.

Perspective rendering

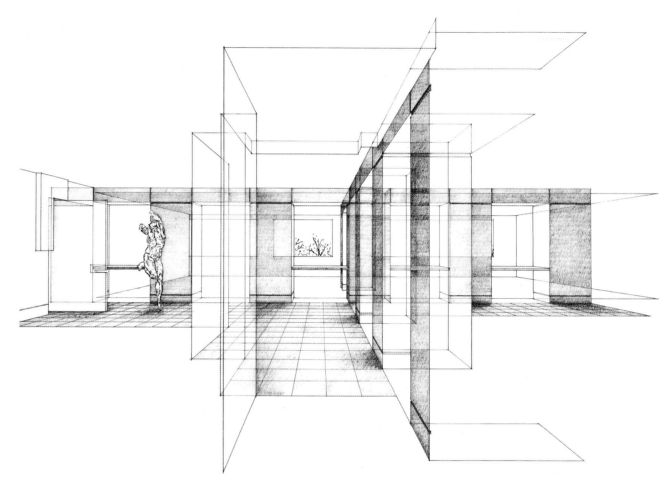

The columns, also functioning as cabinets, visually support the weight of the ceiling while engaging the imagination through the intimate spaces of their cavities. The cabinets' contents were determined by their positions in the apartment. Ranging from a wardrobe and drawers to the enigmatic figures that flank the living and dining area, each cabinet was given a name —Adam and Eve, The Fates, Pandora's Box—to reflect a relationship between the objects inside and their immediate environment.

Two years after completion of the initial construction, the architect designed an addition through an adjacent unit. The new space was conceived as an exposed "anatomical setting" populated with architectural fragments. The passage between the earlier completed unit and the addition occurs along the exterior building wall, cutting the interior free from the existing perimeter. This incision is "stitched" with sliding door panels, floating soffits, and an aluminum and glass window wall.

Construction
Painted ash veneer casework defines one wall of the study, while the figure and pivoting mask of the thirteenth cabinet conceal existing plumbing stacks. Cabinet interiors are composed of wood, aluminum, bronze, acid-etched zinc plate, and glass mirrors. The glass and aluminum window wall and the aluminum, bronze, and plate steel hardware were designed, fabricated, and installed by the architect and assistants.

Existing conditions

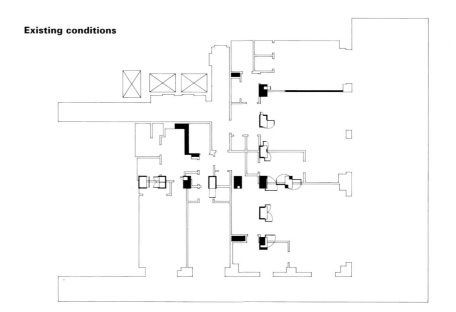

Floor plan

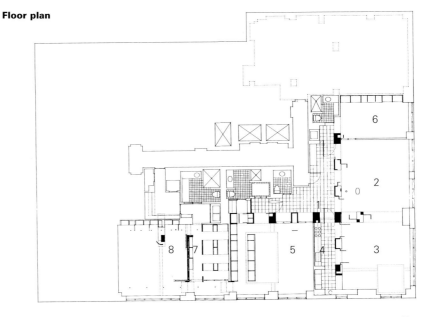

1. ENTRY
2. LIVING ROOM
3. DINING ROOM
4. KITCHEN
5. BEDROOM
6. GUEST BEDROOM
7. DRESSING ROOM
8. STUDY

0 5 10

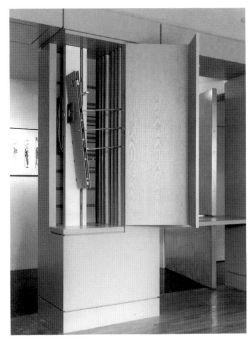

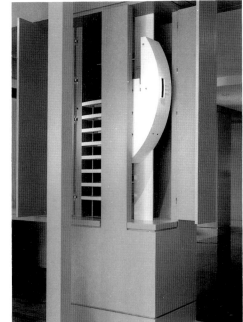

Axonometrics of cabinets

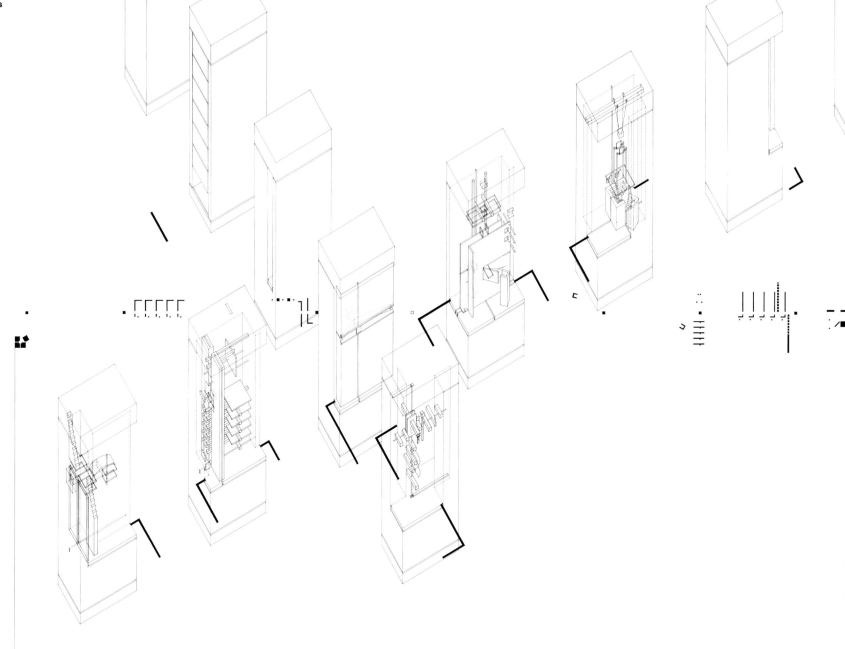

CLOCKWISE FROM TOP LEFT:
Entry to master bedroom with window wall to whirlpool bath; bathroom; view from living room through entry hall to master bedroom pivot door; master bedroom entry wih floating plane above.
FACING PAGE: *Informant cabinet at left with Fates at right*

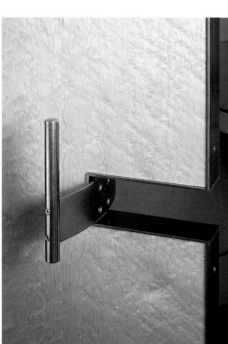

Hardware details and assembly

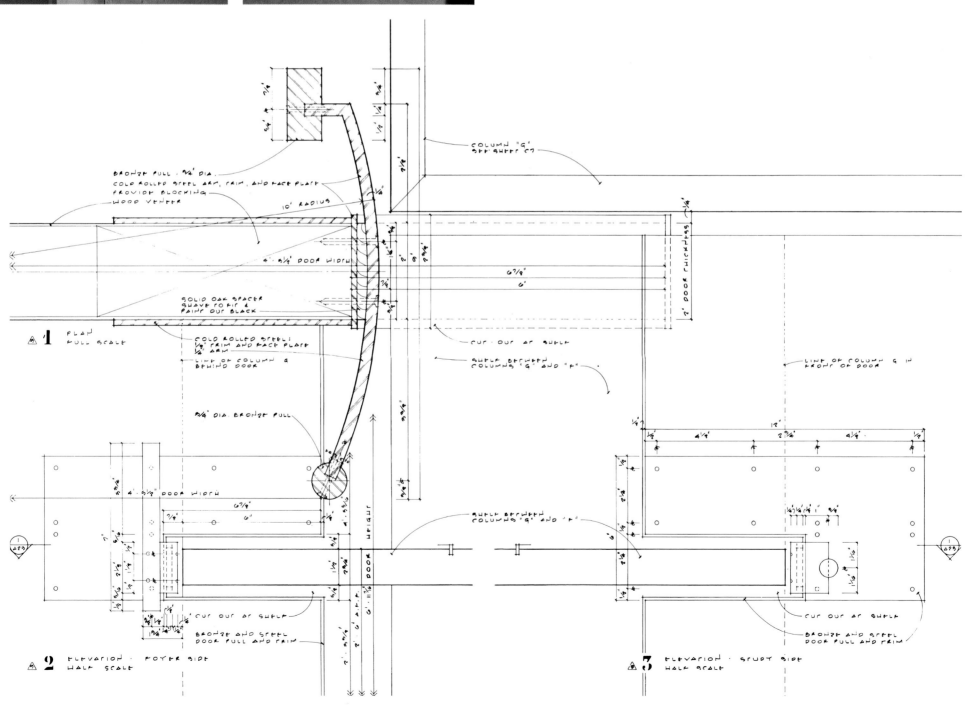

BRONZE PULL · 7/8" DIA.
COLD ROLLED STEEL ARM, TRIM, AND FACE PLATE
PROVIDE BLOCKING
WOOD VENEER

10" RADIUS

COLUMN "G"
SEE SHEET S7

4'-5½" DOOR WIDTH

SOLID OAK SPACER
SHAVE TO FIT &
PAINT OUT BLACK

6 7/8"
6"

2" DOOR THICKNESS

CUT OUT AT SHELF

SHELF BETWEEN
COLUMNS "G" AND "F"

LINE OF COLUMN "G" IN
FRONT OF DOOR

COLD ROLLED STEEL:
1/8" TRIM AND FACE PLATE
1/4" ARM

LINE OF COLUMN G
BEHIND DOOR

⚠ **1** PLAN
FULL SCALE

7/8" DIA. BRONZE PULL

4'-5½" DOOR WIDTH
6 7/8"
6"

SHELF BETWEEN
COLUMNS "G" AND "F"

DOOR HEIGHT

CUT OUT AT SHELF

BRONZE AND STEEL
DOOR PULL AND TRIM

⚠ **2** ELEVATION · FOYER SIDE
HALF SCALE

CUT OUT AT SHELF

BRONZE AND STEEL
DOOR PULL AND TRIM

⚠ **3** ELEVATION · STUDY SIDE
HALF SCALE

Pivoting door details

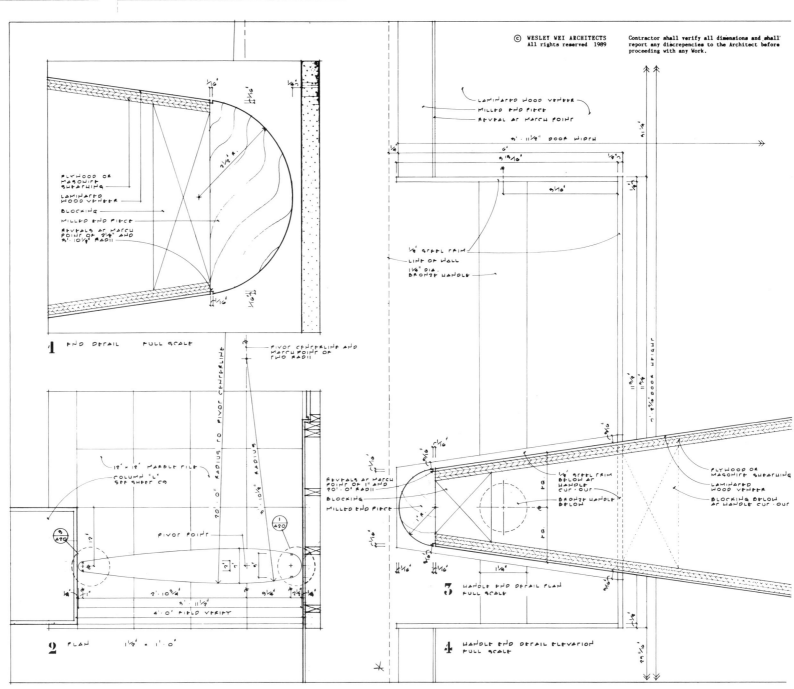

Contractor shall verify all dimensions and shall report any discrepencies to the Architect before proceeding with any Work.

215

Lipschutz/Jones Apartment

1987-1989

FRANK LUPO AND DANIEL ROWEN, ARCHITECTS

Owner: William Lipschutz and Lynnelle Jones
Architect: Frank Lupo and Daniel Rowen, Architects, New York, New York
Design Team: Frank Lupo, Daniel Rowen (partners-in-charge); Alissa Bucher, Richard Blender.
Engineers: Severud Associates (structural), Ambrosino, DePinto & Schmieder (mechanical)
General Contractor: Gordon Construction
Photography: Michael Moran

Site: New York, New York
Program: Foyer, powder room, library, office/guest bedroom, dressing room, eat-in kitchen, living/dining room, master bedroom, master bathroom.
Square Footage: 1500
Structural System: Wood frame with steel beams
Mechanical System: Heat pump/air conditioners
Major Interior Materials: Figured maple (cabinets), Vermont green slate, clear maple planks, white marble, Pirelli rubber, custom V'Soske carpeting (flooring), Absolute black granite, Verde antique marble (counters), cold rolled steel, stainless steel (stair, rails, and heat pump/air conditioning enclosures), stainless steel wire mesh, pigmented plaster (walls and ceilings).
Furnishings and Storage: Built-in cabinetry by architect, Rietveld chair, Eileen Gray chair, Fortuny lamp.
Doors and Hardware: Custom by architects, hardware by Lamp.
Windows: Sun Windows (jalousie), PPG (glass block), Dluback (curved glass).
Fixtures: Speakman (faucets), American Standard (water closets), Jacuzzi (tub).
Appliances and Equipment: Gaggenau (cooktop and oven), Sub-Zero (refrigerator/freezer), Kitchen-Aid (dishwasher).
Cost: $400 per square foot

Site/Context

The apartment is located in a downtown Manhattan industrial building that was joined with both new and old adjacent buildings upon conversion. The owner's unit is housed in the building's older, cast iron warehouse section.

Design

The design combines the organizational principles appropriate to the making of both a large cabinet and a small house. The program called for an open bedroom and a private office that could double as a guest bedroom. Though the space was limited, it was also a programmatic requirement that these two components be as distant from one another as possible. In addition to these two rooms, an entry foyer, powder room, dressing room, eat-in kitchen, library, living room/dining room, and master bathroom were also to be included. This was all to be accomplished without losing the sense of space made possible by fifteen-foot-high ceilings.

RIGHT: *Double height living room with bedroom loft at right*

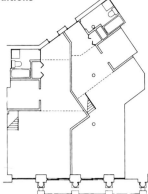

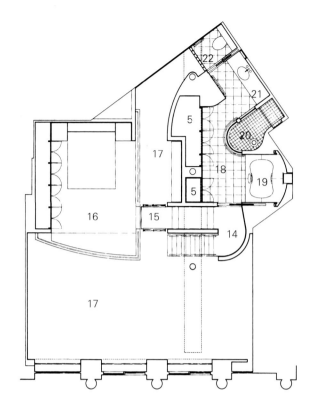

The entire program was consolidated to the corridor side of the plan, thereby creating a large, double-height space along the window wall and exterior balcony. The program mass is divided in two and separated, providing the desired vertical and horizontal distance between the bedroom and office. The resultant space between these two halves yields a tall and narrow double-height library corridor that leads from the entry vestibule, through the apartment, to the wall of natural light at the perimeter of the living/dining room. The large living/dining room is a volume bordered on one side by tall windows showing city views and on the other by the sculptural façade of the bedroom loft and stair/bridge combination. The public space acts like an outdoor room from which the façade of the bedroom loft can be viewed. The intention of this arrangement is to permit an understanding of the entire apartment from within its own boundaries.

Vertical circulation is gathered into a combination of a stainless steel stair ladder, a curved landing, "the dipsy-doodle" (an up-and-down stair mediating an existing beam), and "the bucket" (a stainless steel cantilevered bridge spanning the library corridor and providing access to the bedroom loft).

Construction

The project's compositional simplicity allows the properties of each material used to be expressed as fully as possible; pigmented plaster, figured maple, slate, granite, marble, acid-etched glass, aluminum, and stainless steel enrich the apartment's neutral tonality.

Lower level floor plan

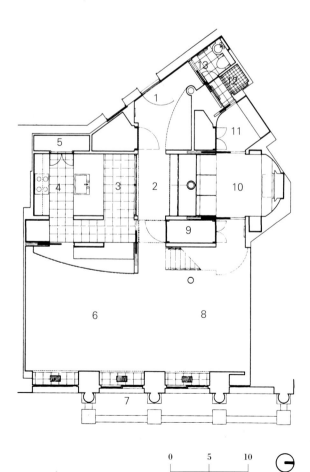

1. ENTRY
2. FOYER
3. BREAKFAST ROOM
4. KITCHEN
5. CLOSET
6. LIVING ROOM
7. BALCONY
8. DINING ROOM
9. STORAGE
10. TRADING ROOM
11. DRESSING ROOM
12. SHOWER ROOM
13. POWDER ROOM
14. LANDING
15. BRIDGE
16. BEDROOM
17. OPEN
18. BATHROOM
19. WHIRLPOOL BATH
20. SHOWER
21. LAVATORY
22. TOILET

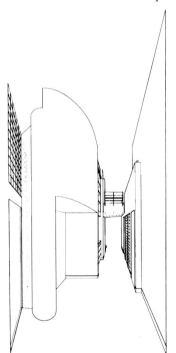

Perspective sketch of entry corridor

0   5   10

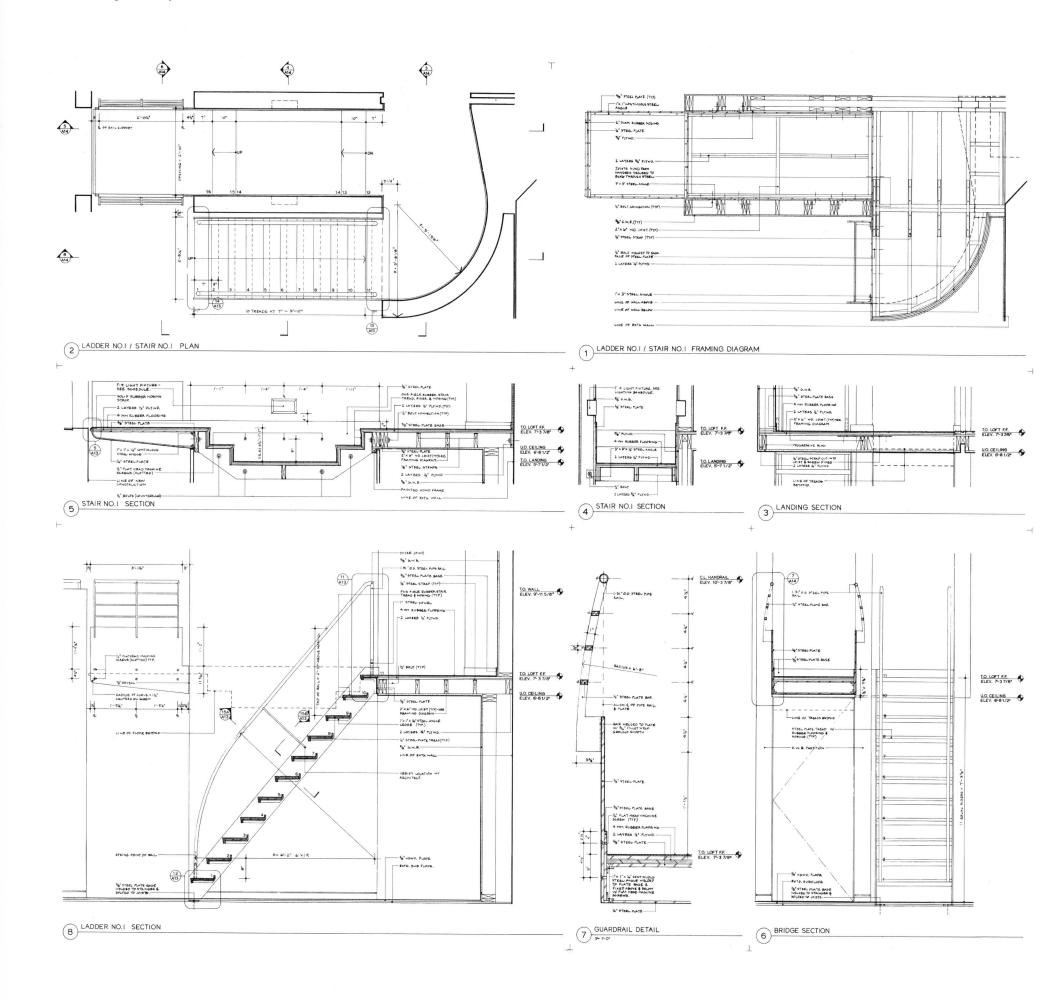

2 LADDER NO.1 / STAIR NO.1 PLAN

1 LADDER NO.1 / STAIR NO.1 FRAMING DIAGRAM

5 STAIR NO.1 SECTION

4 STAIR NO.1 SECTION

3 LANDING SECTION

8 LADDER NO.1 SECTION

7 GUARDRAIL DETAIL

6 BRIDGE SECTION

Melia Warehouse
Renovation *1987-1991*
ANTHONY AMES ARCHITECT

Owner: Deborah and Michael Melia
Architect: Anthony Ames Architect, Atlanta, Georgia
Design Team: Anthony Ames (principal in charge), J. James Strange, Clark Tefft, William Pantsari, Denise Dumais (assistant muralist).
Engineer: Russ Johnson (structural)
General Contractor: S & S Contracting
Photography: Toby Abrams

Site: Atlanta, Georgia
Program: Single-family residence including living room, dining space, kitchen, 2 bedrooms, 2 bathrooms, study/gallery, roof deck, sleeping porch.
Square Footage: 3400
Structural System: Existing post and beam construction with exterior load bearing masonry walls.
Mechanical System: Forced air HVAC
Major Exterior Materials: Masonry
Major Interior Materials: Gypsum board walls and ceilings, hardwood floors.
Furnishings and Storage: Built-in by architect, rug by V'Soske, furniture by Cassina, Knoll, Nienkamper, ICF, and by architect.
Doors and Hardware: Interior doors solid core wood, hardware by Schlage.
Windows: Existing steel frame awning windows
Fixtures: American Standard
Appliances and Equipment: General Electric
Cost: Withheld at owner's request.

Site/Context

The apartment is located in a one-story, L-shaped warehouse northeast of downtown Atlanta and adjacent to the Jimmy Carter Library. A transitional area, the neighborhood is conveniently close to the downtown commercial district. The building offers a panoramic view of the city from the roof.

Design

The clients are a young couple who wanted to convert the raw warehouse space into rental apartments, an office for his graphic design business, and their own living space.

The scheme is quite straightforward. The office and their living space face the street while a long corridor, cut perpendicular to and bisecting the façade, provides access to the rental units to the rear of the L. For reasons of economy and simplicity, the rental units and office are relatively uneventful. The clients' living space, however, allowed for a more inspired solution.

The clients' wants and needs were basic—a living room, dining space, small kitchen, two bedrooms, two bathrooms, a study or gallery, and access to a roof deck and sleeping porch. An attempt was made to provide

RIGHT: *View toward living room with murals on left and right*

LEFT: *View of former warehouse*

Existing conditions

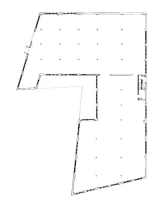

a variety of spatial types and experiences—a rotunda, a vaulted gallery, and an open living area—with the juxtaposition of circulation types—tight carved hallways and free-flowing adjacencies.

Framed views, murals, and natural light direct one along the architectural promenade that commences at the rotunda and culminates on the roof deck with its view of downtown Atlanta.

Construction

The existing warehouse consists of concrete brick exterior walls, steel awning windows, and wood columns. The space was gutted, leaving only the wood columns for physical structure and conceptual and perceptual order. The gypsum-board walls were thus free to assume only the requirements of spatial enclosure. The new floors are wood. Glass block and a skylight were introduced to allow the passage of natural light.

Roof plan

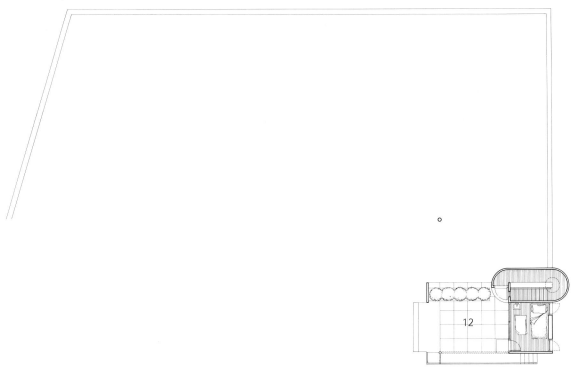

Ground floor plan

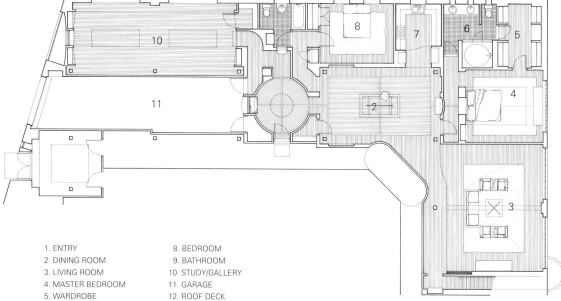

1. ENTRY
2. DINING ROOM
3. LIVING ROOM
4. MASTER BEDROOM
5. WARDROBE
6. MASTER BATHROOM
7. KITCHEN
8. BEDROOM
9. BATHROOM
10. STUDY/GALLERY
11. GARAGE
12. ROOF DECK
13. SLEEPING PORCH (NOT REALIZED)

0   5   10

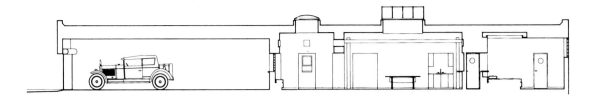

BELOW: *Bedroom with recessed ceiling*

CLOCKWISE FROM TOP LEFT: *View from entry rotunda toward dining room; kitchen; mural connecting living and dining areas* **FACING PAGE:** *Dining room with recessed walls and skylight*

LEFT: *Coffee table by architect*
RIGHT: *Dining room with table by architect*

Coffee table plan and elevations

Dining table plan and elevations

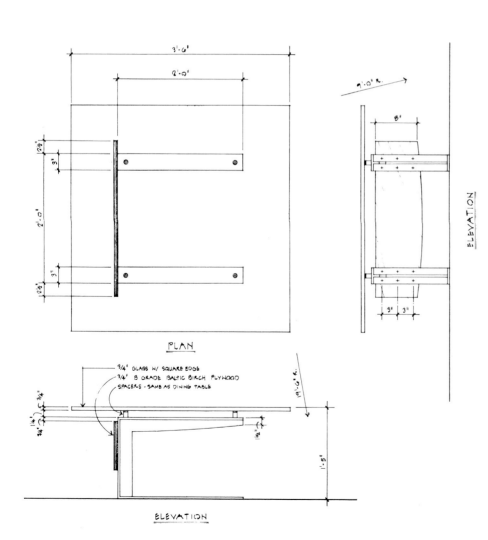

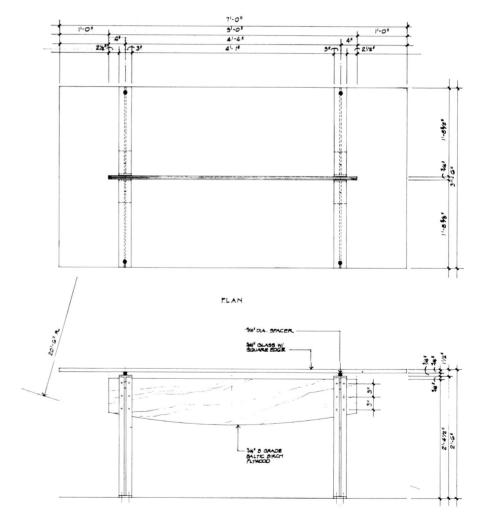

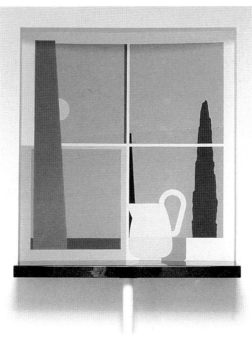

Sideboard plan and elevations

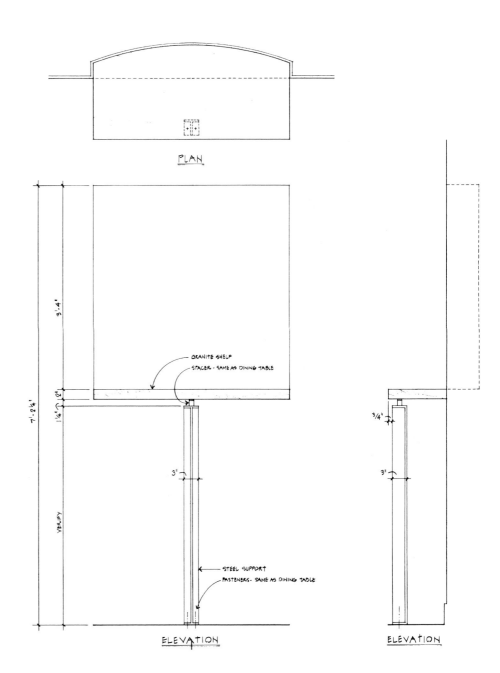

PLAN

GRANITE SHELF

SPACER - SAME AS DINING TABLE

3'-4"

7'-2¼"

1¼" 2"

VERIFY

3"

STEEL SUPPORT

FASTENERS - SAME AS DINING TABLE

ELEVATION

¾"

3"

ELEVATION

Dente Residence *1987*
GABELLINI ASSOCIATES

Owner: Barbara Dente
Architect: Michael Gabellini, Gabellini Associates, New York, New York
Interior Designer: Michael Gabellini, Jay Smith
Design Team: Michael Gabellini, Jay Smith, Chris Howard, Thomas Rose.
Engineers: Severud Associates
Consultants: Chris Howard (lighting)
General Contractor: Cogan, Inc., New York
Photography: Paul Warchol

Site: New York, New York
Program: Penthouse residence on two levels of historically listed building. Upper penthouse level: foyer, living room, kitchen, pantry, guest bathroom, staircase, main terrace. Lower penthouse level: master bedroom, master bathroom, changing room, bedroom terrace.
Square Footage: 2000 in 2 floors
Structural System: Steel and concrete floor construction with French plaster wall and ceiling panels on metal studs connected by horsehair and liquid plaster tendrils.
Mechanical System: Baseboard heating supplemented by forced air.
Major Exterior Materials: Restoration of masonry walls, bluestone paving on terraces.
Major Interior Materials: French plaster with white satin titanium paint (walls), white Yugoslavian Sivec marble (floors and stair), optical water white clear glass (fireplace), white polyester satin lacquer finish (cabinets), honed jet mist black granite (table), natural Greek walnut with bleached leather woven straps (chairs), pearl gray satin leather (chaise).
Furnishings and Storage: Custom designed by Gabellini Associates.
Doors and Hardware: Custom designed by Gabellini Associates.
Windows: Restored windows and terrace doors
Fixtures: Villeroy & Boch, Kroin
Appliances and Equipment: Sub-Zero (refrigerator/freezer), Thermador (oven), Miele (dishwasher), Gaggenau (stove/ventilating hood).
Cost: $600,000

Site/Context

The apartment is on the 20th and 21st penthouse floors in a historically listed building that faces south to views of lower Manhattan and the Hudson River.

Design

The concept driving the design of the space is one of functional simplicity. Two levels, each with their own connecting terraces, are conceived as open, light-filled volumes. These light containers, enveloped with daylight and moonlight, allow the artificially-lit internal spaces to simulate the outside, balancing the ever-changing natural light. Light is rendered as the primary physical, or spatial material, thereby setting a variety of "moods" in an otherwise static area.

LEFT: *View of apartment building*

The material palette of cool whites and natural earth tones further embellishes the desire for reflection and serenity. The stair connecting the floors becomes a suspended, cascading ribbon that provides light, air, and movement.

Construction

The material palette was developed to integrate wall, floor, and ceiling into one tonal volume. The floors are 48" Yugoslavian white marble panels on a concrete and steel slab. Walls and ceiling are constructed with molded tongue and groove plaster panels attached to the structure by horsehair plaster tendrils. The curving stair is based on a helix geometry and constructed of a forged steel string with massive white marble treads. The string is enameled with white titanium paint.

Existing conditions

Upper level floor plan

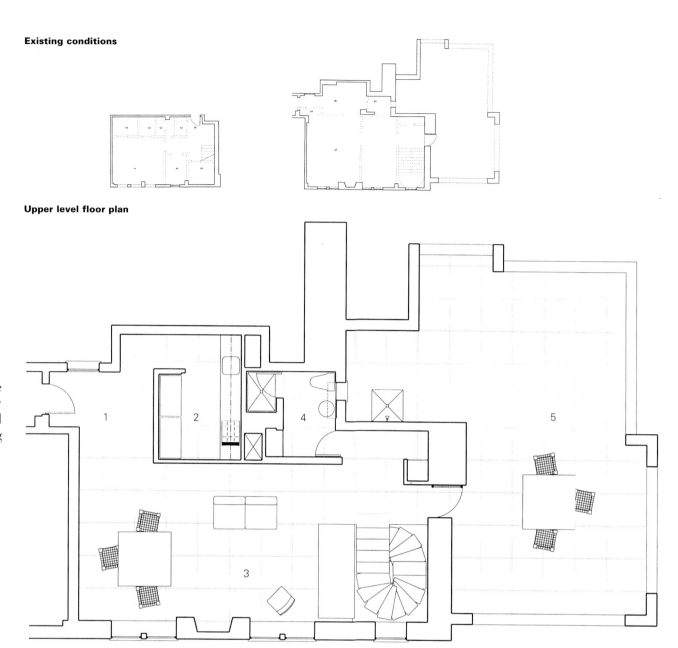

Lower level floor plan

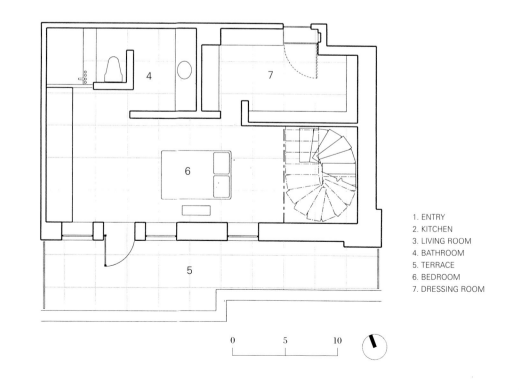

1. ENTRY
2. KITCHEN
3. LIVING ROOM
4. BATHROOM
5. TERRACE
6. BEDROOM
7. DRESSING ROOM

0   5   10

Axonometric

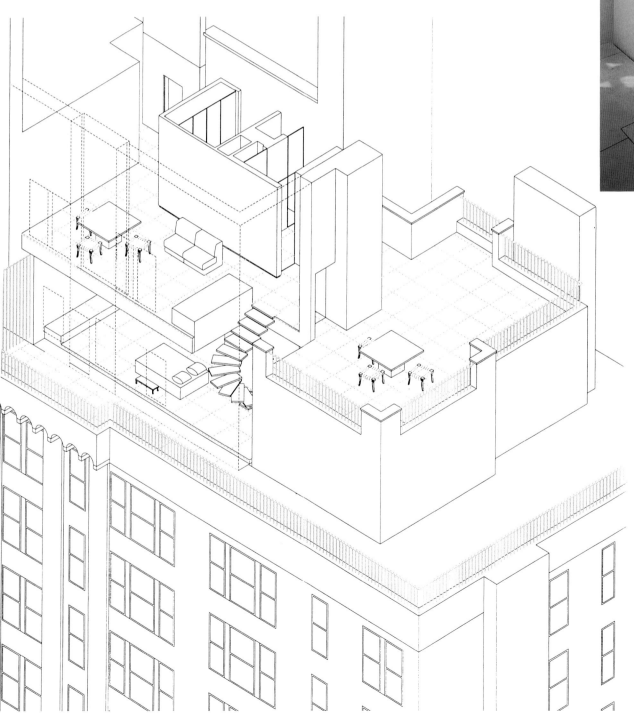

RIGHT: *Stair detail and construction drawings*

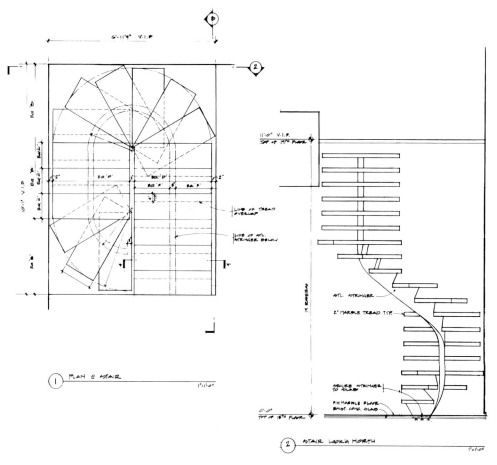

① PLAN @ STAIR

② STAIR LOOK'G NORTH

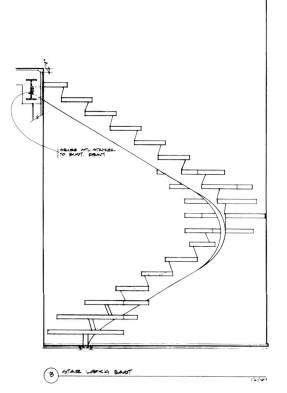

③ STAIR LOOK'G EAST

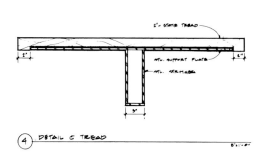

④ DETAIL @ TREAD

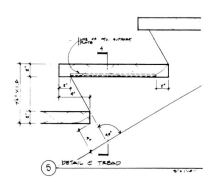

⑤ DETAIL @ TREAD

Master bath sections

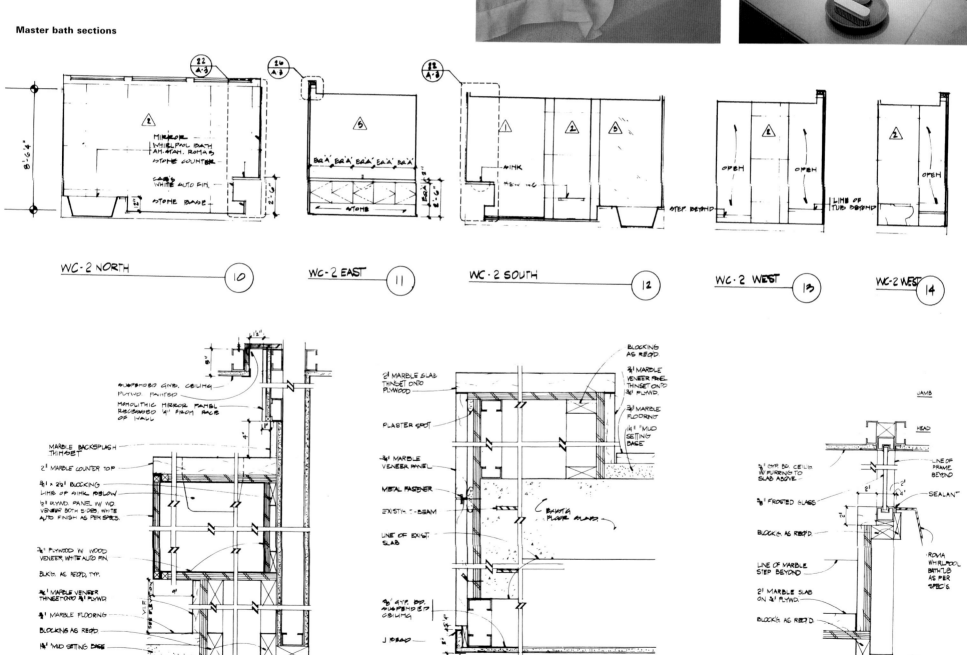

WC-2 NORTH ⑩

WC-2 EAST ⑪

WC-2 SOUTH ⑫

WC-2 WEST ⑬

WC-2 WEST ⑭

㉒ BATHRM. CABINET DETAIL
3" = 1'-0"

㉓ STONE BENCH DETAIL
3" = 1'-0"

㉔ BATHTUB DETAIL
3" = 1'-0"

Corporate Apartment *1994-1995*

GERNER KRONICK + VALCARCEL, ARCHITECTS P.C.

Owner: Name withheld at owner's request.
Architect: Gerner Kronick + Valcarcel, New York, New York
Design Team: Richard Kronick, AIA (design partner), Ruxandra Panaitescu (project manager), Teri Figliuzzi (finishes and furniture), Keitaro Nei, Friedl Streiminster (project architect), Canizaro Trigiani Architects (architects-of-record).
Engineer: Thomas V. Polise
Consultants: Kugler Tillotson Associates (lighting)
General Contractor: Ken Simmons
Photography: Paul Warchol

Site: Southern United States
Program: Corporate entertainment facility and accommodations for company visitors. Entry gallery, living room, wet bar, solarium, dining room, powder room, kitchen, laundry room, library, guest bedroom and bathroom suite, master bedroom, master bathroom, dressing room, 2 terraces.
Square Footage: 2800 plus an additional 1500-square-foot roof terrace
Structural System: Reinforced concrete, metal studs
Mechanical System: Forced air
Major Interior Materials: Stanstead granite tile floors with custom wool carpet inserts, stainless steel and carved float glass partitions (Eric Bauer fabricator), stanstead granite and custom anigre wood cabinet partions (Walter P. Sauer fabricator), skim coat plastered gypsum board (walls and ceilings), stanstead granite bathrooms (floors and walls) with anigre custom millwork cabinets, plastic laminate kitchen cabinets with granite countertops, and custom color tile backsplash.
Furnishings and Storage: Built-ins by architect, Mackintosh ladderback chair by Palazzetti, piano by Steinway, custom sofas and arm chairs by Custom Editions, Le Corbusier chaise longue by Palazzetti, Kjaerholm sofa table by ICF, side tables by Flex Form, Le Corbusier dining table by Palazzetti, tubular Brno chair by Mies van der Rohe from Knoll, solarium furniture by Frank Gehry from Knoll, beds by Avery Boardman.
Doors and Hardware: Custom doors by GKV, hardware by Sargent.
Fixtures: Toilets and bathtubs by Kohler, sinks by Kroin, fittings by Speakman.
Appliances and Equipment: Sub-Zero refrigerator and freezer, Miele dishwasher, oven, and cooktop, GE microwave, Maytag washer/dryer, Traulson wine cooler.
Cost: Withheld at owner's request.

Site/Context

The apartment is one of four penthouse units on top of a ten-story, classically inspired apartment tower in an urban setting. The building faces an intersection between an interstate highway and a major thoroughfare that run through the city. It also borders an affluent residential neighborhood, as well as one of the area's major retail centers.

RIGHT: *View of living room*

Existing conditions

Design

The architect began by laying a 12" x 12" grid over the entire plan of the apartment, and then inserted into the grid floating partitions roughly aligned along the north-south and east-west axes. The north-south partitions are stainless steel and glass; those running east-west are granite and wood. The partitions subdivide the space while they also permit the passage of light.

The entry hall terminates in a juncture defined by a granite and wood partition perpendicular to another of steel and glass. At this point one can either enter the apartment's public area—living room, dining room, and kitchen—or proceed to the private space—master and guest bedrooms and bathrooms. Both types of partitions are used throughout the apartment to delineate space.

Construction

The construction involved was very straightforward, according to the project's design partner, Richard Kronick. The apartment's existing structure was not altered. Granite was used throughout in partitions, floors, walls, and countertops. Walls and ceilings are skim coat plastered gypsum board.

Diagram of floating partitions

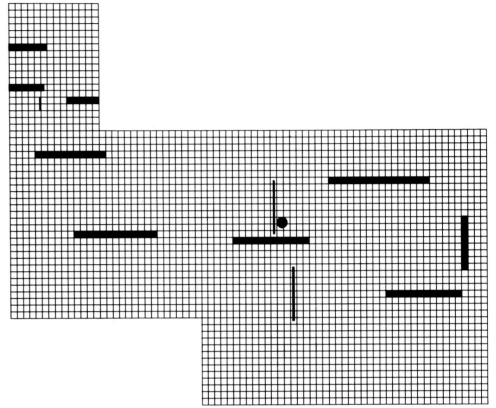

Floor plan

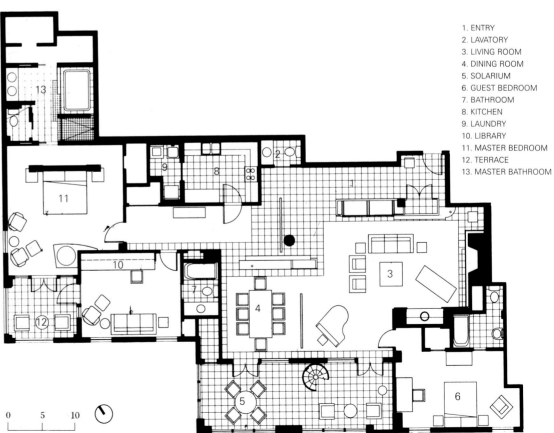

1. ENTRY
2. LAVATORY
3. LIVING ROOM
4. DINING ROOM
5. SOLARIUM
6. GUEST BEDROOM
7. BATHROOM
8. KITCHEN
9. LAUNDRY
10. LIBRARY
11. MASTER BEDROOM
12. TERRACE
13. MASTER BATHROOM

0   5   10

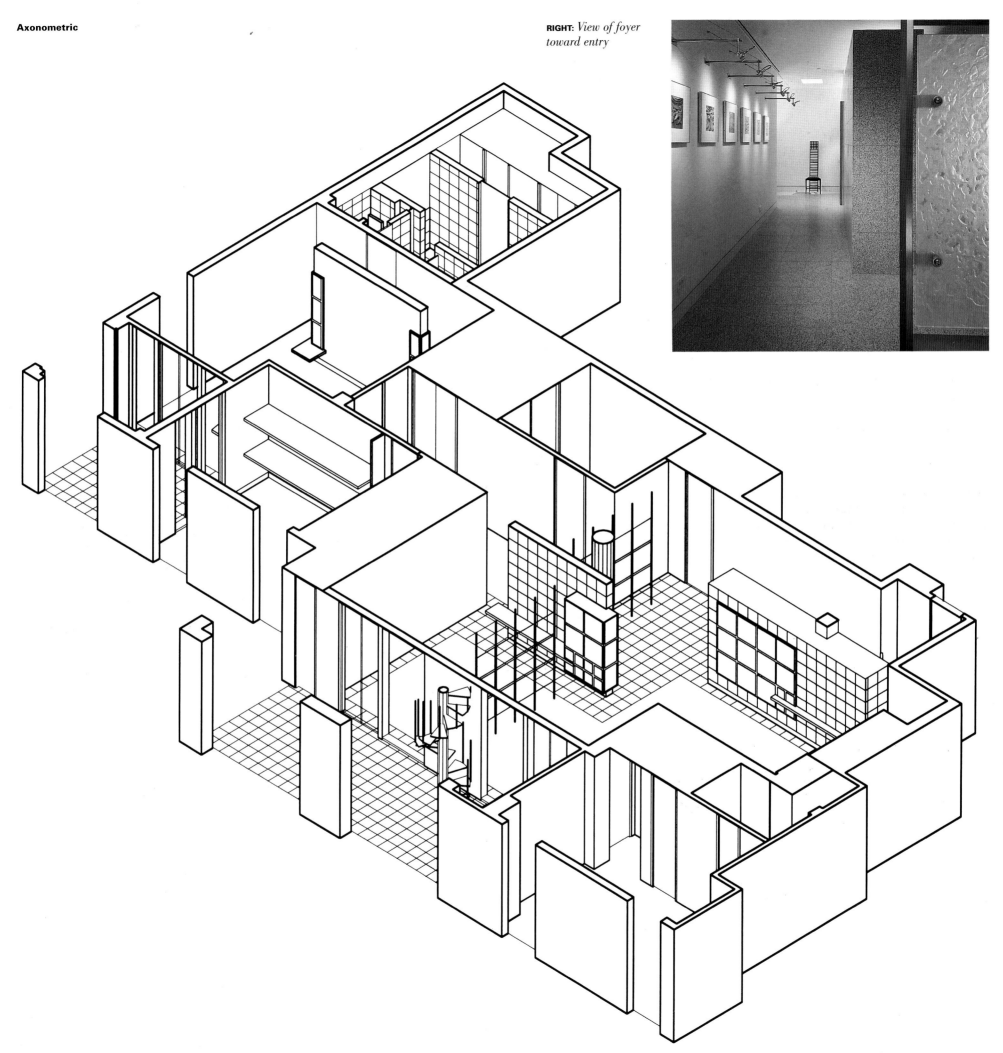

LEFT: *Dining room*
MIDDLE: *Bedroom with custom night table*
BOTTOM: *Bathroom detail*

RIGHT: *Details of stainless steel and glass partitions*

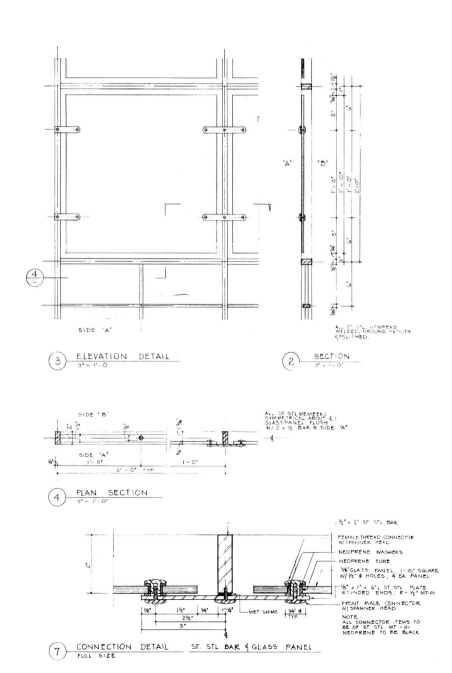

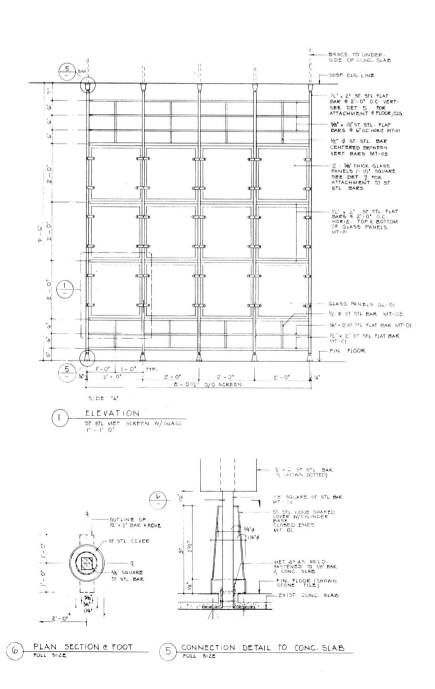

RIGHT: *View of entry's diverse partitions*

Wet bar assembly

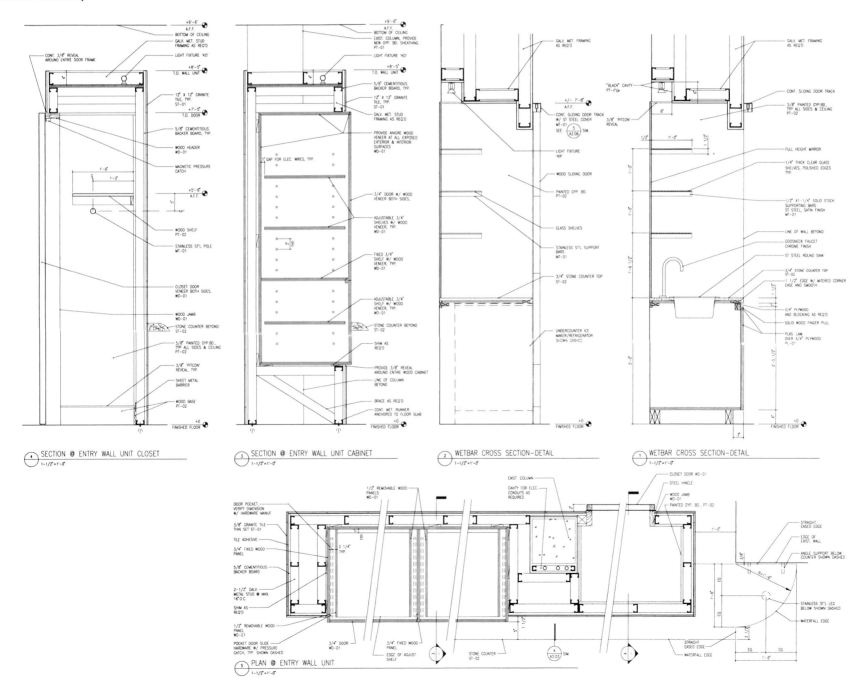

Ludwig / Fineman Loft

1986-1987

LEESER ARCHITECTURE

Owners: Gerd Ludwig and Dana Fineman
Architect: Leeser Architecture, New York, New York
General Contractor: Up-Right Construction
Photography: Jeff Goldberg/Esto

Site: Chelsea, New York, New York
Program: Lobby, office, photo studio, kitchen/dining area, bathroom, bedroom.
Square Footage: 2000
Structural System: Existing sheetrock walls and cast iron columns
Mechanical System: Existing heating and window air conditioning unit
Major Interior Materials: Painted wood, aluminum, graphite plaster, industrial ceramic tile, sandblasted glass.
Furnishings and Storage: Custom by architect.
Doors and Hardware: Custom by architect.
Fixtures: Commercial hospital supply
Appliances and Equipment: Existing
Cost: $65,000

Site/Context

This fifth-floor loft is typical of Manhattan's Chelsea district. All its windows face north.

Design

This apartment design explores the interaction between two architectural systems. The "closed" system is the readymade weathered industrial space, in which secure walls traditionally define volume. Superimposed on it is a pristine, abstract system that defines space through the absence of conventional walls, windows, and columns (the new L-shaped structures do not touch the ceiling). Because neither "system" is entirely autonomous, multiple readings and uses of the space are possible.

Construction

The only on-site construction that was done besides demolition work was the refinishing of the floor and the creation of the L-shaped elements. The latter are made of a plywood substructure with a layer of expanded metal nailed to the plywood. Metal edges are embedded in its seven outer layers of hand-sanded dyed plaster finish. The apartment's other elements were pre-fabricated and delivered to the site for assembly. Finishing of the surfaces was done after installation.

RIGHT:
View of bedroom

LEFT: *View of loft building*

Existing conditions

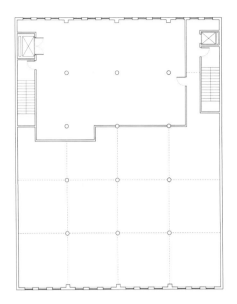

Floor plan

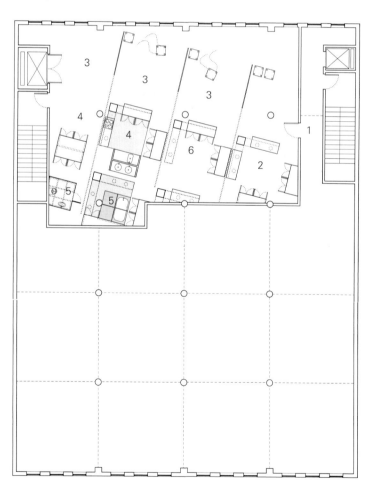

1. ENTRY
2. OFFICE
3. PHOTO STUDIO
4. KITCHEN/DINING ROOM
5. BATHROOM
6. BEDROOM

0   5   10

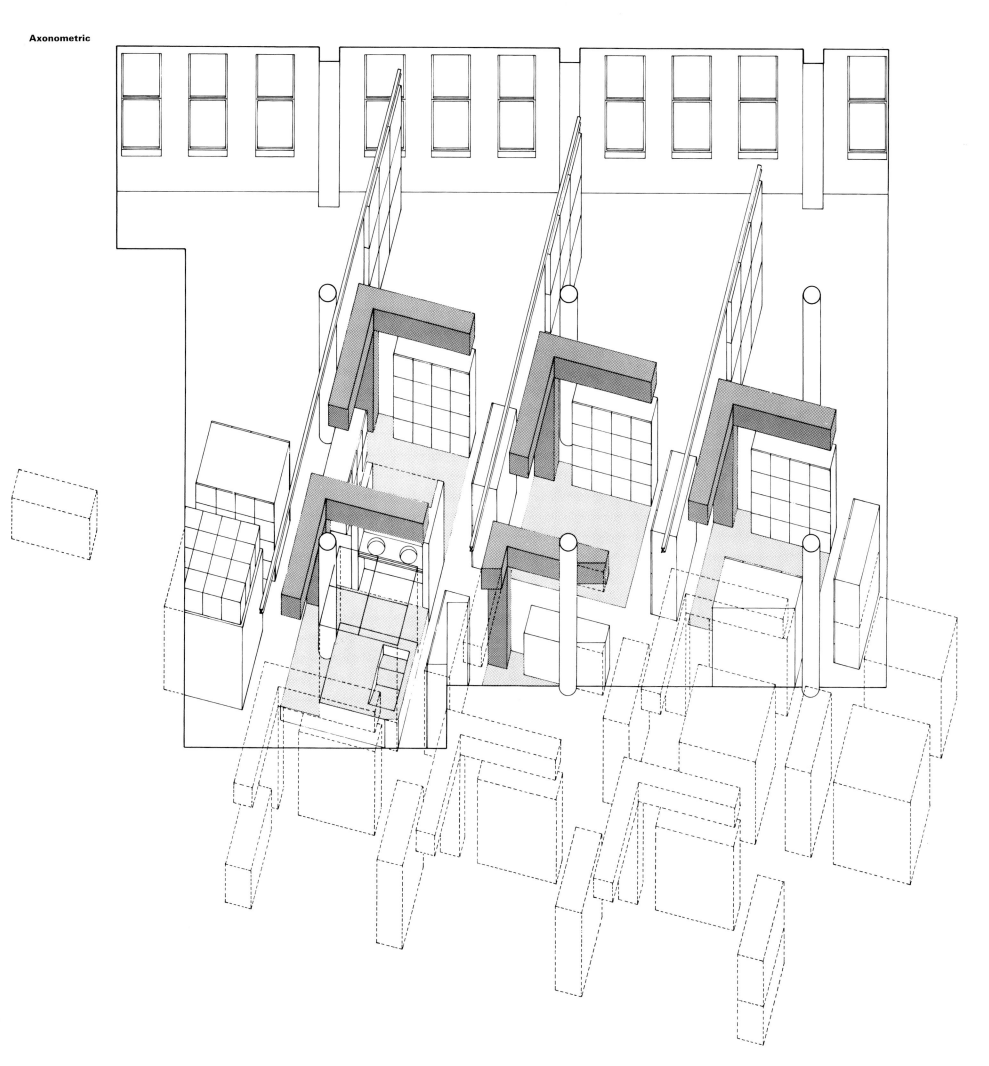

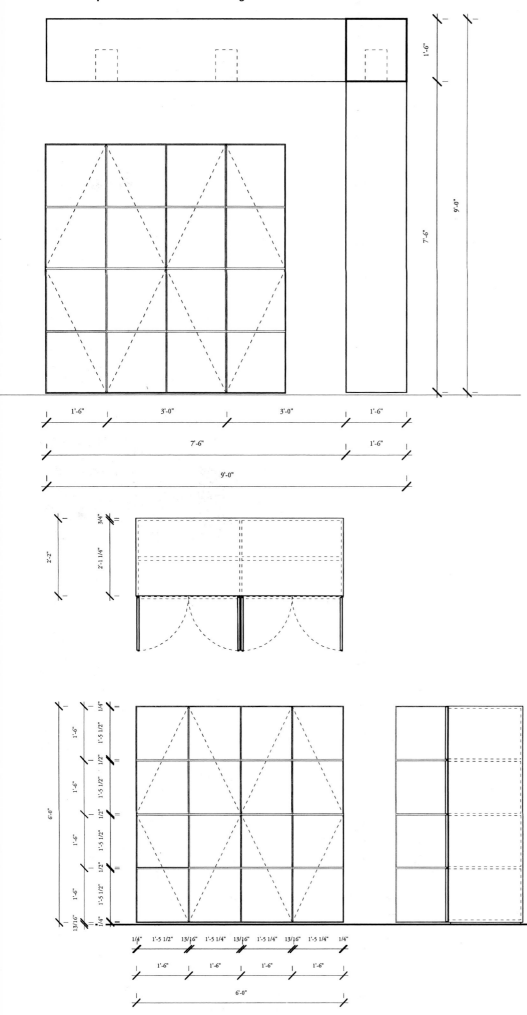

RIGHT: *View of metal and plywood frame*

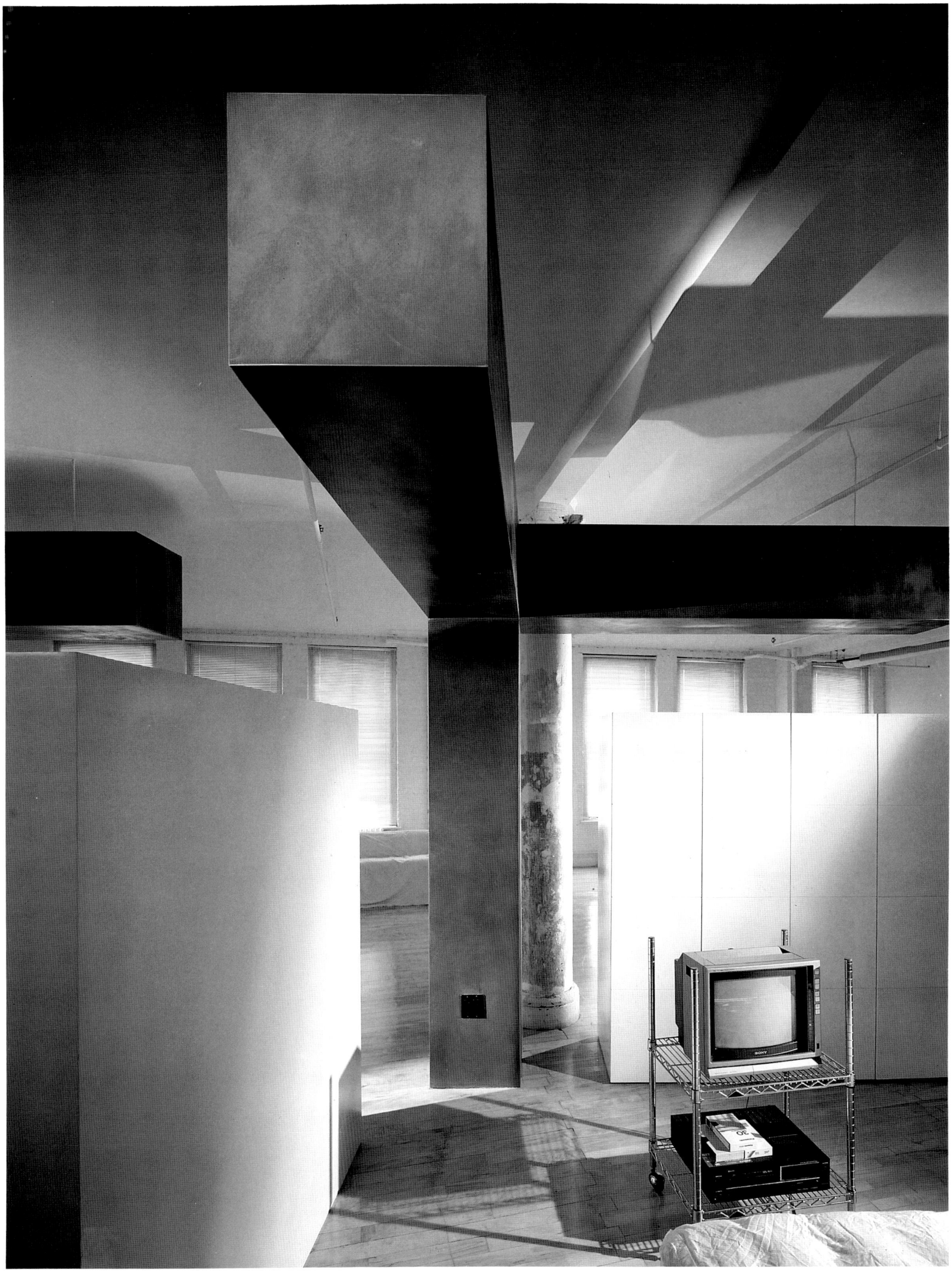

Greene Street Loft *1990–1991*

LAURETTA VINCIARELLI

Owner: Lauretta Vinciarelli
Architect: Lauretta Vinciarelli, New York, New York
Consultant: Alexandr Neratoff (architect)
General Contractor: VRC Tile & Construction
Photography: Carla Breeze

Site: New York, New York
Program: Live/work loft including breakfast room, dining room, living room, office, master bedroom, dressing room, 3 bathrooms, laundry room, guest bedroom, guest living room, and storage.
Square Footage: 3200 including mezzanine
Structural System: Existing brick bearing walls, wooden truss, cast iron columns
Mechanical System: Existing hot water system
Major Interior Materials: Sheetrock
Furnishings and Storage: Custom by architect (desks).
Doors and Hardware: Ordinary hardware store stock.
Fixtures: Ordinary hardware store stock.
Appliances and Equipment: General Electric (refrigerator), Thermador (dishwasher), Magic Chef (stove).
Cost: $100,000 including basic furniture

Site/Context

This loft is in Soho, a Manhattan neighborhood known for its prevalence of cast iron buildings. Built mainly at the end of the nineteenth century for light manufacturing and storage, these buildings are now widely used for residences.

Design

The program called for a live-work space for two people that could comfortably accommodate occasional overnight guests. The owner also wanted to keep the loft's characteristic spatial quality as intact as possible. By relegating certain functions to the apartment's irregular side—the one containing the building stairs—more than half of the loft was left open, preserving essential features like the spatial continuum and cast iron columns.

At 15' 6", the ceiling height allowed the insertion of a mezzanine comprising two bedrooms, closets, and a toilet. Placed directly below are the kitchen, two bathrooms, and various storage and utility spaces. This configuration permits the interplay of compressed and expansive spaces and establishes a clear hierarchy in an apartment type that is by nature unarticulated.

Construction

The building work involved in the project was basic wooden frame and gypsum board construction. The architect and owner refers to the process as "honest," adding that "the only fancy thing is the space: it's large and well-proportioned."

RIGHT: *View of living area*

Existing conditions

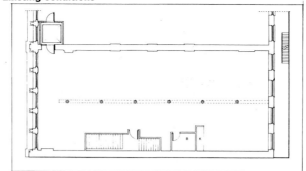

Upper level floor plan

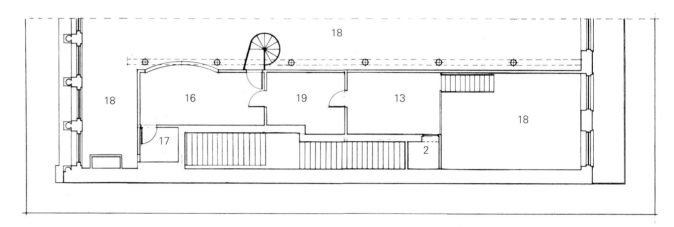

Lower level floor plan

1. ENTRY
2. STORAGE
3. DINING ROOM
4. LIVING ROOM
5. STUDIO/OFFICE
6. BREAKFAST ROOM
7. KITCHEN
8. BATHROOM
9. SHOWER
10. LAUNDRY
11. BACK ENTRY
12. HALL
13. GUEST BEDROOM
14. GUEST BATHROOM
15. GUEST LIVING ROOM
16. MASTER BEDROOM
17. MASTER BATHROOM
18. OPEN
19. DRESSING ROOM

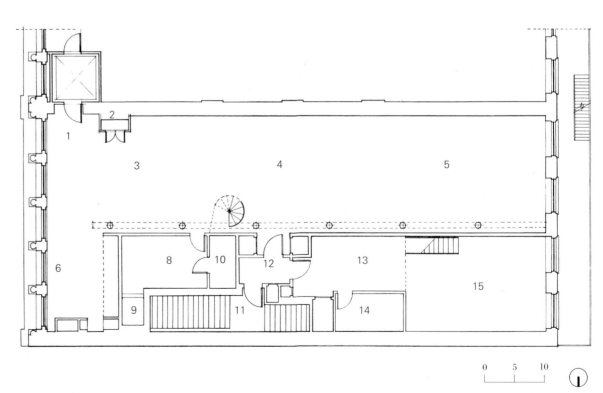

0   5   10

Index